Italian Verb

HANDBOOK

Carole Shepherd

Italian Verb Handbook

The Author:
Carole Shepherd is an experienced teacher, author and language consultant.

The Series Editor:
Christopher Wightwick is a former UK representative on the Council of Europe Modern Languages Project and principal Inspector of Modern Languages for England.

Other titles in the Berlitz Language Handbook Series:

French Grammar Handbook
German Grammar Handbook
Spanish Grammar Handbook
Italian Grammar Handbook
French Verb Handbook
German Verb Handbook
Spanish Verb Handbook
French Vocabulary Handbook
German Vocabulary Handbook
Spanish Vocabulary Handbook
Italian Vocabulary Handbook

Published by Berlitz Publishing Co., Ltd.,
Peterley Road, Oxford OX4 2TX

1st printing 1994

Printed in England by Clays Ltd, St Ives plc

CONTENTS

How to use this Handbook

How to use this Handbook

This book aims to provide a full description of the Italian verb system for all learners and users of the Italian language. It provides the following information:
• a chapter explaining the Italian verb system;
• the conjugation of 106 verbs, grouped to show the common patterns underlying the system;
• a subject index to *The verb system in Italian*;
• a verb index, containing over 2,200 verbs with their English meanings and references to the pattern(s) they follow.

An important feature of the book is that examples, showing many of the verbs in use, are given throughout *The verb system in Italian* and *Model verbs*.

THE VERB SYSTEM IN ITALIAN

Use the *Contents* and *Subject index* to find your way around this section, which describes the functions and forms of verbs in general. Information is given on the use of tenses, word order, the way verbs govern other parts of speech and the way verbs are formed. Methods of avoiding the passive are described, and features such as the reflexive forms, the subjunctive, and the auxiliary verbs are explained. The main features of predictability and irregularity are explained, and key irregular verbs are illustrated.

THE MODEL VERBS

Use the *Verb index* to find your way around this section, which gives the full conjugation of two key model verbs, **comprare** and **entrare,** in all tenses. Models are provided for all three conjugations of regular verbs as well as the full range of spelling change verbs, followed by all useful irregular verbs. This makes 106 model verbs in total.

The conjugation of each verb is given in all tenses. Tenses which have an irregularity are given in full, with the irregularity in bold type. For tenses which are predictable, particularly compound tenses, only the first person singular form is given, as this is sufficient to allow you to predict the remaining forms within those tenses. Therefore if a tense is not given in full you can assume that it is regular.

For simple tenses, just look at one of the four regular verb models to work out the endings you need. For compound tenses, check which auxiliary is necessary, then look up the appropriate auxiliary verb (**avere** or **essere** for the past, **stare** for the present and imperfect continuous tenses) in the *Model verbs*.

Where appropriate, the model verb pages also contain the following:
• A list of other verbs following the same pattern. If possible, all such verbs are given. If, however, they are too numerous to list, a selection of the most useful ones is given. There are, of course, verbs which have no others following their model.

• Notes indicating the main features of this pattern, and any variations or additional features affecting any of the verbs which basically follow that model.

• Short dialogues, narratives or sentences which illustrate some of the different tenses and uses of these verbs.

For further information on how the verb system works, refer to *The verb system in Italian*.

THE SUBJECT INDEX

The *Subject index* gives section references for all the main grammatical terms used in *The verb system in Italian*.

VERB INDEX

For each of the 2,200 or so verbs listed, information is given on whether it is transitive (*tr*), intransitive (*intr*) or reflexive (*refl*), together with its English meaning. Common secondary meanings are also listed, as are the main idiomatic expressions based on common verbs. Finally each entry is referred to the model verb whose pattern it follows.

acquistare (tr)   acquire, get 3

There are verbs which have more than one predictable or unpredictable variation from the norm. Such verbs have two numbers after them and both model verb pages should be consulted in these cases.

assorbire (tr)   to absorb, soak up 5, 6

HOW TO FIND THE INFORMATION YOU WANT

If you want to check on the form, meaning or use of a verb, first look it up in the *Verb index*. This shows:

• which verbs are model verbs (indicated by **[M]**);

vendere *(tr)*   retail, sell 4 **[M]**

• which verbs take **essere** (indicated by *)

*andare *(intr)*   go, ride (in car) 21 **[M]**

• which verbs take **avere** when transitive, and **essere** when intransitive (indicated by a †)

†salire *(tr/intr)*   go up, climb, mount, come in (tide) 77 **[M]**

• any preposition normally accompanying the verb;

*abituarsi a *(intr/refl)*   become accustomed to, get used to 7

• whether the verb is transitive *(tr)*, intransitive *(intr)* or reflexive *(refl)*;

camminare *(intr)*   step, tread, walk 3

• the main English meaning of the verb, along with any important idiomatic uses;

colpire *(tr)*   impress, knock against, shock, smack, strike, hit 6

colpire a morte *(tr)*   shoot dead 6

• a number indicating the model verb which gives further information about the verb, how it is formed and others that follow the same or a similar pattern.

chiudere *(tr)*   close, shut, zip up 30

If you want further information on the form or use of the verb, turn to the verb reference given.

Note: *The rules regarding the use of accents in Italian require that there should be an acute accent on closed vowels and a grave accent on open vowels [▶Berlitz Italian Grammar Handbook 2a]. However, modern usage tends to prefer the grave accent, particularly on à, ò, ù and ì, and this usage is employed throughout the Handbook.*

A
THE VERB SYSTEM IN ITALIAN

1 | What verbs do

1a Full verbs

The great majority of verbs tell us about the actions, state of mind or changing situation of the subject of the sentence. These we call full verbs.

Abito in Italia.	*I live* in Italy.
Abbiamo un appartamento.	*We have* a flat.

1b Auxiliary verbs

A much smaller group of verbs is used to add something to the sense of the full verb, for example to make a compound tense or to add a comment on an action. These are called *auxiliary* (helping) verbs.

Sto studiando l'italiano.	I am studying Italian.
Ho comprato una macchina.	I (have) bought a car.
Sono andato in città.	I went into town.

1c Dual-purpose verbs

Most auxiliary verbs can be used either with full meaning or as an auxiliary. For example, the verb **stare**, used mostly to express position or the state or condition of something or somebody, is also used as an auxiliary verb to form the present continuous tense – this describes an action actually in progress.

Sta in casa.	He is in the house.
Sta preparando da mangiare.	He is preparing something to eat.

2 What verbs govern

A sentence can contain many items of information other than what is given by the subject and the main verb. Some of these items depend directly on the main verb and cannot be removed without leaving the sentence incomplete. These are said to be governed by the verb.

2a Intransitive verbs

Some verbs do not normally govern an object [➤2c], though the sentence may, of course, contain expressions which add to the meaning. These verbs are called intransitive verbs and are usually marked in verb lists and dictionaries as (intr) or (i).

Torno subito.	I'll come back straightaway.

'I'll come back' makes sense in itself. The 'straightaway' gives us some extra information.

2b Verbs linking equals: the complement

A small number of verbs act as a link between the subject and another word or phrase, which is called the complement of the verb. Usually the complement is a noun or a phrase, in which case it refers to the same person or thing as the subject.

Mio padre *è* dottore.	My father is a doctor.

2c Transitive Verbs

Many verbs take a *direct* object. These verbs are *transitive*. They are usually marked in dictionaries and verb lists as (tr). A direct object answers the question *what?* or *whom?* Intransitive verbs cannot have a direct object.

Giorgio ha comprato *un cane*.	Giorgio bought *a dog*.

Here the dog was what Giorgio bought, so it is the direct object of 'bought'.

2d   Verbs which can be both transitive and intransitive

Many Italian verbs can be both transitive and intransitive. They may be listed as *(intr/tr)* in verb lists.

Maria parla troppo.	Maria talks too much.
Giovanna parla inglese.	Giovanna speaks English.

2e   Verbs with two objects: direct and indirect

Some transitive verbs describe the transfer of the direct object to another person (or possibly thing). This person is then the *indirect object* of the verb. The idea can be extended with some verbs to include people indirectly affected by the action of the verb. The indirect object answers the question *to whom?* or *for whom?*, but in English the 'to' or the 'for' are not always stated.

Sandro ha comprato dei fiori per la mamma.	Sandro bought some flowers for his mother.
Le ha comprato dei fiori.	He bought her some flowers.
Ha dato i fiori alla mamma.	He gave the flowers to his mother.
Le ha dato i fiori.	He gave her the flowers.

Here the flowers are the direct object and the mother/her – the recipient – is the indirect object.

2f   Reflexive verbs

(i)   Some verbs express an action which is turned back on the subject, in other words the object is the same person or the same thing as the subject. These are called *reflexive* verbs [➤10]. In English, these verbs may use one of the '-self' pronouns.

Mi diverto sempre in Italia.	I always enjoy myself in Italy.
Ci siamo divertiti molto.	We enjoyed ourselves a lot.

(ii)   Sometimes people are doing the action not to themselves but to each other, in which case the subject is usually plural. As a result it is only possible to use the plural forms **noi**, **voi** and **loro**.

| Si sono incontrati ieri. | They met (each other) yesterday. |
| Ci telefoniamo spesso. | We often phone each other. |

(iii) In many cases the Italian reference to '-self' or 'each other' is not expressed in English.

Mi sveglio alle sette.	I wake up at 7:00 a.m.
Mi alzo subito.	I get up immediately.
Mi lavo nel bagno.	I get washed in the bathroom.

(iv) With some verbs the reflexive idea has largely disappeared in English, but the grammatical form still applies.

| Me ne sono accorta che l'uomo mi guardava. | I noticed that the man was looking at me. |
| Non si rende conto che sono straniera. | He does not realize that I am a foreigner. |

(v) Normally reflexive verbs do not have another direct object, but if they do the past participle agrees with that object rather than the reflexive pronoun, which then becomes an indirect object.

Mi sono tagliato il dito.	I cut my finger.
Mi sono rotta la gamba.	I have broken my leg.
Mi sono lavate le mani.	I washed my hands.

However, usage varies and you may find that Italians make a past participle agree with the subject, even when there is a direct object.

| Alberto s'è tolto la camicia. | Antonio took off his shirt. |

In these examples, the English uses a possessive whereas Italian uses a reflexive pronoun.

(vi) Reflexive verbs are often used where a passive would be used in English.

5

| Qui si vendono mele.
Qui si parla inglese. | Apples are sold here.
English is spoken here. |

2g Verbs governing verbs
(i) Verbs followed by an infinitive

This is quite a common structure in Italian, which has many expressions based on a *modal* auxiliary verb [➤ 3].

| *Vorrei* partire alle otto.
Devo essere in città alle nove.
Sai nuotare?
Possiamo andare in piscina insieme. | *I'd like* to leave at 8:00.
I must be in town at 9:00.
Can you swim?
We can go to the swimming pool together. |

(ii) Verbs followed by a preposition and an infinitive

Italian also has a number of these structures, which are very similar to (i), but with a preposition between the auxiliary verb and the main verb. The *Verb index* lists which verbs take which prepositions.

Andiamo *a* mangiare adesso !	Let's go to have something to eat now!
T'invito *a* cenare stasera.	I'm inviting you to dinner this evening.
Ho dimenticato *di* comprare il giornale.	I forgot to buy the paper.
Sono usciti *senza* salutarmi.	They went out without saying good-bye to me.

(iii) Use of the gerund

As in English, Italian has a way of describing an action in progress. In English the verb 'to be' and the present participle is used, while in Italian the verb **stare** and the gerund can be used.

| *Sto* studiando l'italiano.
Stavo leggendo quando è arrivato Luigi. | I am studying Italian.
I was reading when Luigi arrived. |

2h   Position of verbs in the sentence

(i)   Subject pronouns

Generally speaking, the position of verbs in an Italian sentence is similar to that in English. However, one important difference is that Italian verbs are usually found without a subject pronoun. This is because each verb ending is clear and distinct, not just in the written but also in the spoken form. The pronouns are, however, used, when necessary, for emphasis, contrast or to avoid ambiguity.

Io vado in città, ma *tu* devi rimanere qui.	*I* am going into town, but *you* must stay here.
– Chi ha rotto il bicchiere? – L'ha rotto *lui*, mamma.	– Who broke the glass? – *He* broke it, mum/mom.

In the last example the pronoun comes after the verb for greater emphasis on the person who broke the glass.

(ii)   Questions

Questions in English are usually formed by inverting the verb and the subject, or by the use of the verb 'to do'. Such inversion is not so common in Italian, as the subject pronoun is rarely used, except for emphasis. Instead, questions often look exactly the same as statements but are indicated by voice intonation – the voice is raised at the end of the question. In written form, the question is made visible, as in English, by the question mark.

Tuo padre ha una macchina nuova.	Your father has a new car.
Tuo padre ha una macchina nuova?	Does your father have a new car?
Hai visto Carlo ieri.	You saw Carlo yesterday.
Hai visto Carlo ieri?	Did you see Carlo yesterday?

(iii)   Negative expressions

Negative expressions are straightforward in Italian. The English word 'not' is translated by the Italian **non**, which is placed immediately before the verb and any dependent object pronouns.

– *Non* vado al cinema stasera.	– I'm *not* going to the cinema/movies this evening.
– Perché *non* ci accompagni?	– Why are*n't* you coming with us?
– *Non* mi sento bene.	– I do*n't* feel well.
Non lo so.	I do*n't* know.

Non can be combined with other negative expressions (**mai, nessuno, niente**, etc.) usually placed after the main verb.

Non vedo *nessuno* fuori.	I can't see anyone outside.
Non è *niente*, non ti preoccupare.	It's nothing, don't worry.
Non ho *mai* visto quel film.	I have never seen that film.

Note: **Nessuno** can begin a sentence, in which case there is no need for the **non**. This does not affect the position of the verb in the sentence.

Nessuno vuole venire.	Nobody wants to come.

③ Attitudes to action: modal verbs

3a The function of modal verbs

Modal verbs, as mentioned in 2g(i), modify full verbs to express an additional point of view such as possibility, desire or obligation. They create a *mood* for the verb which follows. They are used in the appropriate person and tense form, followed by the infinitive of the full verb.

3b Modal verbs and their meanings

These are the main modal auxiliary verbs used in Italian:

(i) *potere* 'be able'

Non *posso* venire domani.	I *can*'t come tomorrow.

(ii) *volere* 'want, wish'

Non *voleva* andarci.	He *didn*'t *want* to go there.

(iii) *dovere* 'have to, must, be obliged to, ought to'

Dovete ascoltare il professore.	*You should* listen to the teacher.

(iv) *sapere* 'know how to, be able to'

– Sai suonare il flauto? – No, ma so giocare a tennis!	– Do you know how to play the flute? – No, but I can play tennis!

Note: Object pronouns may precede the modal verb or be attached to the end of the infinitive.

Te lo posso dire adesso.	I can tell you now.
Posso dirtelo adesso.	I can tell you now.

④ Verb forms not related to time

Verbs are very important words, in that a single verb form will usually give three pieces of information: *what* is happening, *when* it is happening, and *who* is doing it. However, there are some verb forms which do not specify time or person.

4a   The infinitive

The part of the verb which you will find in a verb list or dictionary and also in the *Verb index* of this book – is the *infinitive*. In English this is the word preceded by 'to', for example 'to love'. In Italian the infinitive form of all regular verbs ends in one of the following: **-are, -ere, -ire** (for example **amare, vendere, capire, dormire**).

4b   The participles and the gerund

(i)   The present participle

The present participle in Italian has lost its verbal force and in most cases is used as an adjective or a noun. It is usually formed by adding **-ante** or **-ente** to the stem of the infinitive.

il capitolo seguente	the following chapter
gli amanti	the lovers

(ii)   The gerund

The gerund is often used to describe an action in progress. Its most common use is with the auxiliary verb **stare** to form the progressive or continuous tenses, usually present, imperfect or sometimes future, but it can be used by itself, provided that its subject and that of the verb in the sentence are the same. The gerund is formed by adding **-ando** or **-endo** to the stem of the infinitive, is invariable and *never* takes a preposition before it. Care must be taken that the action being referred to is/was actually happening in the past.

Sto finendo l'esercizio	*I am finishing* the exercise.
Parlando con Anna cammino lungo la strada.	*While speaking* to Anna, I walk along the road.
Cosa state *facendo*?	What *are you doing*?
Il bambino *sta dormendo* nella culla.	The baby *is sleeping* in the cradle.

Note the difference between the following:

Studio l'italiano a scuola.	I study Italian at school
Sto studiando l'italiano adesso.	I am studying Italian now (i.e. at this precise moment).

(iii)   *The past participle*

This form is used to describe an action which is finished. In Italian it ends in **-ato** (**-are** verbs), **-uto** (**-ere** verbs), or **-ito** (**-ire** verbs). It is mainly used with the verb **avere** or the verb **essere** to form the perfect tense and other compound tenses, but it is also used in other ways, including as an adjective and to form the passive. When used with **avere** in compound tenses, it does not agree with the subject, but can agree with a preceding direct object and *must* agree with a preceding direct object *pronoun*.

When used with **essere** it almost always agrees with the subject [but for reflexive usage ►2f(v)].

Ho comprato una casa nuova.	I have bought a new house.
Fu costruita da Salvatore.	It was built by Salvatore.
L'ho invitata a pranzo.	I invited her to lunch.
La mia amica è partita alle nove.	My friend left at 9:00.
Ho lasciato la porta aperta.	I left the door open.

In the examples given above, the past participle is used as part of a compound tense in all but the second example, where it is used as part of a passive construction. In the final example the second past participle is used as an adjective. When used in the passive or as an adjective or with the verb **essere**, the past participle agrees like an adjective.

4c   *Impersonal verbs*

(i)   *piacere* *'please'*

This verb is used to express the English term 'like', but it is an impersonal verb.

Mi piace cantare.	I like singing.
Ti piacerebbe uscire stasera?	Would you like to go out this evening?

 The use of tenses

5a   *What are tenses?*

Tenses are grammatical structures which record when an event happened. Both the number of tenses and the names given to them vary from language to language. Many tenses are formed from the stem of the infinitive - this is the part which remains when the **-are, -ere** or **-ire** ending has been removed (for example the stem of **parlare** is **parl-**). We may speak of simple and compound tenses.

(i)   Simple tenses

These are formed by adding specific endings to the stem of the verb, which may also change.

(ii)   Compound tenses

These are formed with the help of the auxiliary verbs **avere, essere** and **stare,** a participle or a gerund.

Thus a simple tense is a one-word form, whilst a compound tense uses two or more words.

5b   *Auxiliary verbs*

(i)   The progressive/continuous tenses

These are used to describe actions which are in progress at the time being referred to, present, past (imperfect), or some-times future. In English these are easily identifiable, as they are formed by the appropriate form of the verb 'to be' followed by the main verb in the '-ing' form. Italian uses a similar structure with the verb **stare** in an appropriate tense followed by the gerund of the main verb. The two main tenses of **stare** used in Italian are the present and the imperfect. However, you should note that Italian uses these forms less than in English, and only when the action is in progress at the time being described.

Quando è arrivato stavo leggendo un libro.	When he arrived I was reading a book.

Andare is sometimes used to form the progressive tenses when a cumulative progression is indicated.

Gianna andava parlando di questo progetto per ore e ore.	Gianna went on talking about this project for hours and hours.

(ii) The compound past tenses

In Italian these tenses are formed with the appropriate form of the verb **avere** or the verb **essere** and the past participle.

Ho visto Gianluca ieri.	I saw Gianluca yesterday.
Aveva incontrato Sara.	He had met Sara.
Sono andata in città.	I went into town.
Era partito presto.	He had left early.

(iii) The past gerund

The past gerund is formed by combining the present gerunds of **avere** and **essere** with the past participle of the verb. It is used to translate the English perfect participle (i.e. having bought, having understood, etc.).

Avendo comprato il giornale tornai a casa.	Having bought the newspaper, I returned home.
Essendo partite le mie amiche, andai a dormire.	My friends having left, I went to bed.

Note: As in the second example, the past gerund often has a subject of its own, unlike the present gerund used in the present continuous tense.

6 Statements of probable fact: the indicative

Verb forms and tenses which make a positive statement are said to be *indicative*. [Contrast this with the subjunctive ➤8.]

In all verbs there are some tenses whose stems and endings can be predicted if you know one of the other parts of the verb. Parts which cannot be predicted in this way have to be learned. It is helpful to know how to obtain the stem, to which the endings for each tense are added, and any spelling adjustments that may need to be made. The following sections give a breakdown of the main uses of each tense, and explain how to get the stem and endings for each tense, along with any pitfalls to watch out for.

6a The present tenses

(i) The present tense

The present tense of regular verbs is formed as follows:

First Conjugation   Second conjugation   Third conjugation

amare 'love'	**vendere** 'sell'	**dormire** 'sleep'	**finire** 'finish'
am**o**	vend**o**	dorm**o**	fini**sco**
am**i**	vend**i**	dorm**i**	fini**sci**
am**a**	vend**e**	dorm**e**	fini**sce**
am**iamo**	vend**iamo**	dorm**iamo**	fini**amo**
am**ate**	vend**ete**	dorm**ite**	fin**ite**
am**ano**	vend**ono**	dorm**ono**	fini**scono**

Note that the following groups of verbs undergo spelling changes or other modifications, mainly for pronunciation purposes.

First Conjugation verbs

• verbs whose stem ends in **-c** or **-g** insert an **h** before an **i** or an **e**:

| **pagare** | pago, **paghi, paghiamo,** pagate, pagano |
| **cercare** | cerco, **cerchi,** cerca, **cerchiamo,** cercate, cercano |

• verbs ending in **-iare** have only one **i** in the **tu** form if the **i** of the stem is not stressed:

| studiare | studi | (the stress falls on the first syllable) |

• verbs ending in **-iare** retain the **i** if the stem is stressed:

| sciare | scii | (the stress is on the first **i**) |

Second Conjugation verbs

• verbs ending in **-durre** are not irregular once the first person singular is known, as this is based on a **-ducere** ending:

produrre	**produco,** etc
ridurre	**riduco,** etc.
tradurre	**traduco,** etc

• three verbs **bere, dire,** and **fare** are formed from the obsolete **-ere** infinitives **bevere, dicere** and **facere** and, if classified as second conjugation verbs, are regular in some parts of their present tense:

bere (bevere)	bevo, bevi, beve, beviamo, bevete, bevono
dire (dicere)	dico, dici, dice, diciamo, **dite,** dicono.
fare (facere)	**faccio, fai, fa, facciamo, fate, fanno**

• some verbs add another vowel (turning into a diphthong) in the first, second and third person singular and third person plural:

| **morire** | **muoio, muori, muore,** moriamo, morite, **muoiono** |
| **sedere** | **siedo, siedi, siede,** sediamo, sedete, **siedono** |

For irregular verbs, see Model verbs.

The present tense in Italian can be used to convey the following ideas:

• What the situation is now.

| **Studio l'italiano a una scuola serale.** | I study Italian at night classes. |

• What happens sometimes or usually.

| **Ogni giorno esco alle sette.** | I go out every day at 7:00. |

• What is going to happen soon.

Quest'estate vado in America.	This summer I am going to America.

• What has been happening up to now and may be going to continue.

Abito a Firenze da due anni .	I have been living in Florence for 2 years.
Aspettiamo da una mezz'ora.	We have been waiting for half an hour.

(ii)   The present progressive/continuous

This is formed by using the present tense of **stare** plus the gerund [➤ 5b(i)]:

studiare – studiando   **prendere – prendendo**   **finire – finendo**

There are three irregular gerunds formed from obsolete forms of the **-ere** infinitive.

Verb	Obsolete infinitive	Gerund
dire	**(dicere)**	**dicendo**
fare	**(facere)**	**facendo**
bere	**(bevere)**	**bevendo**

Sto *bevendo* un bicchiere di vino.	I am *drinking* a glass of wine.
Sto *leggendo* il giornale.	I am *reading* the newspaper.

6b   The past tenses

(i)   The imperfect indicative

The imperfect tense of all verbs is formed by taking off the **-re** ending of the infinitive and adding the following endings:

vo, vi, va, vamo, vate, vano

comprare 'buy'	*vendere* 'sell)	*dormire* 'sleep'
compra**vo**	vende**vo**	dormi**vo**
compra**vi**	vende**vi**	dormi**vi**
compra**va**	vende**va**	dormi**va**
compra**vamo**	vende**vamo**	dormi**vamo**
compra**vate**	vende**vate**	dormi**vate**
compra**vano**	vende**vano**	dormi**vano**

The following irregular imperfects are formed from obsolete forms of the infinitive:

Verb	Obsolete infinitive	Imperfect
dire	(dicere)	dicevo etc.
fare	(facere)	facevo etc.
bere	(bevere)	bevevo etc.

Verbs ending in **-durre:**

produrre	producevo etc.
tradurre	traducevo etc.

Verbs ending in **-arre:**

attrarre	attraevo etc.
distrarre	distraevo etc.

The verb **essere** is the only verb to have a completely irregular form:

essere　　　　**ero, eri, era, eravamo, eravate, erano**

The imperfect tense is used for:

• repeated or habitual actions in the past;
• descriptions of things or people in the past;
• ongoing actions in the past, often as a setting to other actions.

Ogni anno *andava* in Spagna.	He *used to go* to Spain every year.
***Era* una ragazza molto povera.**	She *was* a very poor girl.
***Parlava* con Antonio quando sono entrata.**	He *was speaking* to Antonio when I came in.

(ii)　The imperfect progressive/continuous tense

This is formed by using the appropriate form of the imperfect tense of **stare** followed by the gerund [for usage ➤5b(i)]:

Stavo scrivendo quando ha telefonato Leonardo.	I was writing when Leonardo telephoned/called.

(iii)　The past definite

In regular verbs the past definite is formed by adding the following endings to the stem:

-are	–	ai, asti, ò, ammo, aste, arono
-ere	–	ei (-etti), esti, é (ette), emmo, este, erono (ettero)
-ire	–	ii, isti, í, immo, iste, irono

trovare	*vendere*	*capire*
trovai	vendei/vendetti	capii
trovasti	vendesti	capisti
trovò	vendé/vendette	capí
trovammo	vendemmo	capimmo
trovaste	vendeste	capiste
trovarono	venderono/vendettero	capirono

Note: *There is a stress on the ending of the third person plural.*

For irregular verbs, ➤*Model verbs* 17-106. Although there are a considerable number of verbs which are irregular in the past definite, many of these are only irregular in the first and third person singular and third person plural, as in the following example:

chiedere – **chiesi,** chiedesti, **chiese,** chiedemmo, chiedeste, **chiesero**

Note the irregular past definite of **avere** and **essere:**

avere	*essere*
ebbi	fui
avesti	fosti
ebbe	fu
avemmo	fummo
aveste	foste
ebbero	furono

The past definite is used to describe completed actions in the past, which have no further correlation to the present. It is mainly used in literary and formal writing, though in some parts of Italy it is an alternative to the perfect tense.

| Tornando a casa, *incontrai* Carlo. | While I was returning home *I met* Carlo. |
| *Comprai* una macchina due mesi fa. | *I bought* a car 2 months ago. |

Note: The verb **nascere** needs special attention – **è nato** is used for someone still living; **era nato** for someone who has recently died; **nacque** is used for someone long dead.

La bambina è nata stamattina.	The baby girl *was born* this morning.
Il morto era nato novantadue anni fa.	The dead man *was born* 92 years ago.
Dante Alighieri nacque secoli fa.	Dante Alighieri *was born* centuries ago.

(iv)   *Other past tenses*

The remainder of the past tenses in Italian are compound tenses. They are formed using the appropriate tense of the auxiliary verbs **avere** or **essere** and the past participle [➤ 5b(ii)].

(v)   *The perfect tense*

The perfect tense is formed in Italian by using the present tenses of **avere** or **essere** and the past participle of the verb. To form the past participle of regular verbs, remove the infinitive ending and add the appropriate ending:

-are	-ato
-ere	-uto
-ire	-ito

comprare	*vendere*	*finire*
ho comprato	ho venduto	ho finito
hai comprato	hai venduto	hai finito
ha comprato	ha venduto	ha finito
abbiamo comprato	abbiamo venduto	abbiamo finito
avete comprato	avete venduto	avete finito
hanno comprato	hanno venduto	hanno finito

andare	*venire*	*lavarsi*
sono andato/a	sono venuto/a	mi sono lavato/a
sei andato/a	sei venuto/a	ti sei lavato/a
è andato/a	è venuto/a	si è lavato/a
siamo andati/e	siamo venuti/e	ci siamo lavati/e
siete andati/e	siete venuti/e	vi siete lavati/e
sono andati/e	sono venuti/e	si sono lavati/e

Note: Most intransitive verbs, most impersonal verbs and all reflexives take **essere** in their perfect tense. In the *Verb Index* these are marked *****.

Some of the most common verbs taking **essere** are as follows:

andare (andato)	go	**restare (restato)**	stay
arrivare (arrivato)	arrive	**rimanere (rimasto)**	remain
†correre (corso)	run	**riuscire (riuscito)**	succeed
cadere (caduto)	fall	**salire (salito)**	go up
essere (stato)	be	**scendere (sceso)**	go down
morire (morto)	die	**scoppiare (scoppiato)**	burst
nascere (nato)	be born	**sembrare (sembrato)**	seem
parere (parso)	appear	**tornare (tornato)**	return
partire (partito)	leave	**uscire (uscito)**	go out
piacere (piaciuto)	please	**venire (venuto)**	come

Note: †**correre** can take **avere** when used with a direct object:

Giovanni ha corso un grave rischio quel giorno.	Giovanni ran a great risk that day.

All verbs marked † in the *Verb Index* take **essere** when used intransitively and **avere** when used transitively.

 Many past participles are irregular and will need to be learned.

The perfect tense is used to describe:

• a single completed action in the past:

Ho letto il suo libro.	I read his book.

• an action taking place in the past but continuing up to the present:

Fino adesso Anna ha scritto 3 libri.	Up to now Anna has written 3 books.

• an action which has recently taken place:

Oggi Antonio è venuto a trovarmi.	Antonio came to see me today.
Stamattina sono andata al mercato.	I went to the market this morning.
Abbiamo finito i compiti!	We have finished the homework!
Maria ha scritto due lettere stasera.	Maria has written 2 letters this evening.

(vi) The pluperfect tense

The pluperfect tense is formed with the imperfect tense of **avere** or **essere** and the past participle.

comprare	*vendere*	*finire*
avevo comprato	avevo venduto	avevo finito
avevi comprato	avevi venduto	avevi finito
aveva comprato	aveva venduto	aveva finito
avevamo comprato	avevamo venduto	avevamo finito
avevate comprato	avevate venduto	avevate finito
avevano comprato	avevano venduto	avevano finito

andare	*venire*	*lavarsi*
ero andato/a	ero venuto/a	mi ero lavato/a
eri andato/a	eri venuto/a	ti eri lavato/a
era andato/a	era venuto/a	si era lavato/a
eravamo andati/e	eravamo venuti/e	ci eravamo lavati/e
eravate andati/e	eravate venuti/e	vi eravate lavati/e
erano andati/e	erano venuti/e	si erano lavati/e

The pluperfect tense is used to take a step back in time in the past. It corresponds to the English 'had'.

Antonio aveva scritto due righe.	Antonio had written a note (two lines).
Avevo mangiato bene.	I had eaten well.
Ero arrivato tardi.	I had arrived late.

(vii) The past anterior

The past anterior has the same meaning as the pluperfect tense. It also corresponds to the English 'had' and is formed with the past definite tense of **avere** or **essere** and the past participle:

comprare	*vendere*	*finire*
ebbi comprato	ebbi venduto	ebbi finito
avesti comprato	avesti venduto	avesti finito
ebbe comprato	ebbe venduto	ebbe finito
avemmo comprato	avemmo venduto	avemmo finito
aveste comprato	aveste venduto	aveste finito
ebbero comprato	ebbero venduto	ebbero finito

andare	*venire*	*lavarsi*
fui andato/a	fui venuto/a	mi fui lavato/a
fosti andato/a	fosti venuto/a	ti fosti lavato/a
fu andato/a	fu venuto/a	si fu lavato/a
fummo andati/e	fummo venuti/e	ci fummo lavati/e
foste andati/e	foste venuti/e	vi foste lavati/e
furono andati/e	furono venuti/e	si furono lavati/e

  The past anterior is rarely used in speech.

It can only be used in subordinate clauses introduced by a conjunction of time, when the verb of the main clause is in the past definite.

Quando ebbi finito, me ne andai.	When I had finished, I went away.
Appena fu arrivato, cominciò a fumare.	As soon as he arrived he started to smoke.

6c   *The future tenses*

(i)   *The simple future*

The present tense in Italian can be used to denote the future.

Dove vai in vacanza?	Where are you going on holiday/vacation?
Vado in Italia quest'estate.	I am going to Italy this summer.
A che ora arriva Paolo?	What time is Paolo arriving?
Arriva alle otto.	He is arriving at eight.

(ii)   *The future*

The future tense is formed in Italian by attaching these modified forms of the present tense of **avere** to the infinitive without the **-e.**

-ò, -ai, -à, -emo, -ete, -anno

Note: -are verbs change their stem to -er in the future:

comprare	*vendere*	*finire*
comprerò	venderò	finirò
comprerai	venderai	finirai
comprerà	venderà	finirà
compreremo	venderemo	finiremo
comprerete	venderete	finirete
compreranno	venderanno	finiranno

The verbs **avere** and **essere** have irregular future stems:

avr-	avrò		sar-	sarò

The following verbs have contracted stems (i.e. they lose the characteristic vowel of the infinitive ending).

andare	andrò	potere	potrò
cadere	cadrò	sapere	saprò
dovere	dovrò	vedere	vedrò
morire	morrò	vivere	vivrò

Some verbs and their compounds undergo a slight modification to their spelling so that the stem doubles the **-r.**

bere	berrò	valere	varrò
parere	parrò	venire	verrò
rimanere	rimarrò	volere	vorrò
tenere	terrò		

A few verbs retain the vowel of the infinitive ending.

dare	darò	stare	starò
fare	farò		

Verbs ending in **-ciare/-giare** drop the **i** before the **-er** of the future tense.

cominciare	comincerò	mangiare	mangerò

Verbs ending in **-care** and **-gare** will add an **h** after the **c** or the **g** throughout the future tense to retain the hard sound.

cercare	cercherò	pagare	pagherò

The future tense is used to refer to what is going to happen.

Andrò a Roma l'anno prossimo.   I shall go to Rome next year.

It is used after **se** or a conjunction of time if the main verb is future.

Se lo vedrò, glielo spiegherò.	If I see him, I shall explain it to him.
Quando arriverà, gliene parlerò.	When he arrives, I shall speak to him about it.

It can also denote probability.

Sarà un coltello?	Is it (perhaps) a knife?
Saranno i miei genitori alla porta.	It must be my parents at the door.

(iii) The future perfect

The future perfect tense is used to take a step forward from a time in the past. It expresses the idea of 'will have', or indicates probability. It is formed with the future tense of **avere** or **essere** and the past participle.

comprare	*vendere*	*finire*
avrò comprato	avrò venduto	avrò finito
avrai comprato	avrai venduto	avrai finito
avrà comprato	avrà venduto	avrà finito
avremo comprato	avremo venduto	avremo finito
avrete comprato	avrete venduto	avrete finito
avranno comprato	avranno venduto	avranno finito

andare	*venire*	*lavarsi*
sarò andato/a	sarò venuto/a	mi sarò lavato/a
sarai andato/a	sarai venuto/a	ti sarai lavato/a
sarà andato/a	sarà venuto/a	si sarà lavato/a
saremo andati/e	saremo venuti/e	ci saremo lavati/e
sarete andati/e	sarete venuti/e	vi sarete lavati/e
saranno andati/e	saranno venuti/e	si saranno lavati/e

Quando avrò finito i compiti, guarderò la televisione.	When I have finished the exercises, I shall watch television.
Saranno andati al bar.	They will/must have gone to the bar.
Avrà perso la borsa.	She must have lost her bag.

6d   *The conditional*

(i)   *The present conditional*

The present tense of the conditional mood is formed by adding the following endings to the future stem: **-ei, -esti, -ebbe, -emmo, -este, -ebbero.**

comprare	*vendere*	*finire*
comprer**ei**	vender**ei**	finir**ei**
comprer**esti**	vender**esti**	finir**esti**
comprer**ebbe**	vender**ebbe**	finir**ebbe**
comprer**emmo**	vender**emmo**	finir**emmo**
comprer**este**	vender**este**	finir**este**
comprer**ebbero**	vender**ebbero**	finir**ebbero**

Note: The irregular future stems in 6c also apply to the conditional.

The conditional is used to express an English conditional form.

| **Dovrei andare a scuola.** | *I should* go to school. |
| **Vorrei comprare dei fiori.** | *I would like* to buy some flowers. |

It is also used to express a wish more politely.

| **Potrei avere un po' di zucchero?** | *Could I* have some sugar? |
| **Mi *accompagneresti* domani?** | *Will you come with* me tomorrow? |

The verb **gradire** can also be used in the conditional to stress politeness.

| **Gradirei una risposta alla mia lettera.** | *I would like* a reply to my letter. |
| **Gradiremmo sapere i prezzi da Voi praticati.** | *We would like* to know your prices. |

(ii)   *The conditional perfect*

The perfect tense of the conditional mood is used to convey the idea of 'would have' or that the statement reported is hearsay. It is formed with the present conditional of **avere** or **essere** and the past participle.

comprare	*vendere*	*finire*
avrei comprato	avrei venduto	avrei finito
avresti comprato	avresti venduto	avresti finito
avrebbe comprato	avrebbe venduto	avrebbe finito
avremmo comprato	avremmo venduto	avremmo finito
avreste comprato	avreste venduto	avreste finito
avrebbero comprato	avrebbero venduto	avrebbero finito

andare	*venire*	*lavarsi*
sarei andato/a	sarei venuto/a	mi sarei lavato/a
saresti andato/a	saresti venuto/a	ti saresti lavato/a
sarebbe andato/a	sarebbe venuto/a	si sarebbe lavato/a
saremmo andati/e	saremmo venuti/e	ci saremmo lavati/e
sareste andati/e	sareste venuti/e	vi sareste lavati/e
sarebbero andati/e	sarebbero venuti/e	si sarebbero lavati/e

Note: According to the sequence of tenses in Italian, when the main verb is in the past tense, any subordinate conditional clause must also be in the past.

Avrei voluto imparare il giapponese.	I would have liked to have learnt Japanese.
Lasciò detto che sarebbe tornato alle otto.	He left word to say that he would be returning at eight o'clock.
A quanto dicono i giornali, la disoccupazione sarebbe cresciuta durante gli ultimi dieci anni.	From what the newspapers say, unemployment has increased during the last ten years.

7 Requests and commands: the imperative

7a The informal imperative: tu, noi, voi

(i) Apart from the **tu** form of **-are** verbs, the imperative of regular verbs is the same as the present indicative:

tu form	*noi* form	*voi* form
parla	parliamo	parlate
vendi	vendiamo	vendete
dormi	dormiamo	dormite
finisci	finiamo	finite

A few verbs are irregular in the **tu** and, occasionally, the **voi** forms.

andare	va'	andate
avere	abbi'	**abbiate**
dare	da'	date
dire	di'	dite
essere	sii	**siate**
fare	fa'	fate
sapere	sappi	**sappiate**
stare	sta'	state

Pronouns are attached to the end of the informal imperative.

Parla alla mamma!	Speak to mum/mom!
Andiamo in Italia!	Let's go to Italy!
Trovate quei libri!	Find those books!
Fammi un piacere!	Do me a favour/favor!
Digli che venga a casa mia.	Tell him to come to my house.

7b Informal negative imperatives

The informal negative **tu** form is formed by adding **non** before the infinitive. Pronouns are attached to the end of the infinitive, which then drops the **-e.**

The plurals are formed by placing **non** before the **noi** or **voi** form of the informal imperative:

Non parlargli!	Don't speak to him!
Non vendere quella gonna!	Don't sell that skirt!
Non andarci!	Don't go there!
Non facciamo i compiti!	Let's not do our homework!
Non finite l'articolo!	Don't finish the article!

7c   *Polite imperatives:* Lei, Loro

All formal imperatives are formed using the **Lei** or **Loro** form of the present subjunctive. Any irregularity in the present subjunctive will, of course, occur in these imperatives [➤8].

Note: 1) The formal form **Loro** is often now replaced by the less formal **voi** form, which avoids the use of the subjunctive. Therefore in the *Model verb* section the **Loro** form is not given, but can of course be worked out from the **Loro** form of the present subjunctive, if required.

2) With the exception of **loro** 'to them', pronouns come before the imperative form of the verb.

Mi passi il sale, per favore.	(Would you) pass me the salt, please.
Gli dia quella penna per favore.	(Would you) give him that pen, please.
Mi mostri il libro che ha comprato.	(Would you) show me the book you have bought.
Finiscano adesso.	Finish now.

8 Areas of uncertainty: the subjunctive

8a The present subjunctive

(i) The present subjunctive of regular verbs is formed by adding the following endings to the stem:

-are	**-i, -i, -i, -iamo, -iate, -ino**
-ere	**-a, -a, -a, -iamo, -iate, -ano**
-ire	**-a, -a, -a, -iamo, -iate, -ano** (**dormire** type verbs)
-ire	**-isca, -isca, -isca, -iamo, -iate, -iscano**
	(**finire** type verbs)

parlare	*vendere*	*dormire*	*finire*
parl**i**	vend**a**	dorm**a**	fin**isca**
parl**i**	vend**a**	dorm**a**	fin**isca**
parl**i**	vend**a**	dorm**a**	fin**isca**
parl**iamo**	vend**iamo**	dorm**iamo**	fin**iamo**
parl**iate**	vend**iate**	dorm**iate**	fin**iate**
parl**ino**	vend**ano**	dorm**ano**	fin**iscano**

(ii) There are a number of irregular verbs.

Most irregular verbs are formed from the first person singular of the irregular present indicative.

andare	vada, vada, vada, andiamo, andiate, vadano
bere	beva, beva, beva, beviamo, beviate, bevano
dire	dica, dica, dica, diciamo, diciate, dicano
dovere	debba, debba, debba, dobbiamo, dobbiate, debbano
fare	faccia, faccia, faccia, facciamo, facciate, facciano
morire	muoia, muoia, muoia, moriamo, moriate, muoiano
parere	paia, paiano
potere	possa, possa, possa, possiamo, possiate, possano
rimanere	rimanga, rimanga, rimanga, rimaniamo, rimaniate, rimangano
scegliere	scelga, scelga, scelga, scegliamo, scegliate, scelgano
tenere	tenga, tenga, tenga, teniamo, teniate, tengano
tradurre	traduca, traduca, traduca, traduciamo, traduciate, traducano
uscire	esca, esca, esca, usciamo, usciate, escano
venire	venga, venga, venga, veniamo, veniate, vengano
volere	voglia, voglia, voglia, vogliamo, vogliate, vogliano

However, some are formed from the **noi** form of the present indicative

avere	abbia, abbia, abbia, abbiamo, abbiate, abbiano
dare	dia, dia, dia, diamo, diate, diano
essere	sia, sia, sia, siamo, siate, siano
sapere	sappia, sappia, sappia, sappiamo, sappiate, sappiano
stare	stia, stia, stia, stiamo, stiate, stiano

8b   The imperfect subjunctive

The imperfect subjunctive is formed by adding the following endings to the stem of the infinitive.

-are	**-assi, -assi, -asse, -assimo, -aste, -assero**
-ere	**-essi, -essi, -esse, -essimo, -este, -essero**
-ire	**-issi, -issi, -isse, -issimo, -iste, -issero**

comprare	*vendere*	*finire*
comprassi	vendessi	finissi
comprassi	vendessi	finissi
comprasse	vendesse	finisse
comprassimo	vendessimo	finissimo
compraste	vendeste	finiste
comprassero	vendessero	finissero

The following verbs are irregular:

dare	**dessi** etc.	**stare**	**stessi** etc.
essere	**fossi** etc.		

All verbs with contracted infinitives revert to their obsolete forms.

bere	**bevessi** etc.	**fare**	**facessi** etc.
dire	**dicessi** etc.		

Note also verbs in **-durre** and **-arre:**

produrre	**producessi** etc.	**trarre**	**traessi** etc.

8c   Compound subjunctive tenses

The compound subjunctive tenses are formed by using the appropriate subjunctive tense of the auxiliary verb, followed by the past participle of the main verb.

(i) *The perfect subjunctive*

This is formed by using the present subjunctive of **avere** or **essere** with the past participle.

| parlare | abbia parlato etc. | capire | abbia capito etc. |
| accorgersi | mi sia accorto etc. | | |

(ii) *The pluperfect subjunctive*

The pluperfect subjunctive is formed by using the imperfect subjunctive of **avere** or **essere** with the past participle.

parlare	avessi parlato etc.
capire	avessi capito etc.
accorgersi	mi fossi accorto etc.

8d   Use of the subjunctive

The subjunctive is used:

• as a polite imperative [➤7c]

| Mi dia un piatto per favore. | (Would you) give me a plate, please. |
| Venga pure ! | Please do come ! |

• in many subordinate clauses introduced by **che**

(i)   *expressing commands, following these verbs:*

dire	tell
ordinare	order
proibire	forbid, prohibit

Ha ordinato che io venga con te.	He has ordered me to come with you.
Digli che debba accompagnarci al teatro.	Tell him that he must accompany us to the theatre.
Proibisco che tu esca stasera.	I forbid you to go out tonight.

(ii)   *expressing preference, desire or insistence, following the verbs:*

| aspettare | await | lasciare | let |
| aspettarsi | expect | permettere | permit, allow |

attendere	await	**piacere**	like (impersonal)
augurarsi	wish, hope	**preferire**	prefer
desiderare	want	**sperare**	hope
impedire	prevent	**suggerire**	suggest
insistere	insist	**volere**	want, wish

Ha voluto che si parlasse inglese qui.	He wanted English to be spoken here.
Preferisce che tu rimanga in Italia.	He prefers you to stay in Italy.
Non permetto che tu esca stasera!	I won't allow you to go out tonight!
Impedì che visitassero la nonna.	He prevented them from visiting grandmother.

(iii) *expressing opinion, doubt, ignorance or denial following the verbs:*

credere	believe	**(non) dire**	(not) say
dubitare	doubt	**negare**	deny
pensare	think	**(non) sapere**	(not) know
ritenere	consider, think		

Penso che Domenico abbia ragione.	I think Domenico is right.
Dubito che Gianni venga stasera.	I doubt whether Gianni will come this evening.
Non dico che Antonia abbia ragione.	I am not saying that Antonia is right.
Non so se abbia molto denaro.	I do not know whether he has much money.
Nego che Gianni abbia rotto quella finestra.	I deny that Gianni broke that window.
Non dico che non sia vero.	I am not saying it isn't true.

Note: However, if there is no doubt at all, the indicative may be used with verbs expressing positive opinion.

Credo che Luigi potrà aiutarci.	I believe/am sure that Luigi will be able to help us.

(iv) *expressing emotions following the verbs:*

avere paura	be afraid	**essere sconvolto**	be upset
dispiacere	be sorry, regret	**essere sorpreso**	be surprised
essere arrabbiato	be angry	**essere spiacente**	be sorry
essere contento	be happy, pleased	**essere triste**	be sad
essere deluso	be disappointed	**meravigliarsi**	be amazed
essere felice	be happy, pleased	**rincrescere**	regret
essere infelice	be unhappy, displeased	**stupirsi**	be surprised
		temere	fear
essere scontento	be unhappy, displeased		

Mi dispiace che Giovanni non ci accompagni.	I am sorry that Giovanni is not coming with us.
Sono contenta che tu sia venuta ad incontrarmi.	I am pleased that you have come to meet me.
Mi meraviglio che tu sia riuscito ad aprirla.	I am amazed that you managed to open it.

If the subject is the same in both halves of the sentence, an infinitive construction is preferred.

Sono contenta di incontrarti.	I am pleased to meet you.

(v) *after many impersonal verbs followed by* ***che:***

accade	it happens	**è possibile**	it is possible
basta	it is enough	**è preferibile**	it is preferable
bisogna	it is necessary	**è probabile**	it is probable
capita	it happens	**è strano**	it is strange
conviene	it is better/advisable	**è un peccato**	it is a pity
è bene	it is a good thing	**è utile**	it is useful
è difficile	it is difficult	**importa**	it matters/is important
è facile	it is easy	**occorre**	it is necessary
è impossibile	it is impossible	**pare**	it seems/appears
è improbabile	it is unlikely	**può darsi**	it may be
è inutile	it is useless/pointless	**è necessario**	it is necessary
è male	it is a bad thing	**sembra**	it seems

è meglio	it is better	**succede**	it happens
è naturale	it is natural	**vale la pena**	it is worth it
è peggio	it is worse		

Note that the verbs are given here in the present tense, but they may well be found in other tenses.

Pare che abbia ragione.	It appears that he/she is right/you are right.
Bisogna che vadano subito a vedere Giuliana.	They must go to see Giuliana immediately.
È meglio che esca adesso.	It's better that he/she goes out/you go out now.
È un peccato che tu non sia qui.	It's a pity that you are not here.
Sembrava che avesse già visto quel film.	It seemed that he had already seen that film.
Non è possibile che Simone sia uscito a quest'ora.	It is not possible that Simone has gone out at this time.

Note that many of these impersonal expressions may be followed by the infinitive in Italian, as in English.

È meglio uscire adesso.	It is better to go out now.

(vi) *after certain conjunctions:*

a condizione che	on condition that	**per paura che (non)**	for fear that
a meno che (non)	unless	**perché**	so that, in order that
a patto che	on condition that	**prima che**	before
affinché	so that	**purché**	provided that, on condition that
benché	although, even though, even if	**qualora**	in case, if
caso mai	should, in the event that	**quand'anche**	even if
come se	as if	**salvo che (non)**	unless, provided that
finché non	until	**sebbene**	although, even though, even if
in maniera che	so that	**senza che**	without

in/di modo che	so that	**seppure**	even though, even if
malgrado che	in spite of the fact that	**supposto che**	supposing that
nel caso che	in case	**se, quando, qualora**	if
nonostante che	in spite of the fact that		

Telefonagli prima che esca.	Call him before he goes out.
Benché abbiano ragione, non voglio partire.	Although they are right, I do not want to leave.
Caso mai faccia brutto tempo domani, possiamo andare al cinema.	Should the weather be bad tomorrow, we can go to the cinema/movies.
Gli ho dato i soldi perché andasse al cinema.	I gave him some money so that he could go to the cinema/movies.

Note   **Perché** takes the indicative when it means 'because'. **in modo che** and **in maniera che** also take the indicative when they mean 'with the result that' (i.e. when the action has clearly happened).

Se often takes the indicative in the present and future tenses, and when it means 'whether', but it can *never* be followed by a conditional. When the main verb is in the present or perfect conditional, the verb of the **se** conditional clause must be in the imperfect or the pluperfect subjunctive, according to the sense.

Se mi avesse parlato, avrei detto di sì.	If he had spoken to me, I would have said yes.
Se andasse a trovare la nonna, sarei molto contenta.	If she were to go and see her grandmother, I would be very pleased.

(vii)   *in indirect statements expressing doubt and in some indirect questions, though it is not always obligatory:*

Si dice che il professore sia un uomo alto e bello.	They say that the teacher is a tall, handsome man.
Mi hanno chiesto come fossi venuto in Italia.	They asked me how I had come to Italy.

Il capitano domandò dove andassero i ragazzi.	The captain asked where the boys were going.
Mi domando perché Anna abbia parlato così.	I wonder why Ann spoke like that.
Chi ha chiesto se Antonella potesse venire alla festa?	Who asked whether Antonella could come to the party?

(viii)   after indefinite pronouns and adjectives:

chiunque	whoever
comunque	however, no matter how
dovunque	wherever
qualunque	whichever
qualunque cosa	whatever
qualsiasi cosa	whatever

Chiunque venga con me, deve essere disposto a guidare.	Whoever comes with me must be willing to drive.
Qualunque decisione prenda, fammela sapere domani.	Whichever decision you take, let me know tomorrow.
Qualunque cosa io faccia, trovo sempre difficoltà.	Whatever I do, I always find difficulties.

(ix)   after a negative, comparitive or a superlative in the previous clause:

Non c'è nessuno qui che sappia parlare tedesco.	There is no-one here who can speak German.
Questa donna è più intelligente che *non* sembri.	This woman is more intelligent than she appears.
Giovanni è l'uomo più pigro che io abbia mai conosciuto.	Giovanni is the laziest man I have ever known.
Anna è l'unica persona che sia in grado di scrivere una tale lettera.	Anna is the only person capable of writing such a letter.

Note that, in the second example, the word **non** must be inserted before the verb. Note also that the words **primo, ultimo, unico,** and **solo** are treated as superlatives for this purpose.

(x)   *in certain exclamations:*

Fossi pazzo!	If I were mad!
Volesse il cielo!	Would to heaven!
Fosse possibile!	If only it were possible!

8e   *The sequence of tenses with the subjunctive*

The most usual combination of tenses are as follows:

(i)   *Main clause in present, future or perfect –*

subordinate clause in present or perfect subjunctive.

Spero che tu abbia ragione.	I hope you are right.
Mi ha chiesto come abbiano viaggiato.	He asked me how they had travelled.

(ii)   *Main clause in imperfect, perfect, past definite, pluperfect, conditional, conditional perfect –*

subordinate clause in imperfect or pluperfect subjunctive.

Pensavano che arrivasse alle otto.	They thought he was arriving at eight.
Bisognerebbe che lo studente cambiasse corso.	It would be necessary for the student to change course.
Impedì che venissero domani.	He stopped them from coming tomorrow.
Sperò che fossero partiti l'altro ieri.	He hoped that they had left the day before yesterday.

[For a more detailed explanation ➤Berlitz *Italian Grammar Handbook*.]

⑨ Things done to you: the passive

9a The true passive

The passive is formed when the object of the sentence becomes the subject:

L'uomo ha costruito la casa.	The man built the house.
La casa fu costruita (dall'uomo).	The house was built (by the man).

The object of the first sentence 'the house' has become the subject of the second.

(i) The passive with *essere*

In Italian the passive is usually formed by using an appropriate tense of the verb **essere** and the past participle of the verb. Here are the passive first person singular forms of the verb **lodare** 'praise' [➤ **comprare 1** for full passive forms].

PRESENT
sono lodato/a

IMPERFECT
ero lodato/a

PLUPERFECT
ero stato/a lodato/a

FUTURE
sarò lodato/a

CONDITIONAL
sarei lodato/a

PRESENT SUBJUNCTIVE
sia lodato/a

IMPERFECT SUBJUNCTIVE
fossi lodato/a

PERFECT
sono stato/a lodato/a

PAST DEFINITE
fui lodato/a

PAST ANTERIOR
fui stato/a lodato/a

FUTURE PERFECT
sarò stato/a lodato/a

CONDITIONAL PERFECT
sarei stato/a lodato/a

PERFECT SUBJUNCTIVE
sia stato/a lodato/a

PLUPERFECT SUBJUNCTIVE
fossi stato/a lodato/a

THE VERB SYSTEM IN ITALIAN

Note: The past participle always agrees in number and gender with the subject of the sentence, as in the following examples:

Il pranzo è servito.	Lunch is (being) served.
La cena è servita.	Dinner is (being) served.
La finestra fu rotta ieri.	The window was broken yesterday.
I ladri sono stati visti in città.	The thieves have been seen in town.

(ii) *The use of* **venire**

With verbs of action **venire** very often replaces **essere** as an auxiliary verb, but this is only possible in simple, not compound tenses.

La porta era chiusa.	The door was closed. (state)
La porta venne chiusa.	The door was (had just been) closed. (action)

Note:

Io vengo lodato/io sono lodato	I am praised.
But **Sono stato lodato**	I have been praised.

As **sono stato lodato** is a compound tense, **venire** cannot be used.

(iii) *The use of* **andare**

With verbs of losing, wasting, destroying, **andare** can be used to form the passive.

Una buona parola non va mai sprecata.	A good word is never wasted.
Andarono perduti dei documenti importantissimi.	Important documents went missing/were lost.

However, **andare** is more often used to indicate obligation.

Quella sedia va messa nell'angolo.	That chair should be put in the corner.
Costruirò la scuola come va costruita.	I shall build the school as it should be built.

9b   *Alternatives to the passive*

There are several ways of avoiding the passive.

• Use a reflexive verb.

Come si scrive il tuo nome?	How is your name written?

• Use the indefinite pronoun **si**

Si dice che sia fuggito.	It is said (They say) that he has fled.

• Use the third person plural form of the verb

Dicono che la bottega sia aperta oggi.	It is said that the shop is open today.

10 Reflexive verbs

In section 2f you will find a general explanation of reflexive verbs. Many verbs can be used both reflexively and as ordinary transitive verbs.

10a Reflexive pronouns

The full set of reflexive pronouns can be seen in the present tense of this reflexive verb

lavarsi	to wash oneself/get washed
mi lavo	I wash myself
ti lavi	you wash yourself (informal)
si lava	s/he washes her/himself
	you wash yourself (formal)
ci laviamo	we wash ourselves
vi lavate	you wash yourselves
si lavano	they wash themselves

Note: The pronouns can be abbreviated to **m'**, **t'**, **s'** in front of a vowel, although this is not obligatory.

10b Position of reflexive pronouns

Reflexive pronouns obey the same rules as other pronouns:

• they come *before* the verb in all tenses of the indicative and subjunctive:
• they come *after* the verb with the infinitive; and with the **tu, noi** and **voi** forms of the imperative.

Mi alzo alle sette ogni mattina.	I always get up at 7:00.
Bisogna alzarsi quando entra il maestro.	You need (It is necessary) to stand up when the teacher comes in.
Siediti qui accanto a me !	Sit down here next to me!
Sedetevi, ragazzi!	Sit down, boys!

10c Reflexive verbs and ne

Some verbs are not only reflexive, but also take **ne** as well, for example:

andarsene		to go away/leave
me	ne	**vado**
te	ne	**vai**
se	ne	**va**
ce	ne	**andiamo**
ve	ne	**andate**
se	ne	**vanno**

Note how the **-i** of the reflexive pronoun becomes an **-e** when followed by **ne**.

Verbs with **ne** are very often used colloquially:

prendersene	worry	**sedersene**	sit
scapparsene	slip away		

Sono stanca, me ne vado adesso!	I am tired, I am going now!
Se ne sta seduta senza aiutare la mamma !	She just sits there without helping mum/mom!

10d   Other uses of the reflexive

(i)   The reflexive is often used in Italian when a possessive adjective would be used in English:

Si lavano le mani.	They wash their hands.
Vi asciugate i capelli	You dry your hair.

(ii)   Plural reflexive verbs can be used to describe actions done to 'each other':

Si amano tanto.	They love each other so much.
Si scrivono ogni giorno.	They write to each other every day.

(iii)   A number of idiomatic phrases are formed with the reflexive verb and the feminine pronoun **la**:

Quel professore se la prende con tutti.	That teacher argues with everyone.
Ce la godiamo sempre qui alla spiaggia.	We always enjoy (it) here at the beach.

11 Types of Italian verbs

11a Predictability

Within each tense in Italian there are 6 different forms of the verb, each one corresponding to a particular person as follows:

first person singular	**io**	I
second person singular	**tu**	you (informal singular)
third person singular	**lui**	he
	lei	she
	Lei	you (formal singular)
first person plural	**noi**	we
second person plural	**voi**	you (informal/formal plural)
third person plural	**loro**	they
	Loro	you (formal plural)

Note: He, she, and you (formal singular) share the same verb form. **Loro** is rarely found nowadays and is frequently replaced by **voi**.

11b Regular verbs

Regular verbs are those verbs for which you can predict any part of any tense from the spelling of the infinitive. Infinitives in Italian end in **-are, -ere,** and **-ire**. Verbs in which some parts cannot be predicted in this way are *irregular*. Many common **-ere** verbs are irregular in Italian, but often only in their past participle and past definite forms. Some verbs also have an irregular, shortened, future stem and an irregular present subjunctive/formal imperative form.

11c Spelling change verbs

Some verbs make spelling changes in certain tenses.

(i) Verbs ending in **-care** and **-gare** insert an **h** after the **c** and the **g** when these letters are followed by **e** or **i.**

dimenticare	**dimentichi, dimentichiamo, dimenticherò,** etc.
pregare	**preghi, preghiamo, pregherò,** etc.

(ii) Verbs ending in **-ciare** and **-giare** drop the **i** before another **i** or an **e.**

lasciare	**lasci; lascerò** etc.
mangiare	**mangi; mangerò** etc.
viaggiare	**viaggi; viaggerò** etc.

(iii)   Other verbs in **-iare** which have an unstressed **i** in the first person singular drop the **i** before another **i.**

fischiare	**fischi, fischiamo** etc.
studiare	**studi, studiamo** etc.
imbrogliare	**imbrogli, imbrogliamo** etc.

(iv)   Verbs in **-iare** which have an stressed **i** in the first person singular keep the **i** when it is stressed before another **i.**

rinviare	**rinvii,** but **rinviamo** etc.
sciare	**scii,** but **sciamo** etc.

(v)   Verbs ending in **-scere** insert **i** before the **u** of the past participle only.

consoscere	**conosciuto,** but **conoscono** etc
mescere	**mesciuto,** but **mescono** etc
pascere	**pasciuto,** but **pascono** etc.

(vi)   Some verbs change their stem vowels in ceratin persons of the present tense, in order to facilitate pronunciation:

sedersi	**mi siedo, ti siedi, si siede,** ci sediamo, vi sedete, **si siedono**
muoversi	mi muovo, ti muovi, si muove, **ci moviamo, vi movete,** si muovono

11d   Compound verbs

Prefixes can be added to any verb as long as it makes sense. The following are the most common prefixes:

(i)   **ri-** can be used to indicate repetition, like 're-' in English:

cominciare	begin	**ricominciare**	begin again
fare	do	**rifare**	redo
leggere	read	**rileggere**	reread

(ii)   **s-** can sometimes be added to create the opposite meaning:

chiudere	close	**schiudere**	open

coprire	cover	**scoprire**	uncover, discover
gelare	freeze	**sgelare**	thaw

(iii) **mal-** gives the meaning of bad, badly or evil

trattare	treat	**maltrattare**	mistreat
intendere	understand	**malintendere**	misunderstand

(iv) Some common base verbs have a variety of prefixes, which often correspond to similar prefixes in English.

The verb **porre** 'place/put' has many compounds.

comporre	compose	**posporre**	postpone
decomporre	decompose	**presupporre**	presuppose
disporre	dispose	**proporre**	propose
imporre	impose	**supporre**	suppose
opporre	oppose		

The verb **tenere** 'hold' has many compounds which correspond to the English ending '-tain'.

contenere	contain	**ritenere**	retain
detenere	detain	**sostenere**	sustain
mantenere	maintain	**trattenere**	detain

Similarly the verb **venire** 'come' has a number of compounds.

avvenire	happen	**provenire**	come from, originate from
convenire	agree, suit	**sopravvenire**	arrive, happen
divenire	become	**svenire**	faint
intervenire	intervene		

Finally there are a number of verbs ending in **-durre.**

condurre	lead, drive	**ridurre**	reduce
dedurre	deduce	**riprodurre**	reproduce
indurre	induce, induct	**sedurre**	seduce
introdurre	introduce	**tradurre**	translate
produrre	produce		

B
MODEL VERBS

Index of model verbs

An * before a verb indicates that this verb takes **essere.**

A † before a verb indicates that this verb takes **essere** when intransitive, but **avere** when transitive.

If the verb is usually used impersonally, this is indicated by *(Imp.)*

The complete system of tenses in Italian		*Number*
comprare	buy	1
*entrare	enter	2

Regular verbs

parlare	speak	3
vendere	sell	4
dormire	sleep	5
finire	finish	6
*lavarsi	get washed	7

Verbs with obsolete infinitives

bere	drink	8
dire	say	9
fare	do	10

Spelling-change verbs

dimenticare	forget	11
mangiare	eat	12
fischiare	whistle	13
*sedersi	sit down	14
muovere	move	15
nuocere	harm	16

Irregular verbs

accendere	light	17
affiggere	stick, attach	18
affliggere	afflict	19
alludere	allude	20
*andare	go	21
annettere	annex	22

*apparire	appear	23	†potere	be able	65
aprire	open	24	prendere	take	66
assistere	assist, attend	25	proteggere	protect	67
assumere	assume	26	pungere	sting, prick	68
avere	have	27	radere	shave	69
*cadere	fall	28	reggere	rule, support	70
chiedere	ask	29	rendere	give back	71
chiudere	close	30	ridere	laugh	72
cogliere	gather	31	*rimanere	remain	73
comprimere	compress	32	risolvere	resolve	74
concedere	concede	33	rispondere	reply	75
conoscere	know	34	rompere	break	76
†correre	run	35	†salire	go up	77
crescere	grow	36	sapere	know	78
cuocere	cook	37	†scendere	go down	79
dare	give	38	scorgere	perceive	80
decidere	decide	39	scrivere	write	81
dirigere	direct	40	scuotere	shake	82
discutere	discuss	41	*solere	be used to	83
distinguere	distinguish	42	spargere	scatter	84
dividere	divide	43	spegnere	switch off	85
*dolere	ache	44	spingere	push	86
†dovere	have to	45	*stare	stand, to be	87
espellere	expel	46	stringere	squeeze	88
esplodere	explode	47	struggere	melt	89
*essere	be	48	tacere	be silent	90
*evadere	evade, escape	49	tendere	tend	91
fondere	melt	50	tenere	hold	92
*giacere	lie	51	tingere	dye	93
*giungere	reach	52	torcere	twist	94
leggere	read	53	tradurre	translate	95
mettere	put	54	trarre	pull	96
mordere	bite	55	uccidere	kill	97
*morire	die	56	udire	hear	98
*nascere	be born	57	*uscire	go out	99
*parere	appear	58	*valere	be worth	100
perdere	lose	59	vedere	see	101
persuadere	persuade	60	*venire	come	102
*piacere	please (Imp.)	61	vincere	win	103
piangere	cry	62	†vivere	live	104
†piovere	rain	63	†volere	want	105
porre	place	64	volgere	turn	106

Example of a verb using **avere** in the compound tenses

GERUND	*PAST PARTICIPLE*
comprando	comprato

PRESENT	*PERFECT*
compro	ho comprato
compri	hai comprato
compra	ha comprato
compriamo	abbiamo comprato
comprate	avete comprato
comprano	hanno comprato

PRESENT CONTINUOUS	*IMPERFECT CONTINUOUS*
sto comprando	stavo comprando
stai comprando	stavi comprando
sta comprando	stava comprando
stiamo comprando	stavamo comprando
state comprando	stavate comprando
stanno comprando	stavano comprando

IMPERFECT	*PAST DEFINITE*
compravo	comprai
compravi	comprasti
comprava	comprò
compravamo	comprammo
compravate	compraste
compravano	comprarono

PLUPERFECT	*PAST ANTERIOR*
avevo comprato	ebbi comprato
avevi comprato	avesti comprato
aveva comprato	ebbe comprato
avevamo comprato	avemmo comprato
avevate comprato	aveste comprato
avevano comprato	ebbero comprato

IMPERATIVE
compra (tu)   compriamo (noi)   comprate (voi)   compri (Lei)   comprino (Loro)

FUTURE
comprerò
comprerai
comprerà
compreremo
comprerete
compreranno

FUTURE PERFECT
avrò comprato
avrai comprato
avrà comprato
avremo comprato
avrete comprato
avranno comprato

CONDITIONAL
comprerei
compreresti
comprerebbe
compreremmo
comprereste
comprerebbero

CONDITIONAL PERFECT
avrei comprato
avresti comprato
avrebbe comprato
avremmo comprato
avreste comprato
avrebbero comprato

PRESENT SUBJUNCTIVE
compri
compri
compri
compriamo
compriate
comprino

PERFECT SUBJUNCTIVE
abbia comprato
abbia comprato
abbia comprato
abbiamo comprato
abbiate comprato
abbiano comprato

IMPERFECT SUBJUNCTIVE
comprassi
comprassi
comprasse
comprassimo
compraste
comprassero

PLUPERFECT SUBJUNCTIVE
avessi comprato
avessi comprato
avesse comprato
avessimo comprato
aveste comprato
avessero comprato

PASSIVE VOICE

For notes on other ways of expressing the passive ➤9b *The verb system in Italian.*

PRESENT
sono comprato/a
sei comprato/a
è comprato/a
siamo comprati/e
siete comprati/e
sono comprati/e

PERFECT
sono stato/a comprato/a
sei stato/a comprato/a
è stato/a comprato/a
siamo stati/e comprati/e
siete stati/e comprati/e
sono stati/e comprati/e

IMPERFECT
ero comprato/a
eri comprato/a
era comprato/a
eravamo comprati/e
eravate comprati/e
erano comprati/e

PAST DEFINITE
fui comprato/a
fosti comprato/a
fu comprato/a
fummo comprati/e
foste comprati/e
furono comprati/e

PLUPERFECT
ero stato/a comprato/a
eri stato/a comprato/a
era stato/a comprato/a
eravamo stati/e comprati/e
eravate stati/e comprati/e
erano stati/e comprati/e

PAST ANTERIOR
fui stato/a comprato/a
fosti stato/a comprato/a
fu stato/a comprato/a
fummo stati/e comprati/e
foste stati/e comprati/e
furono stati/e comprati/e

Notes ➤*The verb system in Italian* for explanations of the tenses. It is important to remember that all forms have the basic part or stem **compr-**, which contains the meaning of the verb. Many tenses are simple tenses, in which endings are added to this stem to form one word; other tenses are compound tenses, in which an auxiliary verb is used in the appropriate tense and form in front of the appropriate gerund or past participle of the verb.

FUTURE
sarò comprato/a
sarai comprato/a
sarà comprato/a
saremo comprati/e
sarete comprati/e
saranno comprati/e

FUTURE PERFECT
sarò stato/a comprato/a
sarai stato/a comprato/a
sarà stato/a comprato/a
saremo stati/e comprati/e
sarete stati/e comprati/e
saranno stati/e comprati/e

CONDITIONAL
sarei comprato/a
saresti comprato/a
sarebbe comprato/a
saremmo comprati/e
sareste comprati/e
sarebbero comprati/e

CONDITIONAL PERFECT
sarei stato/a comprato/a
saresti stato/a comprato/a
sarebbe stato/a comprato/a
saremmo stati/e comprati/e
sareste stati/e comprati/e
sarebbero stati/e comprati/e

PRESENT SUBJUNCTIVE
sia comprato/a
sia comprato/a
sia comprato/a
siamo comprati/e
siate comprati/e
siano comprati/e

PERFECT SUBJUNCTIVE
sia stato/a comprato/a
sia stato/a comprato/a
sia stato/a comprato/a
siamo stati/e comprati/e
siate stati/e comprati/e
siano stati/e comprati/e

IMPERFECT SUBJUNCTIVE
fossi comprato/a
fossi comprato/a
fosse comprato/a
fossimo comprati/e
foste comprati/e
fossero comprati/e

PLUPERFECT SUBJUNCTIVE
fossi comprato/a
fossi comprato/a
fosse stato/a comprato/a
fossimo stati/e comprati/e
foste stati/e comprati/e
fossero stati/e comprati/e

Remember that, in Italian, the subject pronouns (**io, tu** etc.) are not normally needed because the verb endings are so clear in both spoken and written forms. Pronouns are only used for emphasis, contrast, or to avoid ambiguity.

For notes on other ways of expressing the passive ➤9b *The verb system in Italian.*

Example of a verb using **essere** in its compound tenses

GERUND	PAST PARTICIPLE
entrando	entrato

PRESENT	PERFECT
entro	sono entrato/a
entri	sei entrato/a
entra	è entrato/a
entriamo	siamo entrati/e
entrate	siete entrati/e
entrano	sono entrati/e

PRESENT CONTINUOUS	IMPERFECT CONTINUOUS
sto entrando	stavo entrando
stai entrando	stavi entrando
sta entrando	stava entrando
stiamo entrando	stavamo entrando
state entrando	stavate entrando
stanno entrando	stavano entrando

IMPERFECT	PAST DEFINITE
entravo	entrai
entravi	entrasti
entrava	entrò
entravamo	entrammo
entravate	entraste
entravano	entrarono

PLUPERFECT	PAST ANTERIOR
ero entrato/a	fui entrato/a
eri entrato/a	fosti entrato/a
era entrato/a	fu entrato/a
eravamo entrati/e	fummo entrati/e
eravate entrati/e	foste entrati/e
erano entrati/e	furono entrati/e

Notes 1. All verbs taking **essere** are marked with an * in all the Notes to the model verb pages and in the Verb index.

2. All compound tenses using **essere** require gender agreements of the past participle – this may be masculine singular (**-o**), feminine singular (**-a**), feminine plural (**-e**), or masculine plural (**-i**).

IMPERATIVE
entra (tu)   entriamo (noi)   entrate (voi)   entri (Lei)   entrino (Loro)

FUTURE
entrerò
entrerai
entrerà
entreremo
entrerete
entreranno

FUTURE PERFECT
sarò entrato/a
sarai entrato/a
sarà entrato
saremo entrato
sarete entrato
saranno entrato

CONDITIONAL
entrerei
entreresti
entrerebbe
entreremmo
entrereste
entrerebbero

CONDITIONAL PERFECT
sarei entrato/a
saresti entrato/a
sarebbe entrato/a
saremmo entrati/e
sareste entrati/e
sarebbero entrati/e

PRESENT SUBJUNCTIVE
entri
entri
entri
entriamo
entriate
entrino

PERFECT SUBJUNCTIVE
sia entrato/a
sia entrato/a
sia entrato/a
siamo entrati/e
siate entrati/e
siano entrati/e

IMPERFECT SUBJUNCTIVE
entrassi
entrassi
entrasse
entrassimo
entraste
entrassero

PLUPERFECT SUBJUNCTIVE
fossi entrato/a
fossi entrato/a
fosse entrato/a
fossimo entrati/e
foste entrati/e
fossero entrati/e

Dubito che Gianna sia ancora entrata.

I doubt whether Gianna *has come* in yet.

Le ragazze *sono entrate* in macchina.

The girls *got into* the car.

First conjugation, regular -**are** verb

GERUND	PAST PARTICIPLE
parlando	parlato

PRESENT	PERFECT
parlo	ho parlato
parli	hai parlato
parla	ha parlato
parliamo	abbiamo parlato
parlate	avete parlato
parlano	hanno parlato

PRESENT CONTINUOUS	IMPERFECT CONTINUOUS
sto parlando	stavo parlando

IMPERFECT	PAST DEFINITE
parlavo	parlai
parlavi	parlasti
parlava	parlò
parlavamo	parlammo
parlavate	parlaste
parlavano	parlarono

Notes The regular -**are** verb conjugation is very large. As most regular verbs belong to this conjugation, only a small selection of the most useful verbs of the group are given below. In the verb index the main meanings of each verb are given. Several can also be found in the reflexive form e.g. **lavare** 'to wash', **lavarsi** 'to get washed'.

The only -**are** verbs which are irregular are **andare, dare, fare, stare**. These are dealt with in the irregular verb section.

Similar verbs

accompagnare	accompany	**aiutare**	help
***arrivare**	arrive	**chiamare**	call
***entrare**	enter	**guardare**	look, watch
lavare	wash	**lavorare**	work
portare	carry, wear	**trovare**	find

IMPERATIVE
parla (tu)   parliamo (noi)   parlate (voi)   parli (Lei)

PLUPERFECT
avevo parlato

PAST ANTERIOR
ebbi parlato

FUTURE
parlerò

FUTURE PERFECT
avrò parlato

CONDITIONAL
parlerei

CONDITIONAL PERFECT
avrei parlato

PRESENT SUBJUNCTIVE
parli

PERFECT SUBJUNCTIVE
abbia parlato

IMPERFECT SUBJUNCTIVE
parlassi

PLUPERFECT SUBJUNCTIVE
avessi parlato

– Con chi *stai parlando*?
– *Stavo parlando* con Gianni. Adesso *sto parlando* con Antonia.
– Hai *parlato* con Giuseppe?
– No, ma gli *parlerò* domani.
– Dubito che Giuseppe *abbia parlato* con tuo fratello.

– Guarda, *porta* una valigia molto pesante.
– Lo *chiamerò* ... Ti possiamo *aiutare*?
– Sì, grazie, mi *accompagnerete* a casa?»

– Who *are you speaking* to?
– *I was speaking* to Gianni. Now *I am speaking* to Antonia.
– *Have you spoken* to Giuseppe?
– No, but *I'll speak* to him tomorrow.
– I doubt whether Giuseppe *has spoken* to your brother.

– Look, *he is carrying* a very heavy case.
– *I'll call* him… Can we *help* you?
– Yes, please, *will you come home* with me?

Second conjugation, regular -**ere** verb

GERUND	*PAST PARTICIPLE*
vendendo	venduto

PRESENT	*PERFECT*
vendo	ho venduto
vendi	hai venduto
vende	ha venduto
vendiamo	abbiamo venduto
vendete	avete venduto
vendono	hanno venduto

PRESENT CONTINUOUS	*IMPERFECT CONTINUOUS*
sto vendendo	stavo vendendo

IMPERFECT	*PAST DEFINITE*
vendevo	vendei / vendetti
vendevi	vendesti
vendeva	vendé / vendette
vendevamo	vendemmo
vendevate	vendeste
vendevano	venderono / vendettero

Similar verbs

The following -**ere** verbs are regular and follow the pattern of **vendere**.

battere	beat	**credere**	believe
ricevere	receive	**ripetere**	repeat
temere	fear		

Notes   Many verbs in the -**ere** conjugation are either irregular, often in the past participle and past definite forms, or subject to spelling variations. The three verbs **bere, dire, fare** which are given in full later [➤8,9,10], also belong to this conjugation.

IMPERATIVE
vendi (tu)   vendiamo (noi)   vendete (voi)   venda (Lei)

PLUPERFECT
avevo venduto

PAST ANTERIOR
ebbi venduto

FUTURE
venderò

FUTURE PERFECT
avrò venduto

CONDITIONAL
venderei

CONDITIONAL PERFECT
avrei venduto

PRESENT SUBJUNCTIVE
venda
venda
venda
vendiamo
vendiate
vendano

PERFECT SUBJUNCTIVE
abbia venduto

IMPERFECT SUBJUNCTIVE
vendessi
vendessi
vendesse
vendessimo
vendeste
vendessero

PLUPERFECT SUBJUNCTIVE
avessi venduto

In addition, many **-ere** verbs can have both a reflexive and a non-reflexive form.

Note that the following present tense endings are the same as those of the **-are** verbs:

• the first person singular and plural
• the second person singular

5 dormire sleep

Third conjugation, regular **-ire** verb

GERUND	PAST PARTICIPLE
dormendo	dormito

PRESENT	PERFECT
dormo	ho dormito
dormi	hai dormito
dorme	ha dormito
dormiamo	abbiamo dormito
dormite	avete dormito
dormono	hanno dormito

PRESENT CONTINUOUS	IMPERFECT CONTINUOUS
sto dormendo	stavo dormendo

IMPERFECT	PAST DEFINITE
dormivo	dormii
dormivi	dormisti
dormiva	dormí
dormivamo	dormimmo
dormivate	dormiste
dormivano	dormirono

PLUPERFECT	PAST ANTERIOR
avevo dormito	ebbi dormito

Similar verbs

Some **-ire** verbs conjugate like **dormire**, others like **finire** [➤6]. A few are irregular and you will find these in the verb index.

The most commonly used verbs like **dormire** are:

bollire	boil	**consentire**	consent
***divertirsi**	amuse oneself	**†fuggire**	flee
***partire**	leave	***pentirsi**	repent
seguire	follow	**sentire**	feel, hear
servire	serve	**soffrire**	suffer

Notes 1. The gerund and following present tense endings are the same as those of the **-ere** verbs:

IMPERATIVE
dormi (tu)   dormiamo (noi)   dormite (voi)   dorma (Lei)   dormano (Loro)

FUTURE
dormirò

FUTURE PERFECT
avrò dormito

CONDITIONAL
dormirei

CONDITIONAL PERFECT
avrei dormito

PRESENT SUBJUNCTIVE
dorma
dorma
dorma
dormiamo
dormiate
dormano

PERFECT SUBJUNCTIVE
abbia dormito

IMPERFECT SUBJUNCTIVE
dormissi
dormissi
dormisse
dormissimo
dormiste
dormissero

PLUPERFECT SUBJUNCTIVE
avessi dormito

- the first person singular and plural
- the second person singular
- the third person singular and plural

2. The verb **riempire** follows the **dormire** pattern, with the exception of the gerund **riempiendo** and the present tense, where it adds an **i** before the endings of the first and third person singular and the third person plural:
riempio, riempi, riempie, riempiamo, riempite, riempiono.

– Ti *senti* meglio oggi?	– *Do* you *feel* better today?
– Sì, *ho dormito* molto bene stanotte.	– Yes, *I slept* very well last night.
Riempie le tasche di caramelle.	*He is filling* his pockets with sweets.

6 finire

Third conjugation, regular -**ire** verbs adding -**isc**-

GERUND	PAST PARTICIPLE
finendo	finito

PRESENT	PERFECT
fin**isc**o	ho finito
fin**isc**i	hai finito
fin**isc**e	ha finito
finiamo	abbiamo finito
finite	avete finito
fin**isc**ono	hanno finito

PRESENT CONTINUOUS	IMPERFECT CONTINUOUS
sto finendo	stavo finendo

IMPERFECT	PAST DEFINITE
finivo	finii
finivi	finisti
finiva	finí
finivamo	finimmo
finivati	finisti
finivano	finirono

Similar verbs

Some -**ire** verbs insert -**isc**- between the stem and the ending in the singular and third person plural of the present indicative and subjunctive tenses. These are indicated in the *Verb Index* by 6.

Some -**ire** verbs can follow the pattern of either **dormire** or **finire.** The most common are:

applaudire	applaud	**nutrire**	nourish
assorbire	absorb	**smentire**	deny
inghiottire	swallow	**tossire**	cough
mentire	lie		

IMPERATIVE
finisci (tu)   finiamo (noi)   finite (voi)   finisca (Lei)

PLUPERFECT avevo finito	**PAST ANTERIOR** ebbi finito
FUTURE finirò	**FUTURE PERFECT** avrò finito
CONDITIONAL finirei	**CONDITIONAL PERFECT** avrei finito
PRESENT SUBJUNCTIVE finisca finisca finisca finiamo finiate finiscano	**PERFECT SUBJUNCTIVE** abbia finito
IMPERFECT SUBJUNCTIVE finissi finissi finisse finissimo finiste finissero	**PLUPERFECT SUBJUNCTIVE** avessi finito

---

– *Capisci* **quando parla il tuo corrispondente?**	– *Do you understand* your penfriend when he speaks?
– **Sì, ma lo** *preferisco* **quando mi spedisce una lettera!**	– Yes, but *I prefer* it when *he sends* me a letter!
– **Il mio corrispondente** *ha suggerito* **un buon dizionario .**	– My penfriend *has suggested* a good dictionary.
– *Preferirei* **un buon traduttore.** *Sarebbe* **meno lavoro per me!**	– *I would prefer* a good translator. *It would be* less work for me.

7 lavarsi — wash oneself

Reflexive, regular -**are** verb

GERUND	PAST PARTICIPLE
lavandosi	lavato

PRESENT	PERFECT
mi lavo	mi sono lavato/a
ti lavi	ti sei lavato/a
si lava	si è lavato/a
ci laviamo	ci siamo lavati/e
vi lavate	vi siete lavati/e
si lavano	si sono lavati/e

PRESENT CONTINUOUS	IMPERFECT CONTINUOUS
mi sto lavando	mi stavo lavando

IMPERFECT	PAST DEFINITE
mi lavavo	mi lavai

Notes

Reflexive verbs can be either -**arsi**, -**ersi** or -**irsi** verbs. As such they follow the conjugation of the non-reflexive verb, i.e. -**are**, -**ere**, or -**ire**, whether regular or irregular.

In all cases the pronouns **mi, ti, si, ci, vi, si** will be used. In front of a vowel these can be abbreviated to **m', t', s', c', v', s'**. Before another pronoun they change to : **me, te, se, ce, ve, se.**

These pronouns normally precede the verb. However they follow the verb in the following cases :

• in the **tu, noi** and **voi** imperative forms
• with the past participle
• with the infinitive
• with the gerund

N.B. All reflexive verbs use **essere** in their compound tenses.

IMPERATIVE
lavati (tu) laviamoci (noi) lavatevi (voi) si lavi (Lei)

PLUPERFECT	*PAST ANTERIOR*
mi ero lavato/a	mi fui lavato/a

FUTURE	*FUTURE PERFECT*
mi laverò	mi sarò lavato/a

CONDITIONAL	*CONDITIONAL PERFECT*
mi laverei	mi sarei lavato/a

PRESENT SUBJUNCTIVE	*PERFECT SUBJUNCTIVE*
mi lavi	mi sia lavato/a

IMPERFECT SUBJUNCTIVE	*PLUPERFECT SUBJUNCTIVE*
mi lavassi	mi fossi lavato/a

Similar verbs

There are many reflexive verbs. Only some of the most common are listed here:

*abbronzarsi	tan	*abituarsi	get used to
*accomodarsi	come in, sit down	*alzarsi	get up, stand up
*arrabbiarsi	get angry	*avvicinarsi a	approach
*chiamarsi	be called	*divertirsi	enjoy oneself
*fermarsi	stop	*incontrarsi	meet
*interessarsi a/di	take an interest in	*perdersi	get lost
*pettinarsi	comb one's hair	*preoccuparsi	worry
*sbrigarsi	hurry up	*scusarsi	apologize
*sentirsi	feel	*svegliarsi	wake up
*vergognarsi	be ashamed	*vestirsi	get dressed

– **Vestiti**, Paolo, sono già le sette!	– *Get dressed,* Paolo, it's already 7:00 a.m.
– **Ma, mamma, non voglio svegliarmi!**	– But mum/mom, I don't want *to wake up.*
– **Vergognati, alzati** e **lavati** subito!	– *You should be ashamed* – *get up* and *get washed* immediately!
– **Mi alzerò** alle sette e mezzo.	– *I'll get up* at 7:30.

obsolete infinitive **bevere**

GERUND	PAST PARTICIPLE
bevendo	bevuto

IMPERATIVE
bevi (tu)   beviamo (noi)   bevete (voi)   beva (Lei)

PRESENT	PERFECT
bevo	ho bevuto

PRESENT CONTINUOUS	IMPERFECT CONTINUOUS
sto bevendo	stavo bevendo

IMPERFECT	PAST DEFINITE
bevevo	**bevvi** / bevei /bevetti
	bevesti
	bevve
	bevemmo
	beveste
	bevvero

PLUPERFECT	PAST ANTERIOR
avevo bevuto	ebbi bevuto

FUTURE	FUTURE PERFECT
berrò	avrò bevuto

CONDITIONAL	CONDITIONAL PERFECT
berrei	avrei bevuto

PRESENT SUBJUNCTIVE	PERFECT SUBJUNCTIVE
beva	abbia bevuto

IMPERFECT SUBJUNCTIVE	PLUPERFECT SUBJUNCTIVE
bevessi	avessi bevuto

Note   ►10 **fare** for notes on verbs with obsolete infinitives.

obsolete infinitive **dicere**

GERUND	*PAST PARTICIPLE*
dicendo	**detto**

IMPERATIVE
di' (tu)   diciamo (noi)   **dite** (voi)   dica (Lei)

PRESENT	*PERFECT*
dico	ho detto
dici	
dice	
diciamo	
dite	
dicono	

PRESENT CONTINUOUS	*IMPERFECT CONTINUOUS*
sto dicendo	stavo dicendo

IMPERFECT	*PAST DEFINITE*
dicevo	**dissi**
	dicesti
	disse
	dicemmo
	diceste
	dissero

PLUPERFECT	*PAST ANTERIOR*
avevo detto	ebbi detto

FUTURE	*FUTURE PERFECT*
dirò	avrò detto

CONDITIONAL	*CONDITIONAL PERFECT*
direi	avrei detto

PRESENT SUBJUNCTIVE	*PERFECT SUBJUNCTIVE*
dica	abbia detto

IMPERFECT SUBJUNCTIVE	*PLUPERFECT SUBJUNCTIVE*
dicessi	avessi detto

obsolete infinitive **facere**

GERUND	PAST PARTICIPLE
facendo	**fatto**

PRESENT	PERFECT
faccio	ho fatto
fai	
fa	
facciamo	
fate	
fanno	

PRESENT CONTINUOUS	IMPERFECT CONTINUOUS
sto facendo	stavo facendo

IMPERFECT	PAST DEFINITE
facevo	**feci**
	facesti
	fece
	facemmo
	faceste
	fecero

Similar verbs

contraffare	counterfeit
disfare	undo, unpack
soddisfare	satisfy

Note   The three verbs with obsolete infinitives (**bere** 8, **dire** 9 and **fare** 10) are exceptions. As can be seen above, sometimes the stem returns to the obsolete infinitive, sometimes it is shorter.

– **Dimmi, cosa *hai fatto* ieri sera?**	– Tell me what *did you* do yesterday evening?
– ***Ho detto* a Stefano di venire a trovarmi.**	– *I told* Stefano to come and call on me.
– **E cosa *avete fatto*?**	– And what *did you do*?
– ***Abbiamo bevuto* una birra e mangiato una pizza.**	– *We drank* a beer and ate a pizza.

IMPERATIVE
fa' (tu)   facciamo (noi)   **fate** (voi)   faccia (Lei)

PLUPERFECT avevo fatto	*PAST ANTERIOR* ebbi fatto
FUTURE **farò**	*FUTURE PERFECT* avrò fatto
CONDITIONAL **farei**	*CONDITIONAL PERFECT* avrei fatto
PRESENT SUBJUNCTIVE **faccia** **faccia** **faccia** **facciamo** **facciate** **facciano**	*PERFECT SUBJUNCTIVE* abbia fatto
IMPERFECT SUBJUNCTIVE facessi	*PLUPERFECT SUBJUNCTIVE* avessi fatto

---

To say you are having or getting something done, you use **fare** followed immediately by the infinitive. Note the use of **fare** in the following examples:

Ho fatto **riparare la macchina.**	*I have had* the car repaired.
Hai fatto **tradurre quella lettera?**	*Have you had* that letter translated?
Gianni mi *ha fatto* **aspettare un'ora!**	Gianni *made* me wait one hour.
Fammi **vedere!**	*Let* me see!
Le *faccio* **entrare?**	*Shall I let* the girls in?

-care/-gare verbs

GERUND	PAST PARTICIPLE
dimenticando	dimenticato

PRESENT	PERFECT
dimentico	ho dimenticato
dimentic**hi**	
dimentica	
dimentic**hiamo**	
dimenticate	
dimenticano	

PRESENT CONTINUOUS	IMPERFECT CONTINUOUS
sto dimenticando	stavo dimenticando

IMPERFECT	PAST DEFINITE
dimenticavo	dimenticai

Note   Verbs ending in **-care** or **-gare** insert an **h** after the **c** and the **g** when these letters are followed by **e** or **i**. In all other respects these verbs are regular.

Similar verbs

cercare	search, look for	leccare	lick
pagare	pay	pregare	pray

IMPERATIVE

dimentica (tu)   dimentic**hiamo** (noi)   dimenticate (voi)   dimenti**chi** (Lei)

PLUPERFECT avevo dimenticato	*PAST ANTERIOR* ebbi dimenticato
FUTURE dimenti**cherò**	*FUTURE PERFECT* avrò dimenticato
CONDITIONAL dimenti**cherei**	*CONDITIONAL PERFECT* avrei dimenticato
PRESENT SUBJUNCTIVE dimenti**chi**	*PERFECT SUBJUNCTIVE* abbia dimenticato
IMPERFECT SUBJUNCTIVE dimenticassi	*PLUPERFECT SUBJUNCTIVE* avessi dimenticato

Ho *dimenticato* dove ho messo la mia penna.	*I have forgotten* where I put my pen.
Ho *cercato* dappertutto.	*I have searched* everywhere.
Chi mi *pagherà* una nuova se l'ho persa?	Who *will pay* for a new one for me, if I have lost it?
Adesso *pregherò*.	Now I shall pray.

12 mangiare   eat

-ciare/-giare verbs

GERUND	*PAST PARTICIPLE*
mangiando	mangiato

PRESENT	*PERFECT*
mangio	ho mangiato
mang**i**	
mangia	
mang**iamo**	
mangiate	
mangiano	

PRESENT CONTINUOUS	*IMPERFECT CONTINUOUS*
sto mangiando	stavo mangiando

IMPERFECT	*PAST DEFINITE*
mangiavo	mangiai

Note   Verbs ending in **-ciare** or **-giare** drop the **i** before another **i** or an **e**.

Similar verbs

cominciare	begin	**pronunciare**	pronounce
lasciare	allow, leave	**viaggiare**	travel

IMPERATIVE
mangia (tu)   mang**iamo** (noi)   mangiate (voi)   mang**i** (Lei)

PLUPERFECT avevo mangiato	*PAST ANTERIOR* ebbi mangiato
FUTURE mang**erò**	*FUTURE PERFECT* avrò mangiato
CONDITIONAL mang**erei**	*CONDITIONAL PERFECT* avrei mangiato
PRESENT SUBJUNCTIVE mang**i**	*PERFECT SUBJUNCTIVE* abbia mangiato
IMPERFECT SUBJUNCTIVE mangiassi	*PLUPERFECT SUBJUNCTIVE* avessi mangiato

---

– *Viaggi* spesso in Italia?	– *Do you travel* to Italy often?
– Sì, so che ci *mangerò* molto bene.	– Yes, I know that *I will eat* very well there.
– *Lasci* i figli a casa?	– *Do you leave* your children at home?
– No, *viaggiamo* tutti insieme.	– No, *we* all *travel* together.

Other **-iare** verbs

GERUND	**PAST PARTICIPLE**
fischiando	fischiato

PRESENT	**PERFECT**
fischio	ho fischiato
fisch**i**	
fischia	
fisch**iamo**	
fischiate	
fischiano	

PRESENT CONTINUOUS	**IMPERFECT CONTINUOUS**
sto fischiando	stavo fischiando

IMPERFECT	**PAST DEFINITE**
fischiavo	fischiai

Note All other verbs in **-iare** drop the **i** before another **i**.

Similar verb

pigliare   take, catch

IMPERATIVE
fischia (tu)   fischiamo (noi)   fischiate (voi)   fischi (Lei)

PLUPERFECT avevo fischiato	**PAST ANTERIOR** ebbi fischiato
FUTURE fischierò	**FUTURE PERFECT** avrò fischiato
CONDITIONAL fischierei	**CONDITIONAL PERFECT** avrei fischiato
PRESENT SUBJUNCTIVE fischi	**PERFECT SUBJUNCTIVE** abbia fischiato
IMPERFECT SUBJUNCTIVE fischiassi	**PLUPERFECT SUBJUNCTIVE** avessi fischiato

---

Perché *fischi*?	Why *are you whistling*?
Chi dorme non piglia *pesci*.	The early bird catches the worm. (Lit. He who sleeps *catches* no fish.)

-ersi verb with change of vowel in present indicative and subjunctive tenses

GERUND	PAST PARTICIPLE
sedendosi	seduto

PRESENT	PERFECT
mi siedo	mi sono seduto/a
ti siedi	
si siede	
ci sediamo	
vi sedete	
si siedono	

PRESENT CONTINUOUS	IMPERFECT CONTINUOUS
mi sto sedendo	mi stavo sedendo

IMPERFECT	PAST DEFINITE
mi sedevo	mi sedei

Similar verbs

possedere	possess
sedere	be seated, to sit

Note The main irregular features of the verb are

• the present indicative and subjunctive tenses

IMPERATIVE
siediti (tu)   sediamoci (noi)   sedetevi (voi)   **si sieda** (Lei)

PLUPERFECT mi ero seduto/a	*PAST ANTERIOR* mi fui seduto/a
FUTURE mi sederò	*FUTURE PERFECT* mi sarò seduto/a
CONDITIONAL mi sederei	*CONDITIONAL PERFECT* mi sarei seduto/a
PRESENT SUBJUNCTIVE **mi sieda** **ti sieda** **si sieda** ci sediamo vi sediate **si siedano**	*PERFECT SUBJUNCTIVE* mi sia seduto/a
IMPERFECT SUBJUNCTIVE mi sedessi	*PLUPERFECT SUBJUNCTIVE* mi fossi seduto/a

---

– *Siediti* qui accanto a me!	– *Sit* here next to me!
– No, grazie, non mi *siedo*, ho fretta.	– No thank you, *I'll* not *sit down*, I'm in a hurry.
– Mi dispiace che non ti *sieda*, ho tanto da dirti.	– I am sorry that *you won't sit down*, I have a lot to tell you.
Possiede una memoria prodigiosa.	*He has* a wonderful memory.
Giovanni *sedeva* in una poltrona vicino alla finestra.	Giovanni *was sitting* in an armchair near the window.

-ere verb with change of vowel in present indicative, past definite and subjunctive tenses and past participle

GERUND	*PAST PARTICIPLE*
muovendo	**mosso**

PRESENT	*PERFECT*
muovo	ho mosso
muovi	
muove	
moviamo	
movete	
muovono	

PRESENT CONTINUOUS	*IMPERFECT CONTINUOUS*
sto muovendo	stavo muovendo

IMPERFECT	*PAST DEFINITE*
muovevo	**mossi**
	movesti
	mosse
	movemmo
	moveste
	mossero

Note   A few verbs change their vowels like **muovere**. These are indicated in the *Verb index* by 15.

Similar verbs

commuovere	move, affect
promuovere	promote, pass (exams)
smuovere	shift, displace

IMPERATIVE
muovi (tu)   **moviamo** (noi)   **movete** (voi)   muova (Lei)

PLUPERFECT avevo mosso	*PAST ANTERIOR* ebbi mosso
FUTURE muoverò	*FUTURE PERFECT* avrò mosso
CONDITIONAL muoverei	*CONDITIONAL PERFECT* avrei mosso
PRESENT SUBJUNCTIVE muova muova muova **moviamo** **moviate** muovano	*PERFECT SUBJUNCTIVE* abbia mosso
IMPERFECT SUBJUNCTIVE muovessi	*PLUPERFECT SUBJUNCTIVE* avessi mosso

Ci *moviamo*?	*Shall we move?*
Nessuno si è *mosso*.	No one *moved*.
***Mosse* la sedia.**	*He moved* the chair.
Era veramente *commossa*.	She *was* really *moved*.
Non fu *promosso* quest'anno.	*He did* not *pass* this year.
***Promosse* il nuovo progetto.**	He *promoted* the new project.
Se Stefano ha deciso è difficile *smuoverlo*.	If Stefano has decided it is difficult *to move* him.

-ere verb with change of vowel in present indicative, past definite and present subjunctive tenses

GERUND	*PAST PARTICIPLE*
nuocendo	**nociuto**

PRESENT	*PERFECT*
nuoccio / **noccio**	ho nociuto
nuoci	
nuoce	
nociamo	
nocete	
nuocciono / **nocciono**	

PRESENT CONTINUOUS	*IMPERFECT CONTINUOUS*
sto nuocendo	stavo nuocendo

IMPERFECT	*PAST DEFINITE*
nuocevo	**nocqui**
	nocesti
	nocque
	nocemmo
	noceste
	nocquero

IMPERATIVE
nuoci/**noci** (tu)   **nociamo** (noi)   **nocete** (voi)   **noccia** (Lei)

PLUPERFECT
avevo nociuto

PAST ANTERIOR
ebbi nociuto

FUTURE
nuocerò

FUTURE PERFECT
avrò nociuto

CONDITIONAL
nuocerei

CONDITIONAL PERFECT
avrei nociuto

PRESENT SUBJUNCTIVE
noccia
noccia
noccia
nociamo
nociate
nocciano

PERFECT SUBJUNCTIVE
abbia nociuto

IMPERFECT SUBJUNCTIVE
nuocessi

PLUPERFECT SUBJUNCTIVE
avessi nociuto

Dubito che *noccia* al bambino.	I doubt that *he will hurt* the child.
Non *nuoce* a nessuno.	He *is harming* nobody.
Non gli *nuocerei*.	*I would* not *harm* him.
Non *nuocerà* ripeterglielo.	*It wo*n't *hurt* to tell him again.

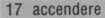
-endere verbs

GERUND	*PAST PARTICIPLE*
accendendo	**acceso**

PRESENT	*PERFECT*
accendo	ho acceso

PRESENT CONTINUOUS	*IMPERFECT CONTINUOUS*
sto accendendo	stavo accendendo

IMPERFECT	*PAST DEFINITE*
accendevo	**accesi**
	accendesti
	accese
	accendemmo
	accendeste
	accesero

Similar verbs

All verbs ending in **-endere**

appendere	hang
difendere	defend
dipendere	depend
intendere	intend
offendere	offend
sospendere	suspend
spendere	spend

For **prendere, rendere, scendere** and their compounds ➤Model Verbs 66, 71 and 79.

Note The main irregular features of the verb are

- the past definite tense
- the past participle

IMPERATIVE
accendi (tu)   accendiamo (noi)   accendete (voi)   accenda (Lei)

PLUPERFECT	*PAST ANTERIOR*
avevo acceso	ebbi acceso

FUTURE	*FUTURE PERFECT*
accenderò	avrò acceso

CONDITIONAL	*CONDITIONAL PERFECT*
accenderei	avrei acceso

PRESENT SUBJUNCTIVE	*PERFECT SUBJUNCTIVE*
accenda	abbia acceso

IMPERFECT SUBJUNCTIVE	*PLUPERFECT SUBJUNCTIVE*
accendessi	avessi acceso

Accese la luce.	He switched *on* the light.
Hai acceso il gas?	Have you switched *on* the gas?
Difesero la patria dal nemico.	They *defended* their country from the enemy.
Sa *difendere* la sua opinione.	He *knows* how to hold his own.
Ho difeso la causa del ragazzo ferito.	I *pleaded* the case for the injured boy.
Non credo che abbiano *difeso* la città.	I don't think that *they defended* the city.
Ho speso 50.000 lire oggi.	I *spent* 50,000 lire today.
Spese 80.000 lire per quella collana.	He *spent* 80,000 lire on that necklace.
Sospesi la lampada al soffitto.	I *hung* the lamp from the ceiling.
L'affare fu *sospeso* a causa della sua partenza.	The business was *adjourned* because of his departure.

GERUND affiggendo	*PAST PARTICIPLE* **affisso**

PRESENT affiggo	*PERFECT* ho affisso
PRESENT CONTINUOUS sto affiggendo	*IMPERFECT CONTINUOUS* stavo affiggendo
IMPERFECT affiggevo	*PAST DEFINITE* **affissi** affiggesti **affisse** affiggemmo affiggeste **affissero**

Note   The main irregular features of the verb are

• the past definite tense
• the past participle

IMPERATIVE
affiggi (tu) affiggiamo (noi) affiggete (voi) affigga (Lei)

PLUPERFECT avevo affisso	**PAST ANTERIOR** ebbi affisso
FUTURE affiggerò	**FUTURE PERFECT** avrò affisso
CONDITIONAL affiggerei	**CONDITIONAL PERFECT** avrei affisso
PRESENT SUBJUNCTIVE affigga	**PERFECT SUBJUNCTIVE** abbia affisso
IMPERFECT SUBJUNCTIVE affiggessi	**PLUPERFECT SUBJUNCTIVE** avessi affisso

---

Affisse lo sguardo sul cane.	*He fixed* his gaze on the dog.
Cosa ha *affisso* ?	What did *he stick up*?
– *Affiggo* il poster qui ?	– *Should I stick* the poster here?
– Lo *affigggerei* laggiù.	– *I would stick it down* there.

GERUND	**PAST PARTICIPLE**
affliggendo	**afflitto**

PRESENT	**PERFECT**
affliggo	ho afflitto

PRESENT CONTINUOUS	**IMPERFECT CONTINUOUS**
sto affliggendo	stavo affliggendo

IMPERFECT	**PAST DEFINITE**
affliggevo	**afflissi**
	affliggesti
	afflisse
	affliggemmo
	affliggeste
	afflissero

Similar verbs

friggere	fry
infliggere	inflict
sconfiggere	defeat
soffriggere	fry lightly
trafiggere	run through, pierce

Note   The main irregular features of the verb are

- the past definite tense
- the past participle

IMPERATIVE
affliggi (tu)   affliggiamo (noi)   affliggete (voi)   affligga (Lei)

PLUPERFECT	*PAST ANTERIOR*
avevo afflitto	ebbi afflitto
FUTURE	*FUTURE PERFECT*
affliggerò	avrò afflitto
CONDITIONAL	*CONDITIONAL PERFECT*
affliggerei	avrei afflitto
PRESENT SUBJUNCTIVE	*PERFECT SUBJUNCTIVE*
affligga	abbia afflitto
IMPERFECT SUBJUNCTIVE	*PLUPERFECT SUBJUNCTIVE*
affliggessi	avessi afflitto

Dubito che sia *afflitto* dai reumatismi.	I doubt whether he is troubled with rheumatism.
Sono *afflitta* dalla sinusite.	I *suffer* from sinusitis.
Inflisse una pena al colpeveole.	He *inflicted* a penalty on the guilty man.
Gli *ha inflitto* un colpo	He *inflicted* a blow on him.
Ho *soffritto* l'olio nella padella.	I *fried* the oil lightly in the pan.
L'olio *frigge* nella padella.	The oil *is frying* in the pan.
Il nemico lo *trafisse* con la spada.	The enemy *pierced* him with a sword.
Le parole le *trafissero* il cuore.	The words *pierced* her heart.

GERUND alludendo	**PAST PARTICIPLE** **alluso**

PRESENT alludo	**PERFECT** ho alluso

PRESENT CONTINUOUS sto alludendo	**IMPERFECT CONTINUOUS** stavo alludendo

IMPERFECT alludevo	**PAST DEFINITE** **allusi** alludesti **alluse** alludemmo alludeste **allusero**

Similar verbs

accludere	enclose
concludere	conclude
deludere	disappoint, delude
disilludere	disillusion
eludere	elude
escludere	exclude
illudere	deceive, delude, fool
includere	include

Note   The main irregular features of the verb are

- the past definite tense
- the past participle

IMPERATIVE
alludi (tu)   alludiamo (noi)   alludete (voi)   alluda (Lei)

PLUPERFECT	*PAST ANTERIOR*
avevo alluso	ebbi alluso
FUTURE	*FUTURE PERFECT*
alluderò	avrò alluso
CONDITIONAL	*CONDITIONAL PERFECT*
alluderei	avrei alluso
PRESENT SUBJUNCTIVE	*PERFECT SUBJUNCTIVE*
alluda	abbia alluso
IMPERFECT SUBJUNCTIVE	*PLUPERFECT SUBJUNCTIVE*
alludessi	avessi alluso

Si *alludeva* a questo durante la discussione ieri.	This *was alluded to* during the discussion yesterday.
Accludiamo un listino prezzi.	*We enclose* a price list.
Inclusi Giovanni nel numero degli invitati.	*I included* Giovanni in the guest list.
Ho escluso alcuni nomi.	*I excluded* some names.
Fu *escluso* dall'elenco.	He was *excluded* from the list.
Non *abbiamo concluso* niente oggi.	*We haven't achieved* anything today.
La faccenda fu *conclusa*.	The matter was *concluded*.

GERUND	**PAST PARTICIPLE**
andando	andato

PRESENT	**PERFECT**
vado	sono andato/a
vai	sei andato/a
va	è andato/a
andiamo	siamo andati/e
andate	siete andati/e
vanno	sono andati/e

PRESENT CONTINUOUS	**IMPERFECT CONTINUOUS**
sto andando	stavo andando

IMPERFECT	**PAST DEFINITE**
andavo	andai

Notes   **andare** is the only verb of this type. The main irregular features of the verb are

- the present indicative and subjunctive tenses
- the future stem

IMPERATIVE
va (tu)   andiamo (noi)   andate (voi)   **vada** (Lei)

PLUPERFECT
ero andato

PAST ANTERIOR
fui andato/a

FUTURE
andrò

FUTURE PERFECT
sarò andato/a

CONDITIONAL
andrei

CONDITIONAL PERFECT
sarei andato/a

PRESENT SUBJUNCTIVE
vada
vada
vada
andiamo
andiate
vadano

PERFECT SUBJUNCTIVE
sia andato/a

IMPERFECT SUBJUNCTIVE
andassi

PLUPERFECT SUBJUNCTIVE
fossi andato/a

– *Vado* in città, vuoi venire anche tu ?

– *I'm going* to town, do you want to come too?

– Grazie no, sono già andata *ieri*.

– No thanks, *I* already *went* yesterday.

– *Va'*, *andiamoci* insieme.

– *Go on*, *let's go* together.

– Certo è un peccato che tu *vada* da sola.

– It's certainly a pity that *you are going* alone.

– Penso che Gianna *sia andata* oggi in città.

– I think Gianna *has gone* to town today.

– Sarà *andata* senz'altro al mercato.

– *She will have gone* to the market.

GERUND	PAST PARTICIPLE
annettendo	**annesso**

PRESENT	PERFECT
annetto	ho annesso

PRESENT CONTINUOUS	IMPERFECT CONTINUOUS
sto annettendo	stavo annettendo

IMPERFECT	PAST DEFINITE
annettevo	**annessi** /annettei
	annettesti
	annesse
	annettemmo
	annetteste
	annessero

Similar verb

connettere   connect

Note   The main irregular features of the verb are

     • the past definite tense
     • the past participle

IMPERATIVE
annetti (tu)   annettiamo (noi)   annettete (voi)   annetta (Lei)

PLUPERFECT
avevo annesso

PAST ANTERIOR
ebbi annesso

FUTURE
annetterò

FUTURE PERFECT
avrò annesso

CONDITIONAL
annetterei

CONDITIONAL PERFECT
avrei annesso

PRESENT SUBJUNCTIVE
annetta

PERFECT SUBJUNCTIVE
abbia annesso

IMPERFECT SUBJUNCTIVE
annettessi

PLUPERFECT SUBJUNCTIVE
avessi annesso

Annettiamo un dépliant.	We *enclose* a brochure.
Dubito che sia stato *annesso*.	I doubt whether it has been *annexed*.
Questi fati sono strettamente *connessi*.	These facts *are* closely *linked*.
Giovanni *connesse* i due fili.	Giovanni *connected* the two wires.

GERUND	PAST PARTICIPLE
apparendo	**apparso**

PRESENT	PERFECT
apparisco/**appaio**	sono apparso/a
apparisci/**appari**	
apparisce/**appare**	
appariamo	
apparite	
appariscono/**appaiono**	

PRESENT CONTINUOUS	IMPERFECT CONTINUOUS
sto apparendo	stavo apparendo

IMPERFECT	PAST DEFINITE
apparivo	**apparvi**
	apparisti
	apparve
	apparimmo
	apparisti
	apparvero

Similar verbs

*comparire	appear
*scomparire	disappear, die
*trasparire	shine forth

Note The verb **apparire** follows a similar pattern to the verb **finire,** but is irregular in the past participle and past definite tenses as well as having optional spelling changes in the present indicative and present subjunctive tenses.

IMPERATIVE
apparisci (tu)   appariamo (noi)   apparite (voi)   apparisca /**appaia** (Lei)

PLUPERFECT avevo apparso	**PAST ANTERIOR** fui apparso/a
FUTURE apparirò	**FUTURE PERFECT** sarò apparso/a
CONDITIONAL apparirei	**CONDITIONAL PERFECT** sarei apparso/a
PRESENT SUBJUNCTIVE apparisca/**appaia** apparisca apparisca appariamo appariate appariscano/**appaiano**	**PERFECT SUBJUNCTIVE** sia apparso/a
IMPERFECT SUBJUNCTIVE apparissi	**PLUPERFECT SUBJUNCTIVE** fossi apparso/a

---

Gli studenti *appaiono* intelligenti.	The students *appear* intelligent.
Non credo che *appaiano* pigri.	I don't think *they appear* lazy.
Apparvero alla riunione.	*They appeared* at the reunion.
Giovanni è *scomparso* due giorni fa.	Giovanni *disappeared/died* two days ago.
La luce *traspariva* dalla finestra.	The light *was shining* through the window.

GERUND	PAST PARTICIPLE
aprendo	**aperto**

PRESENT	PERFECT
apro	ho aperto

PRESENT CONTINUOUS	IMPERFECT CONTINUOUS
sto aprendo	stavo aprendo

IMPERFECT	PAST DEFINITE
aprivo	aprii/**apersi**
	apristi
	aprí /**aperse**
	aprimmo
	apriste
	aprirono/**apersero**

Similar verbs

coprire	cover
offrire	offer
ricoprire	cover, cover again
scoprire	discover, uncover
soffrire	suffer

Note   **aprire** and the similar verbs follow the pattern of **dormire** except for the irregular past participle and optional past definite forms.

IMPERATIVE
apri (tu)   apriamo (noi)   aprite (voi)   apra (Lei)

PLUPERFECT avevo aperto	*PAST ANTERIOR* ebbi aperto
FUTURE aprirò	*FUTURE PERFECT* avrò aperto
CONDITIONAL aprirei	*CONDITIONAL PERFECT* avrei aperto
PRESENT SUBJUNCTIVE apra	*PERFECT SUBJUNCTIVE* abbia aperto
IMPERFECT SUBJUNCTIVE aprissi	*PLUPERFECT SUBJUNCTIVE* avessi aperto

---

– *Apri* la finestra, per piacere.
– Perché ? Ho già *aperto* la porta.

– *Open* the window please.
– Why? I have already *opened* the door.

– *Copri* il bambino, per piacere.
– Perché? Chi l'ha *scoperto*?

– *Cover* the baby, please.
– Why? Who *uncovered* him?

Hai scoperto l'America!

Aren't you clever! (Lit. *You have discovered* America)

La neve *ricopriva* la cima delle montagne.

The snow *covered* the mountain tops.

Quell'uomo *ha sofferto* tanto.

That man *has suffered* so much.

– Gianni ti *ha offerto* da mangiare ?
– Penso che mi *abbia offerto* da mangiare.
– Beh, io ti *offrirei* da mangiare e da bere.

– *Did* Gianni *offer* you something to eat ?
– I think *he offered* me something to eat.
– Well, *I would offer* you something to eat and drink.

Verbs with irregular past participles

GERUND	PAST PARTICIPLE
assistendo	**assistito**

PRESENT	PERFECT
assisto	ho assistito

PRESENT CONTINUOUS	IMPERFECT CONTINUOUS
sto assistendo	stavo assistendo

IMPERFECT	PAST DEFINITE
assistevo	assistei

Similar verbs

25A   All verbs ending in **-istere**

assistere a	attend	***consistere**	consist
esistere	exist	**insistere**	insist

Note   The only irregular feature of these verbs is the past participle.

25B   In addition to verbs ending in **-istere**, there are a number of other verbs which are only irregular in the past participle. These verbs are marked **25B** in the *Verb Index*:

esigere	**(esatto)**	demand, require
transigere	**(transatto)**	compromise
evolvere	**(evoluto)**	evolve
devolvere	**(devoluto)**	transfer
flettere	**(flesso)**	bend
riflettere	**(riflesso)**	reflect
redigere	**(redatto)**	write, compile
seppellire	**(sepolto)**	bury [►6 **finire**]
spandere	**(spanto)**	spread, spill

IMPERATIVE
assisti (tu)   assistiamo (noi)   assistete (voi)   assista (Lei)

PLUPERFECT avevo assistito	*PAST ANTERIOR* ebbi assistito
FUTURE assisterò	*FUTURE PERFECT* avrò assistito
CONDITIONAL assisterei	*CONDITIONAL PERFECT* avrei assistito
PRESENT SUBJUNCTIVE assista	*PERFECT SUBJUNCTIVE* abbia assistito
IMPERFECT SUBJUNCTIVE assistessi	*PLUPERFECT SUBJUNCTIVE* avessi assistito

---

Vi *assisterò* come posso.	*I will give you* all the *help* I can.
Giovanni *ha assistito* ad una partita di calcio.	Giovanni *attended/watched* a soccer match.
Di che cosa è *consistito*?	What *did it consist* of?
***Insisti* perché lei venga!**	*Insist* that she comes!
Ho *insistito* sulla necessità di leggere il libro prima di vedere il film.	*I insisted* on the necessity of reading the book before seeing the film/movie.

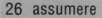

GERUND	PAST PARTICIPLE
assumendo	**assunto**

PRESENT	PERFECT
assumo	ho assunto

PRESENT CONTINUOUS	IMPERFECT CONTINUOUS
sto assumendo	stavo assumendo

IMPERFECT	PAST DEFINITE
assumevo	**assunsi**
	assumesti
	assunse
	assumemmo
	assumeste
	assunsero

Similar verbs

desumere	infer, deduce
presumere	presume

Note The main irregular features of the verb are

- the past definite tense
- the past participle

IMPERATIVE
assumi (tu)   assumiamo (noi)   assumete (voi)   assuma (Lei)

PLUPERFECT avevo assunto	*PAST ANTERIOR* ebbi assunto
FUTURE assumerò	*FUTURE PERFECT* avrò assunto
CONDITIONAL assumerei	*CONDITIONAL PERFECT* avrei assunto
PRESENT SUBJUNCTIVE assuma	*PERFECT SUBJUNCTIVE* abbia assunto
IMPERFECT SUBJUNCTIVE assumessi	*PLUPERFECT SUBJUNCTIVE* avessi assunto

Assunse un'aria innocente.	*He assumed* an air of innocence.
Ho assunto un impiegato ieri.	*I employed* a clerk yesterday.
Fu *assunto* al Pontificato.	He was *raised* to the Papacy.
Penso che sia *assunto* in cielo.	I think that he was *raised* to Heaven.
Presumevo che Stefano fosse ricco.	*I presumed* that Stefano was rich.
Presume troppo dalle sue forze.	*He relies* too much on his strength.

GERUND	PAST PARTICIPLE
avendo	avuto

PRESENT	PERFECT
ho	ho avuto
hai	
ha	
abbiamo	
avete	
hanno	

PRESENT CONTINUOUS	IMPERFECT CONTINUOUS
sto avendo	stavo avendo

IMPERFECT	PAST DEFINITE
avevo	**ebbi**
avevi	avesti
aveva	**ebbe**
avevamo	avemmo
avevate	aveste
avevano	**ebbero**

Note   **avere** is the only verb of this type. It should be learned thoroughly, as it is used to form many compound tenses.

Ho un fratello e due sorelle.	*I have* one brother and two sisters.
Ho ventidue anni.	I am 22 years old. (Lit. I *have* 22 years)

IMPERATIVE
abbi (tu)   abbiamo (noi)   **abbiate** (voi)   **abbia** (Lei)

PLUPERFECT
avevo avuto

PAST ANTERIOR
ebbi avuto

FUTURE
avrò

FUTURE PERFECT
avrò avuto

CONDITIONAL
avrei

CONDITIONAL PERFECT
avrei avuto

PRESENT SUBJUNCTIVE
abbia
abbia
abbia
abbiamo
abbiate
abbiano

PERFECT SUBJUNCTIVE
abbia avuto

IMPERFECT SUBJUNCTIVE
avessi

PLUPERFECT SUBJUNCTIVE
avessi avuto

– Dubito che Carlo *abbia* spedito quella lettera.
– Penso che tu *abbia* ragione.
– Comunque *ha* detto che viene domani.
– *Avremo* tempo a convincerlo allora.
– *Hai* intenzione di spiegargli tutto?
– *Ho* paura di dirgli la verità.
– Ma non *aveva* il diritto di agire così.

– I doubt whether Carlo *has* sent that letter.
– I think you are right.
– However, he said he is coming tomorrow.
– *We'll have* time to convince him, then.
– *Do you* intend to explain everything to him?
– *I am* afraid of telling him the truth.
– But *he did* not *have* the right to act like that.

GERUND	*PAST PARTICIPLE*
cadendo	caduto

PRESENT	*PERFECT*
cado	sono caduto/a

PRESENT CONTINUOUS	*IMPERFECT CONTINUOUS*
sto cadendo	stavo cadendo

IMPERFECT	*PAST DEFINITE*
cadevo	**caddi**
	cadesti
	cadde
	cademmo
	cadeste
	caddero

Similar verbs

*accadere	happen
*ricadere	fall again
*scadere	fall due

Note   The main irregular features of the verb are

  • the past definite tense
  • the future stem

IMPERATIVE
cadi (tu)   cadiamo (noi)   cadete (voi)   cada (Lei)

PLUPERFECT ero caduto/a	**PAST ANTERIOR** fui caduto/a
FUTURE **cadrò**	**FUTURE PERFECT** sarò caduto/a
CONDITIONAL **cadrei**	**CONDITIONAL PERFECT** sarei caduto/a
PRESENT SUBJUNCTIVE cada	**PERFECT SUBJUNCTIVE** sia caduto/a
IMPERFECT SUBJUNCTIVE cadessi	**PLUPERFECT SUBJUNCTIVE** fossi caduto/a

– **Cosa è** *accaduta*?	– What has happened?
– **Ho paura che Chiara** *sia* *ricaduta*.	– I am afraid that Chiara *might have fallen again*.
I prezzi *cadevano* **rapidamente.**	The prices *were falling* quickly.
Gli *sono caduti* **i capelli.**	He *has lost* his hair.
Ho paura che la fattura *scada* **domani.**	I am afraid that the invoice *is due* tomorrow.

GERUND	PAST PARTICIPLE
chiedendo	**chiesto**

PRESENT	PERFECT
chiedo	ho chiesto

PRESENT CONTINUOUS	IMPERFECT CONTINUOUS
sto chiedendo	stavo chiedendo

IMPERFECT	PAST DEFINITE
chiedevo	**chiesi**
	chiedesti
	chiese
	chiedemmo
	chiedeste
	chiesero

Similar verb

richiedere   request

Note   The main irregular features of the verb are

  • the past definite tense
  • the past participle

IMPERATIVE
chiedi (tu)   chiediamo (noi)   chiedete (voi)   chieda (Lei)

PLUPERFECT	*PAST ANTERIOR*
avevo chiesto	ebbi chiesto
FUTURE	*FUTURE PERFECT*
chiederò	avrò chiesto
CONDITIONAL	*CONDITIONAL PERFECT*
chiederei	avrei chiesto
PRESENT SUBJUNCTIVE	*PERFECT SUBJUNCTIVE*
chieda	abbia chiesto
IMPERFECT SUBJUNCTIVE	*PLUPERFECT SUBJUNCTIVE*
chiedessi	avessi chiesto

Ho paura che Carlo *abbia richiesto* l'impossibile.	I am afraid that Carlo *has asked* the impossible.
Cosa *ha chiesto* Luigi?	What *did* Luigi *ask*?
Mi *chiese* di uscire con loro.	*He asked* me to go out with them.
***Chiederò* al professore domani.**	*I shall ask* the teacher tomorrow.

GERUND	PAST PARTICIPLE
chiudendo	**chiuso**

PRESENT	PERFECT
chiudo	ho chiuso

PRESENT CONTINUOUS	IMPERFECT CONTINUOUS
sto chiudendo	stavo chiudendo

IMPERFECT	PAST DEFINITE
chiudevo	**chiusi**
	chiudesti
	chiuse
	chiudemmo
	chiudeste
	chiusero

Similar verbs

dischiudere	diclose, open
racchiudere	contain, imply
richiudere	close again
rinchiudere	shut in, shut up
schiudere	open, disclose
socchiudere	half shut

Note   The main irregular features of the verb are

• the past definite tense
• the past participle

IMPERATIVE
chiudi (tu)   chiudiamo (noi)   chiudete (voi)   chiuda (Lei)

PLUPERFECT avevo chiuso	**PAST ANTERIOR** ebbi chiuso
FUTURE chiuderò	**FUTURE PERFECT** avrò chiuso
CONDITIONAL chiuderei	**CONDITIONAL PERFECT** avrei chiuso
PRESENT SUBJUNCTIVE chiuda	**PERFECT SUBJUNCTIVE** abbia chiuso
IMPERFECT SUBJUNCTIVE chiudessi	**PLUPERFECT SUBJUNCTIVE** avessi chiuso

Ho paura che Antonio *abbia chiuso* a chiave.	I am afraid that Antonio *has locked* up.
Cosa *ha chiuso*?	What *did he close*?
***Socchiuse* la porta**	He *half closed* the door.
***Chiuderei* alle otto.**	*I would close* at eight.
Quella domanda *racchiude* già la risposta.	That question already *implies* the answer.
Elena fu *rinchiusa* nella casa.	Elena was *shut up* in the house.

-iere verbs

GERUND	*PAST PARTICIPLE*
cogliendo	**colto**

PRESENT	*PERFECT*
colgo	ho colto
cogli	
coglie	
cogliamo	
cogliete	
colgono	

PRESENT CONTINUOUS	*IMPERFECT CONTINUOUS*
sto cogliendo	stavo cogliendo

IMPERFECT	*PAST DEFINITE*
coglievo	**colsi**
	cogliesti
	colse
	cogliemmo
	coglieste
	colsero

Similar verbs

accogliere	welcome
disciogliere	dissolve
distogliere	dissuade, distract
prescegliere	choose from
raccogliere	gather, pick
scegliere	choose
sciogliere	dissolve
togliere	remove

Note   The main irregular features of these verbs are

- the present indicative and subjunctive tenses
- the past definite tense
- the past participle

IMPERATIVE
cogli (tu) **cogliamo** (noi) cogliete (voi) **colga** (Lei)

PLUPERFECT avevo colto	*PAST ANTERIOR* ebbi colto
FUTURE coglierò	*FUTURE PERFECT* avrò colto
CONDITIONAL coglierei	*CONDITIONAL PERFECT* avrei colto

PRESENT SUBJUNCTIVE
colga
colga
colga
cogliamo
cogliate
colgano

PERFECT SUBJUNCTIVE
abbia colto

IMPERFECT SUBJUNCTIVE
cogliessi

PLUPERFECT SUBJUNCTIVE
avessi colto

Colgono i fiori.	*They are gathering flowers.*
Lo *colsi* sul fatto.	*I caught him in the act/red handed.*
Anna *sciolse* la corda.	Anna *untied* the rope.
– Aspetta, ti *sciolgo* subito.	– Wait, I'*ll untie* you straight away.
– Grazie è molto meglio *sciolto*!	– Thank you, it is much better *untied*.
– Quale camicia *scegli*?	– Which shirt are you going *to choose*?
– *Scelgo* quella blu, è carina.	– *I'm choosing* the blue one, it's nice.
– Io *avrei scelto* quella rossa!	– I *would have chosen* the red one!
– Adesso non so quale *scegliere*!	– Now I don't know which *to choose*.

111

GERUND comprimendo	*PAST PARTICIPLE* **compresso**

PRESENT comprimo	*PERFECT* ho compresso
PRESENT CONTINUOUS sto comprimendo	*IMPERFECT CONTINUOUS* stavo comprimendo
IMPERFECT comprimevo	*PAST DEFINITE* **compressi** comprimesti **compresse** comprimemmo comprimeste **compressero**

Similar verbs

deprimere	depress
***deprimersi**	become depressed
esprimere	express
imprimere	impress, stamp
***imprimersi**	remain impressed
opprimere	oppress
reprimere	repress
sopprimere	abolish, eliminate, suppress

Note The main irregular features of the verb are

- the past definite tense
- the past participle

La macchina l'*ha compresso*.	The machine *compressed* it.
Vorrei *eprimerti* quanto siamo grati.	I would like *to express* how grateful we are.

IMPERATIVE
comprimi (tu)   comprimiamo (noi)   comprimete (voi)   comprima (Lei)

PLUPERFECT
avevo compresso

PAST ANTERIOR
ebbi compresso

FUTURE
comprimerò

FUTURE PERFECT
avrò compresso

CONDITIONAL
comprimerei

CONDITIONAL PERFECT
avrei compresso

PRESENT SUBJUNCTIVE
comprima

PERFECT SUBJUNCTIVE
abbia compresso

IMPERFECT SUBJUNCTIVE
comprimessi

PLUPERFECT SUBJUNCTIVE
avessi compresso

Il governo *soppresse* il giornale.	The government *suppressed* the newspaper.
L'avvocato *ha soppresso* quella clausola.	The lawyer *deleted* that clause.
Questo tempo lo *deprime*.	This weather *is depressing* him.
Laura si è tanto *depressa* oggi.	Laura has become so *depressed* today.
Il tiranno *oppresse* il popolo.	The tyrant *oppressed* the people.
Il lavoro mi *opprimeva*.	Work *was getting* me *down*.
Ha *impresso* un timbro sul foglio.	He *put* a stamp *on* the paper.
Le sue parole si *impressero* nella sua mente.	His words *remained engraved* in her mind.

GERUND	PAST PARTICIPLE
concedendo	**concesso**/conceduto

PRESENT	PERFECT
concedo	ho concesso

PRESENT CONTINUOUS	IMPERFECT CONTINUOUS
sto concedendo	stavo concedendo

IMPERFECT	PAST DEFINITE
concedevo	**concessi**/concedei/concedetti
	concedesti
	concesse
	concedemmo
	concedeste
	concessero

Note   The main irregular features of the verb are

- the past definite tense
- the past participle

Similar verbs

*accedere	aproach, enter, comply with
*succedere	happen, succeed

IMPERATIVE
concedi (tu)   concediamo (noi)   concedete (voi)   conceda (Lei)

PLUPERFECT avevo concesso	**PAST ANTERIOR** ebbi concesso
FUTURE concederò	**FUTURE PERFECT** avrò concesso
CONDITIONAL concederei	**CONDITIONAL PERFECT** avrei concesso
PRESENT SUBJUNCTIVE conceda	**PERFECT SUBJUNCTIVE** abbia concesso
IMPERFECT SUBJUNCTIVE concedessi	**PLUPERFECT SUBJUNCTIVE** avessi concesso

---

– **Cosa ti è *successo*?**	– What *happened* to you?
– **Non mi *è successo* niente.**	– Nothing *happened* (to me).
– ***Concedi* tutto?**	– *Do you concede* everything ?
– ***Concederei* tutto per l'amore.**	– *I would concede* all for love.

GERUND	***PAST PARTICIPLE***
conoscendo	conos**ci**uto

PRESENT	***PERFECT***
conosco	ho conosciuto

PRESENT CONTINUOUS	***IMPERFECT CONTINUOUS***
sto conoscendo	stavo conoscendo

IMPERFECT	***PAST DEFINITE***
conoscevo	**conobbi**
	conoscesti
	conobbe
	conoscemmo
	conosceste
	conobbero

Similar verb

riconoscere   recognize

Notes   It is important to distinguish between the verbs **conoscere** and **sapere**. **Conoscere** means to know a person or a place, whereas **sapere** means to know a fact or to know how to do something.

The main irregular feature of the verb is

• the past definite tense
• the spelling change in the past participle [➤11c(v)]

IMPERATIVE
conosci (tu)   conosciamo (noi)   conoscete (voi)   conosca (Lei)

PLUPERFECT
avevo conosciuto

PAST ANTERIOR
ebbi conosciuto

FUTURE
conoscerò

FUTURE PERFECT
avrò conosciuto

CONDITIONAL
conoscerei

CONDITIONAL PERFECT
avrei conosciuto

PRESENT SUBJUNCTIVE
conosca

PERFECT SUBJUNCTIVE
abbia conosciuto

IMPERFECT SUBJUNCTIVE
conoscessi

PLUPERFECT SUBJUNCTIVE
avessi conosciuto

– *Conosci* Roma ?	– *Do you know* Rome ?
– *Conosco* Roma molto bene.	– *I know* Rome very well.
– *Conoscevo* una vecchia signora a Roma.	– *I used to know* an old lady in Rome.
– Non so se la signora abiti ancora a Roma.	– I do not know whether the lady still lives in Rome.

Note   In the last example the verb **sapere** is used because the meaning is 'to know a fact'.

GERUND	PAST PARTICIPLE
correndo	**corso**

PRESENT	PERFECT
corro	ho corso/sono corso/a

PRESENT CONTINUOUS	IMPERFECT CONTINUOUS
sto correndo	stavo correndo

IMPERFECT	PAST DEFINITE
correvo	**corsi**
	corresti
	corse
	corremmo
	correste
	corsero

Similar verbs

†accorrere	run, rush
†discorrere	talk, discuss
†incorrerere	incur
†occorrere	be necessary (impersonal)
†percorrere	cover, go along
†ricorrere	resort to, turn to
†scorrere	flow
†soccorrere	aid, assist
††trascorrere	spend (time)

Notes   The main irregular features of the verb are

- the past definite tense
- the past participle

When used transitively, **correre** takes **avere**, otherwise it takes **essere** in its compound tenses.

IMPERATIVE

corri (tu)   corriamo (noi)   correte (voi)   corra (Lei)

PLUPERFECT avevo corso/ero corso/a	*PAST ANTERIOR* ebbi corso/fui corso/a
FUTURE correrò	*FUTURE PERFECT* avrò corso/sarò corso/a
CONDITIONAL correrei	*CONDITIONAL PERFECT* avrei corso/sarei corso/a
PRESENT SUBJUNCTIVE corra	*PERFECT SUBJUNCTIVE* abbia corso/sia corso/a
IMPERFECT SUBJUNCTIVE corressi	*PLUPERFECT SUBJUNCTIVE* avessi corso /fossi corso/a

---

Ho paura che Antonia *sia corsa* troppo velocemente.	I am afraid that Antonia *ran* too fast.
***Corri* ad avvisarlo!**	*Run* to warn him!
La strada *corre* lungo il fiume.	The road *runs* alongside the river.
Il fiume *scorre* vicino alla casa.	The river *flows* near the house.
***Corrono* voci poco rassicuranti sul tuo conto.**	*There are* some less than reassuring rumours/rumors about you.
Abbiamo *corso* il rischio di morire.	We *ran* the risk of dying.
Abbiamo *percorso* tutti gli Stati Uniti.	We have *travelled* all over the United States.
La polizia *percorse* la città in cerca dei ladri.	The police *scoured* the town in search of the thieves.
Ne *discorreremo* dopo cena.	We shall *discuss* it after dinner.

GERUND	*PAST PARTICIPLE*
crescendo	cresciuto

PRESENT	*PERFECT*
cresco	sono cresciuto/a

PRESENT CONTINUOUS	*IMPERFECT CONTINUOUS*
sto crescendo	stavo crescendo

IMPERFECT	*PAST DEFINITE*
crescevo	**crebbi**
	crescesti
	crebbe
	crescemmo
	cresceste
	crebbero

Similar verbs

*accrescere	increase
*decrescere	decrease, go down
*rincrescere	regret, be sorry, mind

Note   The main irregular features of the verb are

- the past definite tense
- the spelling change in the past participle [➤11c(v)]

IMPERATIVE
cresci (tu)   cresciamo (noi)   crescete (voi)   cresca (Lei)

PLUPERFECT
ero cresciuto/a

PAST ANTERIOR
fui cresciuto/a

FUTURE
crescerò

FUTURE PERFECT
sarò cresciuto/a

CONDITIONAL
crescerei

CONDITIONAL PERFECT
sarei cresciuto/a

PRESENT SUBJUNCTIVE
cresca

PERFECT SUBJUNCTIVE
sia cresciuto/a

IMPERFECT SUBJUNCTIVE
crescessi

PLUPERFECT SUBJUNCTIVE
fossi cresciuto/a

I miei capelli non *crescono* molto.	My hair *does* not *grow* much.
Antonio è *cresciuto* molto!	Antonio *has grown* a lot.
L'albero è *cresciuto* poco.	The tree *has grown* very little.
Antonella è *cresciuta* in Sardegna.	Antonella *grew up* in Sardegna.
I prezzi non *decrescono* mai!	Prices never *go down*!
Le *rincresce* di non potervi aiutare.	She *regrets* not being able to help you.
Ti *rincrescerebbe* aprire la porta?	*Would* you *mind* opening the door?

GERUND	*PAST PARTICIPLE*
cuocendo/cocendo	**cotto**

PRESENT	*PERFECT*
cuocio	ho cotto
cuoci	
cuoce	
cociamo/cuociamo	
cocete/cuocete	
cuocciono	

PRESENT CONTINUOUS	*IMPERFECT CONTINUOUS*
sto cuocendo/cocendo	stavo cuocendo/cocendo

IMPERFECT	*PAST DEFINITE*
cuocevo	**cossi**
	cocesti
	cosse
	cocemmo
	coceste
	cossero

Note   The main irregular features of the verb are

- the present indicative and subjunctive tenses
- the past definite tense
- the past participle
- the gerund

IMPERATIVE
cuoci (tu) **cociamo** (noi) **cocete** (voi) **cuocia** (Lei)

PLUPERFECT	**PAST ANTERIOR**
avevo cotto	ebbi cotto
FUTURE	**FUTURE PERFECT**
cuocerò	avrò cotto
CONDITIONAL	**CONDITIONAL PERFECT**
cuocerei	avrei cotto
PRESENT SUBJUNCTIVE	**PERFECT SUBJUNCTIVE**
cuocia	abbia cotto
IMPERFECT SUBJUNCTIVE	**PLUPERFECT SUBJUNCTIVE**
cuocessi	avessi cotto

– **Che cosa *hai cotto*?**	– What *have* you *cooked*?
– **Il sugo *è cotto*, ma sto ancora *cuocendo/cocendo* la pasta.**	– The sauce *is cooked*, but I *am* still *cooking* the pasta.
– **Ma questa pasta *è stracotta*!**	– But this pasta *is overcooked*.

GERUND	**PAST PARTICIPLE**
dando	dato

PRESENT	**PERFECT**
do	ho dato
dai	
dà	
diamo	
date	
danno	

PRESENT CONTINUOUS	**IMPERFECT CONTINUOUS**
sto dando	stavo dando

IMPERFECT	**PAST DEFINITE**
davo	**diedi**
	desti
	diede
	demmo
	deste
	diedero

Note   The main irregular features of the verb are

- the present indicative and subjunctive tenses
- the past definite tense
- the future stem

IMPERATIVE
da' (tu)   diamo (noi)   date (voi)   **dia** (Lei)

PLUPERFECT
avevo dato

PAST ANTERIOR
ebbi dato

FUTURE
darò

FUTURE PERFECT
avrò dato

CONDITIONAL
darei

CONDITIONAL PERFECT
avrei dato

PRESENT SUBJUNCTIVE
dia
dia
dia
diamo
diate
diano

PERFECT SUBJUNCTIVE
abbia dato

IMPERFECT SUBJUNCTIVE
dessi

PLUPERFECT SUBJUNCTIVE
avessi dato

– *Dammi* un po' di pane, per favore.
– Mah, ti *ho* già *dato* il pane.

– Io te ne *darei* senza queste storie!
– Va bene, te lo *do*, basta che stai zitto.

– *Would you give* me some bread please.
– But *I have already given* you the bread.

– *I would give* you some without complaining.
– O.K. *I'll give* you it, as long as you keep quiet.

GERUND	*PAST PARTICIPLE*
decidendo	**deciso**

PRESENT	*PERFECT*
decido	ho deciso

PRESENT CONTINUOUS	*IMPERFECT CONTINUOUS*
sto decidendo	stavo decidendo

IMPERFECT	*PAST DEFINITE*
decidevo	**decisi**
	decidesti
	decise
	decidemmo
	decideste
	decisero

Similar verbs

coincidere	coincide
incidere	cut
recidere	cut off, amputate

Note   The main irregular features of the verb are

- the past definite tense
- the past participle

IMPERATIVE
decidi (tu)   decidiamo (noi)   decidete (voi)   decida (Lei)

PLUPERFECT	**PAST ANTERIOR**
avevo deciso	ebbi deciso

FUTURE	**FUTURE PERFECT**
deciderò	avrò deciso

CONDITIONAL	**CONDITIONAL PERFECT**
deciderei	avrei deciso

PRESENT SUBJUNCTIVE	**PERFECT SUBJUNCTIVE**
decida	abbia deciso

IMPERFECT SUBJUNCTIVE	**PLUPERFECT SUBJUNCTIVE**
decidessi	avessi deciso

Dubito che Marco *abbia* già *deciso*.	I doubt whether Marco *has decided* yet.
Cosa *ha deciso* Carla?	What *has* Carla *decided*?
***Decise* di partire subito.**	*He decided* to leave immediately.
***Decisi* sul rosso.**	*I decided on* the red.
***Incise* il nome di Maria sull'albero.**	*He carved* Maria's name on the tree.
***Ho inciso* un disco l'anno scorso.**	*I cut* a record last year.

GERUND dirigendo	**PAST PARTICIPLE** **diretto**

PRESENT dirigo	**PERFECT** ho diretto
PRESENT CONTINUOUS sto dirigendo	**IMPERFECT CONTINUOUS** stavo dirigendo
IMPERFECT dirigevo	**PAST DEFINITE** **diressi** dirigesti **diresse** dirigemmo dirigeste **diressero**

Similar verbs

*dirigersi   turn one's steps towards
erigere   erect

Note   The main irregular features of the verb are
  • the past definite tense
  • the past participle

IMPERATIVE
dirigi (tu)　dirigiamo (noi)　dirigete (voi)　diriga (Lei)

PLUPERFECT avevo diretto	**PAST ANTERIOR** ebbi diretto
FUTURE dirigerò	**FUTURE PERFECT** avrò diretto
CONDITIONAL dirigerei	**CONDITIONAL PERFECT** avrei diretto
PRESENT SUBJUNCTIVE diriga	**PERFECT SUBJUNCTIVE** abbia diretto
IMPERFECT SUBJUNCTIVE dirigessi	**PLUPERFECT SUBJUNCTIVE** avessi diretto

Diresse la nave verso il porto.	He *steered* the boat towards the port.
La nave *era diretta* a Livorno.	The ship *was heading* for Leghorn.
La lettera *era diretta* a mio padre.	The letter *was addressed* to my father.
Ho diretto lo sguardo verso il mare.	I *turned* my gaze towards to sea.
Lucia *dirige* un'orchestra.	Lucia *conducts* an orchestra.
Mio padre *dirige* una grande società.	My father *manages* a large company.
Eresse un gran monumento.	He *erected* a large monument.
Si *diresse* verso il paese.	He *headed* towards the village.

GERUND	PAST PARTICIPLE
discutendo	**discusso**

PRESENT	PERFECT
discuto	ho discusso

PRESENT CONTINUOUS	IMPERFECT CONTINUOUS
sto discutendo	stavo discutendo

IMPERFECT	PAST DEFINITE
discutevo	**discussi**
	discutesti
	discusse
	discutemmo
	discuteste
	discussero

Similar verb

incutere   rouse, strike

Note   The main irregular features of the verb are

• the past definite tense
• the past participle

IMPERATIVE
discuti (tu) discutiamo (noi) discutete (voi) discuta (Lei)

PLUPERFECT	*PAST ANTERIOR*
avevo discusso	ebbi discusso
FUTURE	*FUTURE PERFECT*
discuterò	avrò discusso
CONDITIONAL	*CONDITIONAL PERFECT*
discuterei	avrei discusso
PRESENT SUBJUNCTIVE	*PERFECT SUBJUNCTIVE*
discuta	abbia discusso
IMPERFECT SUBJUNCTIVE	*PLUPERFECT SUBJUNCTIVE*
discutessi	avessi discusso

– Ho paura che Carlo *abbia discusso* il problema con Carla.	– I am afraid that Carlo *has discussed* the problem with Carla.
– Cosa *hanno discusso* Carlo e Carla?	– What *did* Carlo and Carla *discuss*?
– *Discussero* l'inquinamento.	– *They discussed* pollution.
Discuterò il tema domani.	*I shall discuss* the essay tomorrow.
Incusse terrore nell'anima di Giovanni.	*He struck* terror into Giovanni.

GERUND	*PAST PARTICIPLE*
distinguendo	**distinto**

PRESENT	*PERFECT*
distinguo	ho distinto

PRESENT CONTINUOUS	*IMPERFECT CONTINUOUS*
sto distinguendo	stavo distinguendo

IMPERFECT	*PAST DEFINITE*
distinguevo	**distinsi**
	distinguesti
	distinse
	distinguemmo
	distingueste
	distinsero

Similar verb

estinguere   extinguish

Note   The main irregular features of the verb are

- the past definite tense
- the past participle

IMPERATIVE
distingui (tu)   distinguiamo (noi)   distinguete (voi)   distingua (Lei)

PLUPERFECT
avevo distinto

PAST ANTERIOR
ebbi distinto

FUTURE
distinguerò

FUTURE PERFECT
avrò distinto

CONDITIONAL
distinguerei

CONDITIONAL PERFECT
avrei distinto

PRESENT SUBJUNCTIVE
distingua

PERFECT SUBJUNCTIVE
abbia distinto

IMPERFECT SUBJUNCTIVE
distinguessi

PLUPERFECT SUBJUNCTIVE
avessi distinto

Al telefono non *distinguo* la tua voce da quella di tua madre.	On the telephone *I can't tell the difference* between your voice and your mother's.
Non riuscivo a *distinguere* chi c'era.	I was not able *to make out* who was there.
I vigili del fuoco *estinsero* le fiamme.	The firemen *put out* the flames.
***Distinse* un uomo all'orizzonte.**	He *made out* a man on the horizon.
Le porgo i miei più *distinti* saluti.	Yours faithfully.

GERUND	PAST PARTICIPLE
dividendo	**diviso**

PRESENT	PERFECT
divido	ho diviso

PRESENT CONTINUOUS	IMPERFECT CONTINUOUS
sto dividendo	stavo dividendo

IMPERFECT	PAST DEFINITE
dividevo	**divisi**
	dividesti
	divise
	dividemmo
	divideste
	divisero

Similar verbs

condividere	share
dividersi	separate

Note The main irregular features of the verb are

- the past definite tense
- the past participle

IMPERATIVE
dividi (tu)   dividiamo (noi)   dividete (voi)   divida (Lei)

PLUPERFECT
avevo diviso

PAST ANTERIOR
ebbi diviso

FUTURE
dividerò

FUTURE PERFECT
avrò diviso

CONDITIONAL
dividerei

CONDITIONAL PERFECT
avrei diviso

PRESENT SUBJUNCTIVE
divida

PERFECT SUBJUNCTIVE
abbia diviso

IMPERFECT SUBJUNCTIVE
dividessi

PLUPERFECT SUBJUNCTIVE
avessi diviso

Dividete la torta fra di voi!

Divide the cake amongst you!

Il marmo si divise in tre parti.

The marble *broke up* into 3 parts.

Il Po si divide alla foce.

The Po *divides* at its mouth.

Le lotte interne dividono il partito.

Internal disputes *are tearing* the party *apart*.

I bambini condividevano le caramelle.

The children *shared* the sweets.

GERUND	PAST PARTICIPLE
dolendo	doluto

PRESENT	PERFECT
dolgo	sono doluto/a
duoli	
duole	
doliamo	
dolete	
dolgono	

PRESENT CONTINUOUS	IMPERFECT CONTINUOUS
sto dolendo	stavo dolendo

IMPERFECT	PAST DEFINITE
dolevo	**dolsi**
	dolesti
	dolse
	dolemmo
	doleste
	dolsero

Similar verb

*condolersi   sympathize, condole with

Note   The main irregular features of the verb are

   • the present indicative and subjunctive tenses
   • the past definite tense
   • the future stem

IMPERATIVE
doli (tu)   doliamo (noi)   dolete (voi)   dola (Lei)

PLUPERFECT	**PAST ANTERIOR**
ero doluto/a	fui doluto/a
FUTURE	**FUTURE PERFECT**
dorrò	sarò doluto/a
CONDITIONAL	**CONDITIONAL PERFECT**
dorrei	sarei doluto/a
PRESENT SUBJUNCTIVE	**PERFECT SUBJUNCTIVE**
dolga	sia doluto/a
dolga	
dolga	
doliamo	
doliate	
dolgano	
IMPERFECT SUBJUNCTIVE	**PLUPERFECT SUBJUNCTIVE**
dolessi	fossi doluto/a

– Mi *duole* molto la testa.	– My head *is hurting* a lot.
– Mi dispiace che ti *dolga* tanto.	– I am sorry that it *is hurting* you so much.
– Mi *stava* anche *dolendo* ieri sera.	– It *was* also *aching* yesterday evening.
Si *condolsero* con lui.	They *sympathized* with him.

GERUND	PAST PARTICIPLE
dovendo	dovuto

PRESENT
devo/debbo
devi
deve
dobbiamo
dovete
devono/debbono

PERFECT
ho dovuto/sono dovuto/a

PRESENT CONTINUOUS
sto dovendo

IMPERFECT CONTINUOUS
stavo dovendo

IMPERFECT
dovevo

PAST DEFINITE
dovei

Note   The main irregular features of this modal verb are

• the present indicative and subjunctive tenses
• the future stem

dovere takes **avere** or **essere** according to which one the dependent infinitive takes. However, in practice the auxiliary **avere** is frequently used in speech, when the emphasis is on obligation.

IMPERATIVE
devi (tu)   **dobbiamo** (noi)   dovete (voi)   **debba** (Lei)

PLUPERFECT	PAST ANTERIOR
avevo dovuto/ero dovuto/a	ebbi dovuto/fui dovuto/a

FUTURE	FUTURE PERFECT
dovrò	avrò dovuto/sarò dovuto/a

CONDITIONAL	CONDITIONAL PERFECT
dovrei	avrei dovuto/sarei dovuto/a

PRESENT SUBJUNCTIVE	PERFECT SUBJUNCTIVE
debba	abbia dovuto/sia dovuto/a
debba	
debba	
dobbiamo	
dobbiate	
debbano	

IMPERFECT SUBJUNCTIVE	PLUPERFECT SUBJUNCTIVE
dovessi	ebbi dovuto/fossi dovuto/a

Devono essere le otto.	*It must* be 8:00.
Il treno *deve* arrivare tra poco.	The train *should* arrive soon.
Avrei *dovuto* parlare con la mamma prima di partire.	*I should* have spoken to mother before leaving.
Dovrei tornare a casa ora.	*I should* go home now.
Antonio è *dovuto* andare a casa presto.	Antonio *had* to go home early.

GERUND	PAST PARTICIPLE
espellendo	**espulso**

PRESENT	PERFECT
espello	ho espulso

PRESENT CONTINUOUS	IMPERFECT CONTINUOUS
sto espellendo	stavo espellendo

IMPERFECT	PAST DEFINITE
espellevo	**espulsi**
	espellesti
	espulse
	espellemmo
	espelleste
	espulsero

Note   The main irregular features of the verb are

• the past definite tense
• the past participle

IMPERATIVE
espelli (tu)   espelliamo (noi)   espellete (voi)   espella (Lei)

PLUPERFECT
avevo espulso

PAST ANTERIOR
ebbi espulso

FUTURE
espellerò

FUTURE PERFECT
avrò espulso

CONDITIONAL
espellerei

CONDITIONAL PERFECT
avrei espulso

PRESENT SUBJUNCTIVE
espella

PERFECT SUBJUNCTIVE
abbia espulso

IMPERFECT SUBJUNCTIVE
espellessi

PLUPERFECT SUBJUNCTIVE
avessi espulso

– *Hanno espulso* **quel ragazzo ?**	– *Have they expelled* that boy?
– **Fu** *espulso* **dalla scuola ieri.**	– He was *expelled* from the school yesterday.
– **Io l'***avrei espulso* **l'anno scorso!**	– I *would have expelled* him last year.
– **Sì, ma non è facile** *espellere* **alunni.**	– Yes, but it is not easy *to expel* pupils/students.

GERUND	PAST PARTICIPLE
esplodendo	**esploso**

PRESENT	PERFECT
esplodo	sono esploso/a

PRESENT CONTINUOUS	IMPERFECT CONTINUOUS
sto esplodendo	stavo esplodendo

IMPERFECT	PAST DEFINITE
esplodevo	**esplosi**
	esplodesti
	esplose
	esplodemmo
	esplodeste
	esplosero

Similar verbs

ardere	burn
corrodere	corrode
rodere	gnaw

Note   The main irregular features of the verb are

- the past participle
- the past definite tense

IMPERATIVE
esplodi (tu)   esplodiamo (noi)   esplodete (voi)   esploda (Lei)

PLUPERFECT
ero esploso

PAST ANTERIOR
fui esploso/a

FUTURE
esploderò

FUTURE PERFECT
sarò esploso/a

CONDITIONAL
esploderei

CONDITIONAL PERFECT
sarei esploso/a

PRESENT SUBJUNCTIVE
esploda

PERFECT SUBJUNCTIVE
sia esploso/a

IMPERFECT SUBJUNCTIVE
esplodessi

PLUPERFECT SUBJUNCTIVE
fossi esploso/a

– Sarà *esploso* senz'altro al mercato.
– No, la bomba *esplose* nel negozio.

– It must have *exploded* at the market.
– No, the bomb *went off* in the shop.

Esplosi in una risata.

I burst out laughing.

Poi la sua ira *esplose*.

Then his anger *exploded*.

Ardevano i lumi.

The lights *were shining*.

Il sole *ha arso* la terra.

The sun *has burned* the ground.

I topi *hanno roso* il libro.

The mice *have gnawed* at the book.

GERUND	PAST PARTICIPLE
essendo	**stato**

PRESENT	PERFECT
sono	sono stato/a
sei	sei stato/a
è	è stato/a
siamo	siamo stati/e
siete	siete stati/e
sono	sono stati/e

PRESENT CONTINUOUS	IMPERFECT CONTINUOUS
sto	stavo

IMPERFECT	PAST DEFINITE
ero	**fui**
eri	**fosti**
era	**fu**
eravamo	**fummo**
eravate	**foste**
erano	**furono**

Note It is important that you learn all tenses of **essere** as it is used in so many compound tenses.

IMPERATIVE
sii (tu)   **siamo** (noi)   **siate** (voi)   **sia** (Lei)

PLUPERFECT ero stato	**PAST ANTERIOR** fui stato/a
FUTURE sarò	**FUTURE PERFECT** sarò stato/a
CONDITIONAL sarei	**CONDITIONAL PERFECT** sarei stato/a
PRESENT SUBJUNCTIVE sia sia sia siamo siate siano	**PERFECT SUBJUNCTIVE** sia stato/a
IMPERFECT SUBJUNCTIVE fossi fossi fosse fossimo foste fossero	**PLUPERFECT SUBJUNCTIVE** fossi stato/a

---

Oggi è difficile trovare lavoro.	Nowadays *it is* difficult to find a job.
– **Cosa c'è?**	– What *is the matter*?
– *Sono* **disoccupata.**	– *I'm* unemployed.
– *Sarà* **più facile in un'altra città?**	– *Might it be* easier in another town?
– **Non credo che** *sia* **così facile.**	– I do not think *it is* so easy.
– *Sei* **sempre così pessimista ?**	– *Are you* always such a pessimist?

GERUND	PAST PARTICIPLE
evadendo	**evaso**

PRESENT	PERFECT
evado	sono evaso/a

PRESENT CONTINUOUS	IMPERFECT CONTINUOUS
sto evadendo	stavo evadendo

IMPERFECT	PAST DEFINITE
evadevo	**evasi**
	evadesti
	evase
	evademmo
	evadeste
	evasero

Similar verb

invadere　　　　　　　　invade

Note　　The main irregular features of the verb are

- the past participle
- the past definite tense

IMPERATIVE
evadi (tu)   evadiamo (noi)   evadete (voi)   evada (Lei)

PLUPERFECT ero evaso	*PAST ANTERIOR* fui evaso/a
FUTURE evaderò	*FUTURE PERFECT* sarò evaso/a
CONDITIONAL evaderei	*CONDITIONAL PERFECT* sarei evaso/a
PRESENT SUBJUNCTIVE evada	*PERFECT SUBJUNCTIVE* sia evaso/a
IMPERFECT SUBJUNCTIVE evadessi	*PLUPERFECT SUBJUNCTIVE* fossi evaso/a

Ho paura che l'uomo *sia* già *evaso* dalla prigione.	I am afraid the man *might have* already *escaped* from the prison/jail.
Purtroppo i ladri *evasero*.	Unfortunately the robbers *escaped*.
Le erbacce *invasero* il mio giardino.	My garden *was overrun* with weeds.
Il fiume *invase* i campi.	The river *flooded* the fields.
Hanno *invaso* il campo.	They *invaded* the pitch/field.
L'imperatore *invase* il paese.	The Emperor *invaded* the country.

GERUND	PAST PARTICIPLE
fondendo	**fuso**

PRESENT	PERFECT
fondo	ho fuso

PRESENT CONTINUOUS	IMPERFECT CONTINUOUS
sto fondendo	stavo fondendo

IMPERFECT	PAST DEFINITE
fondevo	**fusi**
	fondesti
	fuse
	fondemmo
	fondeste
	fusero

Similar verbs

diffondere	give out, spread, diffuse
infondere	instil
profondere	squander
***profondersi in**	be profuse in

Note   The main irregular features of the verb are

- the past definite tense
- the past participle

IMPERATIVE
fondi (tu)   fondiamo (noi)   fondete (voi)   fonda (Lei)

PLUPERFECT avevo fuso	*PAST ANTERIOR* ebbi fuso
FUTURE fonderò	*FUTURE PERFECT* avrò fuso
CONDITIONAL fonderei	*CONDITIONAL PERFECT* avrei fuso
PRESENT SUBJUNCTIVE fonda	*PERFECT SUBJUNCTIVE* abbia fuso
IMPERFECT SUBJUNCTIVE fondessi	*PLUPERFECT SUBJUNCTIVE* avessi fuso

Il sole *ha fuso* la neve.	The sun *melted* the snow.
L'artista *fuse* i due colori.	The artist *blended* the two colours/colors.
La notizia è stata *diffusa* per radio.	The news was *broadcast* on the radio.
Claudio *ha infuso* il coraggio a Luigi.	Claudio *instilled* courage into Luigi.
Antonio *profuse* il denaro in divertimenti.	Antonio *squandered* the money on entertainment.
La signora si *profondeva* sempre in lodi.	The lady *was* always *lavish* in her praise.

GERUND	PAST PARTICIPLE
giacendo	**giaciuto**

PRESENT	PERFECT
giaccio	sono giaciuto/a
giaci	
giace	
giaciamo/**giacciamo**	
giacete	
giacciono	

PRESENT CONTINUOUS	IMPERFECT CONTINUOUS
sto giacendo	stavo giacendo

IMPERFECT	PAST DEFINITE
giacevo	**giacqui**
	giacesti
	giacque
	giacemmo
	giaceste
	giacquero

Note   The main irregular features of the verb are

- the present indicative and subjunctive tenses
- the past definite tense
- the insertion of the -i in the past participle

IMPERATIVE
giaci (tu)   giaciamo (noi)   giacete (voi)   **giaccia** (Lei)

PLUPERFECT
ero giaciuto/a

PAST ANTERIOR
fui giaciuto/a

FUTURE
giacerò

FUTURE PERFECT
sarò giaciuto/a

CONDITIONAL
giacerei

CONDITIONAL PERFECT
sarei giaciuto/a

PRESENT SUBJUNCTIVE
giaccia

PERFECT SUBJUNCTIVE
sia giaciuto/a

IMPERFECT SUBJUNCTIVE
giacessi

PLUPERFECT SUBJUNCTIVE
fossi giaciuto/a

- *Giacque* **sulla spiaggia.**
- **Dubito che** *giaccia* **lì nel caldo.**

- *Giacerei* **al sole tutta la giornata!**

– *He lay* on the beach.
– I doubt that *he lay* there in the heat.

– *I would lie* in the sun all day long!

GERUND	*PAST PARTICIPLE*
giungendo	**giunto**

PRESENT	*PERFECT*
giungo	sono giunto/a

PRESENT CONTINUOUS	*IMPERFECT CONTINUOUS*
sto giungendo	stavo giungendo

IMPERFECT	*PAST DEFINITE*
giungevo	**giunsi**
	giungesti
	giunse
	giungemmo
	giungeste
	giunsero

Similar verbs

† **aggiungere**	add
† **congiungere**	join, match
† **disgiungere**	separate
† **raggiungere**	overtake/pass, reach
† **soggiungere**	add

verbs marked † can take **essere** when used intransitively or **avere** when used transitively

Note   The main irregular features of the verb are

- the past definite tense
- the past participle

IMPERATIVE
giungi (tu)   giungiamo (noi)   giungete (voi)   giunga (Lei)

PLUPERFECT ero giunto/a	*PAST ANTERIOR* fui giunto/a
FUTURE giungerò	*FUTURE PERFECT* sarò giunto/a
CONDITIONAL giungerei	*CONDITIONAL PERFECT* sarei giunto/a
PRESENT SUBJUNCTIVE giunga	*PERFECT SUBJUNCTIVE* sia giunto/a
IMPERFECT SUBJUNCTIVE giungessi	*PLUPERFECT SUBJUNCTIVE* fossi giunto/a

---

Giunsi in Italia.	I *arrived* in Italy.
Nessun suono *giungeva* al mio orecchio.	No sound *reached* my ears.
Fino dove lo sguardo può *giungere*, c'è verde.	As far as the eye *can see* there are green fields.
Il nonno *è giunto* all'età di novant'anni.	Grandad *has reached* the age of ninety.
Va' avanti, ti *raggiungo* presto.	Go on ahead, *I'll catch up* soon.
Il prezzo *raggiunge* i tre milioni di lire.	The price *comes to* 3 million lire.
Congiunsero le mani per pregare.	*They joined* their hands to pray.

GERUND	*PAST PARTICIPLE*
leggendo	**letto**

PRESENT	*PERFECT*
leggo	ho letto

PRESENT CONTINUOUS	*IMPERFECT CONTINUOUS*
sto leggendo	stavo leggendo

IMPERFECT	*PAST DEFINITE*
leggevo	**lessi**
	leggesti
	lesse
	leggemmo
	leggeste
	lessero

Similar verb

eleggere   elect

Note   The main irregular features of the verb are

• the past definite tense
• the past participle

IMPERATIVE
leggi (tu) leggiamo (noi) leggete (voi) legga (Lei)

PLUPERFECT avevo letto	*PAST ANTERIOR* ebbi letto
FUTURE leggerò	*FUTURE PERFECT* avrò letto
CONDITIONAL leggerei	*CONDITIONAL PERFECT* avrei letto
PRESENT SUBJUNCTIVE legga	*PERFECT SUBJUNCTIVE* abbia letto
IMPERFECT SUBJUNCTIVE leggessi	*PLUPERFECT SUBJUNCTIVE* avessi letto

---

Lo *leggo* nei tuoi occhi.	*I can read* it in your eyes.
Legga attentamente questa lettera.	*Read* this letter carefully.
La *lesse* a voce alta.	He *read* it out aloud.
Sa *leggere* la musica a prima vista.	He knows how *to sight read* music.
Ho letto fra le righe.	I *read* between the lines.
Leggerei per addormentarmi.	*I would read* myself to sleep.
È stato *eletto* ieri.	He was *elected* yesterday.

GERUND	PAST PARTICIPLE
mettendo	**messo**

PRESENT	PERFECT
metto	ho messo

PRESENT CONTINUOUS	IMPERFECT CONTINUOUS
sto mettendo	stavo mettendo

IMPERFECT	PAST DEFINITE
mettevo	**misi**
	mettesti
	mise
	mettemmo
	metteste
	misero

Similar verbs

ammettere	admit	**permettere**	permit
commettere	commit	**promettere**	promise
compromettere	compromise	**rimettere**	replace
emettere	emit	**scommettere**	bet
frammettere	interpose, insert	**smettere**	stop
immettere	admit, let in	**trasmettere**	transmit
omettere	omit		

Note The main irregular features of the verb are

• the past definite tense
• the past participle

Abbiamo messo il riscaldamento centrale.	*We put in* central heating.
Mise il fazzoletto in tasca.	*He put* the handkerchief in his pocket.

IMPERATIVE
metti (tu)   mettiamo (noi)   mettete (voi)   metta (Lei)

PLUPERFECT
avevo messo

PAST ANTERIOR
ebbi messo

FUTURE
metterò

FUTURE PERFECT
avrò messo

CONDITIONAL
metterei

CONDITIONAL PERFECT
avrei messo

PRESENT SUBJUNCTIVE
metta

PERFECT SUBJUNCTIVE
abbia messo

IMPERFECT SUBJUNCTIVE
mettessi

PLUPERFECT SUBJUNCTIVE
avessi messo

Dubito che *abbia messo* da parte quei soldi.	I doubt whether *he has put* that money aside.
***Ho messo* la tavola all'asta.**	*I put* the table up for auction.
***Ha messo* indietro l'orologio.**	*He put* his watch back.
Quanto tempo ci *hai messo* a farlo?	How long *did it take you* to do it?
***Ammettiamo* pure che tu abbia ragione.**	*Let's suppose* (*admit*) you are right.
Luigi *emise* un grido forte.	Luigi *let out* a loud cry.
Mi *promise* un bel regalo!	He *promised* me a beautiful present.
***Ho smesso* di fumare!**	*I've stopped* smoking!
***Scommetto* che non lo sa!**	*I bet* he does not know!
***Ho omesso* di leggere quel libro.**	*I have omitted* reading that book.

GERUND	PAST PARTICIPLE
mordendo	**morso**

PRESENT	PERFECT
mordo	ho morso

PRESENT CONTINUOUS	IMPERFECT CONTINUOUS
sto mordendo	stavo mordendo

IMPERFECT	PAST DEFINITE
mordevo	**morsi**
	mordesti
	morse
	mordemmo
	mordeste
	morsero

Similar verbs

*mordersi	bite oneself
rimordere	bite back, prick

Note The main irregular features of the verb are

- the past definite tense
- the past participle

IMPERATIVE
mordi (tu)   mordiamo (noi)   mordete (voi)   morda (Lei)

PLUPERFECT avevo morso	**PAST ANTERIOR** ebbi morso
FUTURE morderò	**FUTURE PERFECT** avrò morso
CONDITIONAL morderei	**CONDITIONAL PERFECT** avrei morso
PRESENT SUBJUNCTIVE morda	**PERFECT SUBJUNCTIVE** abbia morso
IMPERFECT SUBJUNCTIVE mordessi	**PLUPERFECT SUBJUNCTIVE** avessi morso

Il cane mi *ha morso* il braccio.	The dog *bit* my arm.
Pulci e zanzare *mordono*.	Fleas and mosquitoes *bite*.
Un vento gelido gli *mordeva* il viso.	He *felt* an icy wind on his face.
***Mordeva* il freno.**	*He was champing* at the bit.
***Morsero* la polvere.**	*They bit* the dust.
Mi sono *morsa* la lingua.	I *bit* my tongue.
Mi sarei *morsa* la lingua.	I could have kicked myself.
***Gli rimorse* la coscienza.**	His conscience *pricked* him.

GERUND	PAST PARTICIPLE
morendo	**morto**

PRESENT	PERFECT
muoio	sono morto/a
muori	
muore	
moriamo	
morite	
muoiono	

PRESENT CONTINUOUS	IMPERFECT CONTINUOUS
sto morendo	stavo morendo

IMPERFECT	PAST DEFINITE
morivo	morii

Note   The main irregular features are

• the present indicative and subjunctive tenses
• the past participle

IMPERATIVE
muori (tu)   moriamo (noi)   morite (voi)   **muoia** (Lei)

PLUPERFECT
ero morto/a

PAST ANTERIOR
fui morto/a

FUTURE
morirò

FUTURE PERFECT
sarò morto/a

CONDITIONAL
morirei

CONDITIONAL PERFECT
sarei morto/a

PRESENT SUBJUNCTIVE
muoia
muoia
muoia
moriamo
moriate
muoiano

PERFECT SUBJUNCTIVE
sia morto/a

IMPERFECT SUBJUNCTIVE
morissi

PLUPERFECT SUBJUNCTIVE
fossi morto/a

– *Muoio* **dal caldo!**	– *I'm dying* from the heat.
– **Dubito che** *muoia* **dal caldo!**	– I doubt whether *you'll die* from the heat.
– **Ma sono anche stanca** *morta*!	– But I am also *dead tired*.

GERUND	**PAST PARTICIPLE**
nascendo	**nato**

PRESENT	**PERFECT**
nasco	sono nato/a

PRESENT CONTINUOUS	**IMPERFECT CONTINUOUS**
sto nascendo	stavo nascendo

IMPERFECT	**PAST DEFINITE**
nascevo	**nacqui**
	nascesti
	nacque
	nascemmo
	nasceste
	nacquero

Similar verb

rinascere   be born again

Note   The main irregular features of the verb are

   • the past definite tense
   • the past participle

IMPERATIVE
nasci (tu)   nasciamo (noi)   nascete (voi)   nasca (Lei)

PLUPERFECT
ero nato/a

PAST ANTERIOR
fui nato/a

FUTURE
nascerò

FUTURE PERFECT
sarò nato/a

CONDITIONAL
nascerei

CONDITIONAL PERFECT
sarei nato/a

PRESENT SUBJUNCTIVE
nasca

PERFECT SUBJUNCTIVE
sia nato/a

IMPERFECT SUBJUNCTIVE
nascessi

PLUPERFECT SUBJUNCTIVE
fossi nato/a

La bambina *è nata* stamattina.	The baby girl *was born* this morning.
Il morto *era nato* ottantatré anni fa.	The dead man *was born* 83 years ago.
Boccaccio *nacque* secoli fa.	Boccaccio *was born* centuries ago.
Deve ancora *nascere* chi saprà risolvere tali problemi.	The man who can solve such problems is yet *to be born*.
Mi sento *rinascere*.	I feel a new person (*reborn*).
Quando lo rividi, mi *rinacque* l'odio.	When I saw him my feelings of hatred *began again*.
Gli *nascono* i denti.	He *is cutting* his first teeth.
Il Po *nasce* dal Monviso.	The river Po *has its source* on Monviso.

GERUND	PAST PARTICIPLE
parendo	**parso**

PRESENT	PERFECT
paio	sono parso/a
pari	
pare	
paiamo	
parete	
paiono	

PRESENT CONTINUOUS	IMPERFECT CONTINUOUS
sto parendo	stavo parendo

IMPERFECT	PAST DEFINITE
parevo	**parvi/parsi**
	paresti
	parve/parse
	paremmo
	pareste
	parvero/parsero

Notes The verb **parere** is mostly used impersonally and is consequently rare except for the third persons.

The main irregular features of the verb are

• the present indicative and subjunctive tenses
• the future stem
• the past definite tense
• the past participle

There are also some similarities with the verb **apparire** [➤23].

IMPERATIVE
pari (tu) **paiamo** (noi) parete (voi) **paia** (Lei)

PLUPERFECT	*PAST ANTERIOR*
ero parso/a	fui parso/a

FUTURE	*FUTURE PERFECT*
parrò	sarò parso/a

CONDITIONAL	*CONDITIONAL PERFECT*
parrei	sarei parso/a

PRESENT SUBJUNCTIVE	*PERFECT SUBJUNCTIVE*
paia	sia parso/a
paia	
paia	
paiamo	
pariate	
paiano	

IMPERFECT SUBJUNCTIVE	*PLUPERFECT SUBJUNCTIVE*
paressi	fossi parso/a

Mi *pare* importante.	It *seems* important to me.
Non mi *pareva* semplice.	It *did* not *seem* easy.
Gli *paiono* grandi.	They *seem* big to him.
Ti *parevano* stretti ?	*Did you think* they were narrow?

GERUND	*PAST PARTICIPLE*
perdendo	**perso**/perduto

PRESENT	*PERFECT*
perdo	ho perso

PRESENT CONTINUOUS	*IMPERFECT CONTINUOUS*
sto perdendo	stavo perdendo

IMPERFECT	*PAST DEFINITE*
perdevo	**persi**/perdei/perdetti
	perdesti
	perse
	perdemmo
	perdeste
	persero

Similar verb

*perdersi   get lost

Note   The main irregular features of the verb are

    • the past definite tense
    • the past participle (although it is possible to use the regular past
    participle)

IMPERATIVE
perdi (tu)   perdiamo (noi)   perdete (voi)   perda (Lei)

PLUPERFECT avevo perso	*PAST ANTERIOR* ebbi perso
FUTURE perderò	*FUTURE PERFECT* avrò perso
CONDITIONAL perderei	*CONDITIONAL PERFECT* avrei perso
PRESENT SUBJUNCTIVE perda	*PERFECT SUBJUNCTIVE* abbia perso
IMPERFECT SUBJUNCTIVE perdessi	*PLUPERFECT SUBJUNCTIVE* avessi perso

Ho perduto la penna.	*I lost* the pen.
L'*ho persa* ieri.	*I lost* it (the pen) yesterday.
Gianna *ha perso* un figlio.	Gianna *has lost* a son (through death).
Ha perso un anno l'anno scorso perché era ammalata.	*She is* a year *behind* because last year she was ill/sick.
Antonio *ha perso* il treno.	Antonio *has missed* the train.
Questo secchio *perde* acqua.	This bucket *is leaking* water.
Mi sono *perso* a Firenze.	I got *lost* in Florence.
È inutile spiegarmi queste cose, mi ci *perdo*.	It's no use explaining these things to me, I *can't make head or tail of* them.

GERUND	**PAST PARTICIPLE**
persuadendo	**persuaso**

PRESENT	**PERFECT**
persuado	ho persuaso

PRESENT CONTINUOUS	**IMPERFECT CONTINUOUS**
sto persuadendo	stavo persuadendo

IMPERFECT	**PAST DEFINITE**
persuadevo	**persuasi**
	persuadesti
	persuase
	persuademmo
	persuadeste
	persuasero

Similar verbs

dissuadere	dissuade
evadere	escape
invadere	invade

Note   The main irregular features of the verb are

- the past definite tense
- the past participle

IMPERATIVE

persuadi (tu)   persuadiamo (noi)   persuadete (voi)   persuada (Lei)

PLUPERFECT avevo persuaso	*PAST ANTERIOR* ebbi persuaso
FUTURE persuaderò	*FUTURE PERFECT* avrò persuaso
CONDITIONAL persuaderei	*CONDITIONAL PERFECT* avrei persuaso
PRESENT SUBJUNCTIVE persuada	*PERFECT SUBJUNCTIVE* abbia persuaso
IMPERFECT SUBJUNCTIVE persuadessi	*PLUPERFECT SUBJUNCTIVE* avessi persuaso

Ho avuto difficoltà a *persuaderla*.	I had difficulty in *persuading* her.
Finii per *persuaderla* a farlo.	*I finally persuaded* her to do it.
La *persuasi* che aveva torto.	*I persuaded* her that she was wrong.
L'*ho persuaso* dell'innocenza di Gianni.	*I convinced* him of Gianni's innocence.
***Dissuadila* dal venire!**	*Dissuade* her from coming!
Nulla la *dissuaderà* dal provare ancora una volta.	Nothing *will dissuade* her from trying one more time.

GERUND	PAST PARTICIPLE
piacendo	**piaciuto**

PRESENT	PERFECT
piaccio	sono piaciuto/a
piaci	
piace	**è piaciuto/a**
piacciamo/piaciamo	
piacete	
piacciono	**sono piaciuti/e**

PRESENT CONTINUOUS	IMPERFECT CONTINUOUS
sto piacendo	stavo piacendo

IMPERFECT	PAST DEFINITE
piacevo	**piacqui**
	piacesti
	piacque
	piacemmo
	piaceste
	piacquero

Similar verbs

*compiacere	please
*dispiacere	displease

Notes The verb **piacere** is mostly used impersonally and is consequently mainly found in the third person singular or plural.

The main irregular features of the verb are

- the present indicative and subjunctive tenses
- the past definite tense
- the addition of the **i** in the past participle

IMPERATIVE
piaci (tu)   piaciamo (noi)   piacete (voi)   **piaccia** (Lei)

PLUPERFECT
ero piaciuto/a

PAST ANTERIOR
fui piaciuto/a

FUTURE
piacerò

FUTURE PERFECT
sarò piaciuto/a

CONDITIONAL
piacerei

CONDITIONAL PERFECT
sarei piaciuto/a

PRESENT SUBJUNCTIVE
piaccia
piaccia
piaccia
piacciamo
piacciate
piacciano

PERFECT SUBJUNCTIVE
sia piaciuto/a

IMPERFECT SUBJUNCTIVE
piacessi

PLUPERFECT SUBJUNCTIVE
fossi piaciuto/a

– Ti *piace* la pasta?
– Sì, molto, e mi *piacciono* soprattutto gli spaghetti.
– *Piacciono* anche a Giovanni?

– Beh, penso che non gli *dispiacciano*.
– So che gli *piacciono* di più i tortellini.

Mi *dispiace*, ma non posso venire stasera.

L'*ho compiaciuto* nei suoi capricci.

– *Do you like* pasta?
– Yes, a lot, and *I* particularly *like* spaghetti.
– *Does* Giovanni *like* it (spaghetti) too?

– Well, I don't think *he doesn't like* spaghetti.
– I know he prefers tortellini.

I am *sorry*, but I cannot come this evening.

I humoured/humored him.

GERUND	***PAST PARTICIPLE***
piangendo	**pianto**

PRESENT	***PERFECT***
piango	ho pianto

PRESENT CONTINUOUS	***IMPERFECT CONTINUOUS***
sto piangendo	stavo piangendo

IMPERFECT	***PAST DEFINITE***
piangevo	**piansi**
	piangesti
	pianse
	piangemmo
	piangeste
	piansero

Similar verbs

compiangere	pity
rimpiangere	regret

Note   The main irregular features of the verb are

• the past definite tense
• the past participle

IMPERATIVE
piangi (tu)   piangiamo (noi)   piangete (voi)   pianga (Lei)

PLUPERFECT avevo pianto	*PAST ANTERIOR* ebbi pianto
FUTURE piangerò	*FUTURE PERFECT* avrò pianto
CONDITIONAL piangerei	*CONDITIONAL PERFECT* avrei pianto
PRESENT SUBJUNCTIVE pianga	*PERFECT SUBJUNCTIVE* abbia pianto
IMPERFECT SUBJUNCTIVE piangessi	*PLUPERFECT SUBJUNCTIVE* avessi pianto

---

Luisa *pianse* dal dolore.	Luisa *cried* with pain.
Mi *piangono* gli occhi per il fumo.	My eyes *are watering* because of the smoke.
Rimpiango di non esserci andata.	*I regret* not having gone.
Compiango il tuo dolore.	*I sympathize* with you in your grief.
Piansi di rabbia.	*I cried* with anger.
Piange la giovinezza perduta.	He *weeps* for his lost youth.
Beati quelli che *piangono*.	Blessed are those that *mourn*.
Chi è causa del suo mal, *pianga* se stesso.	You have made your bed, now lie in it. *(Proverb)*

GERUND	*PAST PARTICIPLE*
piovendo	piovuto

PRESENT	*PERFECT*
piove	ha piovuto/è piovuto/a
piovono	hanno piovuto/sono piovuti/e

PRESENT CONTINUOUS	*IMPERFECT CONTINUOUS*
sta piovendo	stava piovendo
stanno piovendo	stavano piovendo

IMPERFECT	*PAST DEFINITE*
pioveva	**piovve**
piovevano	**piovvero**

Notes   **piovere** and all impersonal verbs associated with weather terms take either **avere** or **essere** almost indifferently. In addition **piovere** takes **essere** when it is used figuratively to mean 'to pour in' or 'to turn up unexpectedly'. It is only irregular in the past definite tense.

PLUPERFECT
aveva piovuto/era piovuto/a
avevano piovuto/erano piovuti/e

PAST ANTERIOR
ebbe piovuto/fu piovuto/a
ebbero piovuto/furono piovuti/e

FUTURE
pioverà
pioveranno

FUTURE PERFECT
avrà piovuto/sarà piovuto/a
avranno piovuto/saranno piovuti/e

CONDITIONAL
pioverebbe
pioverebbero

CONDITIONAL PERFECT
avrebbe piovuto/sarebbe piovuto/a
avrebbero piovuto/sarebbero piovuti/e

PRESENT SUBJUNCTIVE
piova

PERFECT SUBJUNCTIVE
abbia piovuto/sia piovuto/a

IMPERFECT SUBJUNCTIVE
piovesse

PLUPERFECT SUBJUNCTIVE
ebbe piovuto/fosse piovuto/a

Ha piovuto./È piovuto.	*It has rained.*
Piovve a catinelle.	*It poured* with rain.
Non ci *piove* sopra.	There's no doubt about it.
Le *piovvero* inviti da ogni parte.	Invitations *showered* upon her from all sides.
La luce *pioveva* nella stanza dalla finestra aperta.	The light *poured into* the room through the open window.
Lettere gli *piovevano* da ogni lato.	Letters *poured in* for him from all sides.

GERUND	PAST PARTICIPLE
ponendo	**posto**

PRESENT	PERFECT
pongo	ho posto
poni	
pone	
poniamo	
ponete	
pongono	

PRESENT CONTINUOUS	IMPERFECT CONTINUOUS
sto ponendo	stavo ponendo

IMPERFECT	PAST DEFINITE
ponevo	**posi**
	ponesti
	pose
	ponemmo
	poneste
	posero

Similar verbs

There are many compounds of **porre** which follow this pattern.

apporre	affix	**comporre**	compose, dial (number)
decomporre	decompose	**disporre**	dispose
esporre	expose	**frapporre**	insert
imporre	impose	**interporre**	interpose
opporre	oppose	**posporre**	postpone
preporre	prefer	**presupporre**	presuppose
proporre	propose	**riporre**	put again
supporre	suppose		

Note The main irregular features of these verbs are

- the present indicative and subjunctive tenses
- the past definite tense
- the past participle
- the future stem

IMPERATIVE
poni (tu)   poniamo (noi)   ponete (voi)   ponga (Lei)

PLUPERFECT	**PAST ANTERIOR**
avevo posto	ebbi posto
FUTURE	**FUTURE PERFECT**
porrò	avrò posto
CONDITIONAL	**CONDITIONAL PERFECT**
porrei	avrei posto
PRESENT SUBJUNCTIVE	**PERFECT SUBJUNCTIVE**
ponga	abbia posto
ponga	
ponga	
poniamo	
poniate	
pongano	
IMPERFECT SUBJUNCTIVE	**PLUPERFECT SUBJUNCTIVE**
ponessi	avessi posto

– Allora cosa *proponi* tu?	– So what do you *propose*?
– *Porrei* la sedia qui ed il divano lì.	– I *would put* the chair here and the settee there.
– No, non mi piace così. Perché non *poniamo* la sedia accanto al divano?	– No, I don't like it like that. Why *don't we put* the chair next to the settee?
– *Suppongo* che devo spostare anche la televisione?	– I *suppose* I'll have to move the television as well?
Spensierata, *composi* il numero.	Without thinking, I *dialled* the number.
Ha esposto delle camicie in vetrina.	He *displayed* some shirts in the window.
Esporrò le mie idee dopodomani.	I *will explain* my ideas the day after tomorrow.

GERUND	PAST PARTICIPLE
potendo	potuto

PRESENT	PERFECT
posso	ho potuto/sono potuto/a
puoi	
può	
possiamo	
potete	
possono	

PRESENT CONTINUOUS	IMPERFECT CONTINUOUS
sto potendo	stavo potendo

IMPERFECT	PAST DEFINITE
potevo	potei

PLUPERFECT	PAST ANTERIOR
avevo potuto/ero potuto/a	ebbi potuto/fui potuto/a

Notes   The verb **potere** is a frequently used modal verb. It is important to distinguish between **potere** and **sapere,** both of which can translate the English word 'can'. The verb **potere** denotes physical capability rather than skill.

The main irregular features of the verb are

- the present indicative and subjunctive tenses
- the past definite tense
- the future stem

The imperative is never used

FUTURE
potrò

CONDITIONAL
potrei

PRESENT SUBJUNCTIVE
possa
possa
possa
possiamo
possiate
possano

IMPERFECT SUBJUNCTIVE
potessi

FUTURE PERFECT
avrò potuto/sarò potuto/a

CONDITIONAL PERFECT
avrei potuto/sarei potuto/a

PERFECT SUBJUNCTIVE
abbia potuto/sia potuto/a

PLUPERFECT SUBJUNCTIVE
avessi potuto/fossi potuto/a

– Mi dispiace, non *posso* andare in città.
– Ma mi hai detto che *potevi* venire!
– Sì, è vero, ma ho tanto da fare. Non ne *posso* più.
– Nemmeno Carlo è *potuto* venire.
– Mi avresti *potuto* dirlo prima !

– I'm sorry, *I can*'t go into town.
– But you said *you could* come!
– Yes, it's true, but I have so much to do. I am completely exhausted.
– Not even Carlo *has been able* to come.
– *You could have* told me before now.

Note In the last two examples the auxiliary used depends on the auxiliary normally used by the dependent infinitive, not **potere**. Thus in **è potuto/a venire** the auxiliary is **essere** because **venire** takes **essere**, and in the final sentence **avere** is used because **dire** takes **avere**.

GERUND	PAST PARTICIPLE
prendendo	**preso**

PRESENT	PERFECT
prendo	ho preso

PRESENT CONTINUOUS	IMPERFECT CONTINUOUS
sto prendendo	stavo prendendo

IMPERFECT	PAST DEFINITE
prendevo	**presi**
	prendesti
	prese
	prendemmo
	prendeste
	presero

Similar verbs

apprendere	learn	**comprendere**	understand, consist of
intraprendere	undertake	**sorprendere**	surprise

Note   The main irregular features of the verb are

• the past definite tense
• the past participle.

***Hanno preso* il ladro.**	*They caught* the thief.
***Prendo* lezioni d'italiano.**	*I take* Italian lessons.
Lo *presi* per il collo.	*I took* him by the scruff of his neck.
***Fu preso* dalla paura.**	*He was seized* by fear.
Devi andare a *prendere* la zia.	You've got to go and *get* auntie.
***Ho preso* un appartamento in affitto.**	I rented a flat/an apartment.
Stefano *ha preso* un raffreddore.	Stephen *has got/gotten* a cold.
Tu mi *sorprendi* spesso!	You often *surprise* me!

IMPERATIVE
prendi (tu)   prendiamo (noi)   prendete (voi)   prenda (Lei)

PLUPERFECT avevo preso	**PAST ANTERIOR** ebbi preso
FUTURE prenderò	**FUTURE PERFECT** avrò preso
CONDITIONAL prenderei	**CONDITIONAL PERFECT** avrei preso
PRESENT SUBJUNCTIVE prenda	**PERFECT SUBJUNCTIVE** abbia preso
IMPERFECT SUBJUNCTIVE prendessi	**PLUPERFECT SUBJUNCTIVE** avessi preso

Comprese il suo errore.	He *understood* what he had done wrong.
La casa *comprende* un salotto, due camere, un bagno e una cucina.	The house *consists of* a lounge, two bedrooms, a bathroom and a kitchen.
Gianni l'*ha sorpreso* mentre fumavo.	Gianni *caught* him smoking.
Il ragazzo le *prese* da suo padre.	The boy *was smacked* by his father.
Prende sempre brutti voti.	He always *gets* bad marks.
Non *ha appreso* nulla a scuola.	He *has* not *learned/learnt* anything at school.
Quanto *prendi* al mese?	How much *do you earn* a month?
Per chi mi *prendi*?	Who *do you take* me for?
Che ti *prende*?	What*'s the matter* with you?
Non *prendertela*!	*Do*n't *worry about it*.
Se l'*ha preso* a cuore.	He*'s taken* it to heart.

GERUND	PAST PARTICIPLE
proteggendo	**protetto**

PRESENT	PERFECT
proteggo	ho protetto

PRESENT CONTINUOUS	IMPERFECT CONTINUOUS
sto proteggendo	stavo proteggendo

IMPERFECT	PAST DEFINITE
proteggevo	**protessi**
	proteggesti
	protesse
	proteggemmo
	proteggeste
	protessero

Note   The main irregular features of the verb are

• the past definite tense
• the past participle

IMPERATIVE
proteggi (tu)   proteggiamo (noi)   proteggete (voi)   protegga (Lei)

PLUPERFECT
avevo protetto

PAST ANTERIOR
ebbi protetto

FUTURE
proteggerò

FUTURE PERFECT
avrò protetto

CONDITIONAL
proteggerei

CONDITIONAL PERFECT
avrei protetto

PRESENT SUBJUNCTIVE
protegga

PERFECT SUBJUNCTIVE
abbia protetto

IMPERFECT SUBJUNCTIVE
proteggessi

PLUPERFECT SUBJUNCTIVE
avessi protetto

Quest'ombrello ti *proteggerà* dalla pioggia.	This umbrella *will protect* you from the rain.
Il cane *protesse* la casa.	The dog *protected* the house.
Un angelo *protegge* il bambino.	An angel *is protecting* the baby.
Che Dio ti *protegga* !	May God *protect* you !
La fortuna *protegge* gli audaci.	Fortune *favours/favors* the brave.

GERUND	**_PAST PARTICIPLE_**
pungendo	**punto**

PRESENT	**_PERFECT_**
pungo	ho punto

PRESENT CONTINUOUS	**_IMPERFECT CONTINUOUS_**
sto pungendo	stavo pungendo

IMPERFECT	**_PAST DEFINITE_**
pungevo	**punsi**
	pungesti
	punse
	pungemmo
	pungeste
	punsero

Similar verbs

fungere	act as
mungere	milk
ungere	oil, grease, lubricate, anoint

Note   The main irregular features of the verb are

- the past definite tense
- the past participle

IMPERATIVE
pungi (tu)   pungiamo (noi)   pungete (voi)   punga (Lei)

PLUPERFECT avevo punto	**PAST ANTERIOR** ebbi punto
FUTURE pungerò	**FUTURE PERFECT** avrò punto
CONDITIONAL pungerei	**CONDITIONAL PERFECT** avrei punto
PRESENT SUBJUNCTIVE punga	**PERFECT SUBJUNCTIVE** abbia punto
IMPERFECT SUBJUNCTIVE pungessi	**PLUPERFECT SUBJUNCTIVE** avessi punto

Le rose *pungono*.	Roses *prick*.
Le vespe *pungono*.	Wasps *sting*.
Mi *punsi* la mano.	I *pricked* my hand.
Gli *punge* il desiderio di vederla.	He *was spurred on* by the wish to see her.
Il freddo mi *pungeva* il viso.	The cold *stung* my face.
Fu *punto* dal rimorso.	He was *pricked* with remorse.
Mi *punse* la coscienza.	My conscience *pricked* me.
***Munse* la vacca.**	*He milked* the cow.
***Unsero* le ruote.**	*They oiled* the wheels.
Fu *unto* re.	He *was anointed* King.
L'uomo *funse* da capo.	The man *acted* as leader.

GERUND	*PAST PARTICIPLE*
radendo	**raso**

PRESENT	*PERFECT*
rado	ho raso

PRESENT CONTINUOUS	*IMPERFECT CONTINUOUS*
sto radendo	stavo radendo

IMPERFECT	*PAST DEFINITE*
radevo	**rasi**
	radesti
	rase
	rademmo
	radeste
	rasero

Similar verb

*radersi   shave oneself

Note   The main irregular features of the verb are

   • the past definite tense
   • the past participle

IMPERATIVE
radi (tu)   radiamo (noi)   radete (voi)   rada (Lei)

PLUPERFECT avevo raso	**PAST ANTERIOR** ebbi raso
FUTURE raderò	**FUTURE PERFECT** avrò raso
CONDITIONAL raderei	**CONDITIONAL PERFECT** avrei raso
PRESENT SUBJUNCTIVE rada	**PERFECT SUBJUNCTIVE** abbia raso
IMPERFECT SUBJUNCTIVE radessi	**PLUPERFECT SUBJUNCTIVE** avessi raso

---

Mi *ha raso* male.	*He shaved* me badly.
La città fu *rasa* al suolo.	The city was *razed* to the ground.
Rase la superficie dell'acqua.	*It skimmed* the surface of the water.
Mi *rado* ogni mattina.	I *shave* every morning.

GERUND	*PAST PARTICIPLE*
reggendo	**retto**

PRESENT	*PERFECT*
reggo	ho retto

PRESENT CONTINUOUS	*IMPERFECT CONTINUOUS*
sto reggendo	stavo reggendo

IMPERFECT	*PAST DEFINITE*
reggevo	**ressi**
	reggesti
	resse
	reggemmo
	reggeste
	ressero

Similar verbs

correggere	correct
soreggere	support, hold up

Note   The main irregular features of the verb are

- the past definite tense
- the past participle

IMPERATIVE
reggi (tu)   reggiamo (noi)   reggete (voi)   regga (Lei)

PLUPERFECT avevo retto	*PAST ANTERIOR* ebbi retto
FUTURE reggerò	*FUTURE PERFECT* avrò retto
CONDITIONAL reggerei	*CONDITIONAL PERFECT* avrei retto
PRESENT SUBJUNCTIVE regga	*PERFECT SUBJUNCTIVE* abbia retto
IMPERFECT SUBJUNCTIVE reggessi	*PLUPERFECT SUBJUNCTIVE* avessi retto

Regge il governo.	He *is the head of* the government.
Le gambe non mi *reggono*.	I *cannot stand* on my feet.
Quella corda non lo *reggerà*.	That rope *will* not *hold* him.
La mensola non *reggerà* quei libri.	The shelf *will* not *support* those books.
Non *reggo* il vino.	I *cannot take* wine.
Questo materiale *regge* il fuoco.	This material is fireproof.
Non *reggo* più.	I *cannot go on*.
Bisogna *correggere* quel bambino.	That child *should be corrected*.
Hai corretto i compiti?	*Have you corrected* the homework?
Correggerò il tuo caffè col cognac.	*I'll lace* your coffee with brandy.
I genitori *hanno sorretto* il bambino.	The parents *supported/held up* the child.

GERUND	PAST PARTICIPLE
rendendo	**reso**

PRESENT	PERFECT
rendo	ho reso

PRESENT CONTINUOUS	IMPERFECT CONTINUOUS
sto rendendo	stavo rendendo

IMPERFECT	PAST DEFINITE
rendevo	**resi**
	rendesti
	rese
	rendemmo
	rendeste
	resero

Similar verbs

*arrendersi	surrender
*rendersi conto di	realize

Note The main irregular features of the verb are

- the past definite tense
- the past participle

IMPERATIVE
rendi (tu)   rendiamo (noi)   rendete (voi)   renda (Lei)

PLUPERFECT avevo reso	**PAST ANTERIOR** ebbi reso
FUTURE renderò	**FUTURE PERFECT** avrò reso
CONDITIONAL renderei	**CONDITIONAL PERFECT** avrei reso
PRESENT SUBJUNCTIVE renda	**PERFECT SUBJUNCTIVE** abbia reso
IMPERFECT SUBJUNCTIVE rendessi	**PLUPERFECT SUBJUNCTIVE** avessi reso

Mi *ha reso* il libro ieri.	He *gave* me the book *back* yesterday.
Rendimi la penna che ti ho prestata.	*Give* me *back* the pen that I lent you.
Questo lavoro non *rende* molto.	This job is not well paid.
L'amore *rende* felici.	Love *makes* you happy.
Questa notizia lo *rese* incapace di parlare.	This piece of news *left* him speechless.
È difficile *rendere* il senso dell'originale in una traduzione.	It is difficult *to render* the sense of the original in a translation.
Non *mi sono reso conto* di ciò che è successo.	I *did* not *realize* what happened.
I soldati si *sono arresi*.	The soldiers *surrendered*.

GERUND	***PAST PARTICIPLE***
ridendo	**riso**

PRESENT	***PERFECT***
rido	ho riso

PRESENT CONTINUOUS	***IMPERFECT CONTINUOUS***
sto ridendo	stavo ridendo

IMPERFECT	***PAST DEFINITE***
ridevo	**risi**
	ridesti
	rise
	ridemmo
	rideste
	risero

Similar verbs

deridere	deride
sorridere	smile

Note The main irregular features of the verb are

- the past definite tense
- the past participle

IMPERATIVE
ridi (tu)   ridiamo (noi)   ridete (voi)   rida (Lei)

PLUPERFECT
avevo riso

PAST ANTERIOR
ebbi riso

FUTURE
riderò

FUTURE PERFECT
avrò riso

CONDITIONAL
riderei

CONDITIONAL PERFECT
avrei riso

PRESENT SUBJUNCTIVE
rida

PERFECT SUBJUNCTIVE
abbia riso

IMPERFECT SUBJUNCTIVE
ridessi

PLUPERFECT SUBJUNCTIVE
avessi riso

Non c'è da *ridere*!	It's not a laughing matter!
Non ci vedo niente da *ridere*.	I can't see anything *to laugh about*.
Ma non farmi *ridere*!	But don't make me *laugh*!
Quella bambina *sorride* sempre.	That girl's always *smiling*.
Gianni mi *sorrise*.	Gianni *smiled* at me.
La fortuna gli *sorride*.	Good fortune *smiles* on him.
L'*hanno deriso*.	*They ridiculed* him.
Risero alle sue spalle.	*They laughed* behind his back.
I suoi occhi *risero* di gioia.	Her eyes *sparkled* with happiness.
Ride bene chi *ride* ultimo.	He who *laughs* last *laughs* longest.
La fortuna gli *ride*.	Good luck *smiles* at him.
Chi *ride* il venerdì, piange la domenica.	*Laugh* today, for tomorrow you may cry.

GERUND	PAST PARTICIPLE
rimanendo	**rimasto**

PRESENT	PERFECT
rimango	sono rimasto/a
rimani	
rimane	
rimaniamo	
rimanete	
rimangono	

PRESENT CONTINUOUS	IMPERFECT CONTINUOUS
sto rimanendo	stavo rimanendo

IMPERFECT	PAST DEFINITE
rimanevo	**rimasi**
	rimanesti
	rimase
	rimanemmo
	rimaneste
	rimasero

Note The main irregular features of the verb are

- the present indicative and subjunctive tenses
- the past definite tense
- the past participle
- the future stem

IMPERATIVE
rimani (tu)   rimaniamo (noi)   rimanete (voi)   **rimanga** (Lei)

PLUPERFECT	*PAST ANTERIOR*
ero rimasto/a	fui rimasto/a

FUTURE	*FUTURE PERFECT*
rimarrò	sarò rimasto/a

CONDITIONAL	*CONDITIONAL PERFECT*
rimarrei	sarei rimasto/a

PRESENT SUBJUNCTIVE	*PERFECT SUBJUNCTIVE*
rimanga	sia rimasto/a
rimanga	
rimanga	
rimaniamo	
rimaniate	
rimangano	

IMPERFECT SUBJUNCTIVE	*PLUPERFECT SUBJUNCTIVE*
rimanessi	fossi rimasto/a

– **Quanto tempo *rimani* in Italia?**
– *Rimango* **due settimane.**
– **Che ti *rimane* da fare?**
– **Mi *rimane* soltanto la conclusione del tema.**
– **Dubito che tu *rimanga* fino alla festa allora.**

– How long *are you staying* in Italy?
– *I am staying* 2 weeks.
– What *have you left* to do?
– *I have* only the essay's conclusion *left* to do.
– I doubt whether *you are staying* until the party then.

GERUND	PAST PARTICIPLE
risolvendo	**risolto**

PRESENT	PERFECT
risolvo	ho risolto

PRESENT CONTINUOUS	IMPERFECT CONTINUOUS
sto risolvendo	stavo risolvendo

IMPERFECT	PAST DEFINITE
risolvevo	**risolsi**/risolvei/risolvetti
	risolvesti
	risolse
	risolvemmo
	risolveste
	risolsero

Similar verbs

assolvere	absolve, acquit
dissolvere	dissolve
*risolversi	decide, make up one's mind

Note   The main irregular features of the verb are

- the past definite tense
- the past participle

IMPERATIVE
risolvi (tu) risolviamo (noi) risolvete (voi) risolva (Lei)

PLUPERFECT avevo risolto	**PAST ANTERIOR** ebbi risolto
FUTURE risolverò	**FUTURE PERFECT** avrò risolto
CONDITIONAL risolverei	**CONDITIONAL PERFECT** avrei risolto
PRESENT SUBJUNCTIVE risolva	**PERFECT SUBJUNCTIVE** abbia risolto
IMPERFECT SUBJUNCTIVE risolvessi	**PLUPERFECT SUBJUNCTIVE** avessi risolto

---

Risolse di farlo lui stesso.	*He resolved* to do it himself.
Hai risolto l'equazione?	*Have you solved* the equation?
Dubito che quel problema *sia stato risolto.*	I doubt whether that problem *has been resolved.*
Si *risolse* di andare via.	He *made up* his *mind* to go away.
Il ladro fu *assolto.*	The thief was *acquitted.*

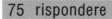
GERUND	PAST PARTICIPLE
rispondendo	**risposto**

PRESENT	PERFECT
rispondo	ho risposto

PRESENT CONTINUOUS	IMPERFECT CONTINUOUS
sto rispondendo	stavo rispondendo

IMPERFECT	PAST DEFINITE
rispondevo	**risposi**
	rispondesti
	rispose
	rispondemmo
	rispondeste
	risposero

Similar verbs

corrispondere	correspond
nascondere	hide
***nascondersi**	hide (oneself)

Note   The main irregular features of the verb are

- the past definite tense
- the past participle

IMPERATIVE
rispondi (tu)   rispondiamo (noi)   rispondete (voi)   risponda (Lei)

PLUPERFECT	*PAST ANTERIOR*
avevo risposto	ebbi risposto
FUTURE	*FUTURE PERFECT*
risponderò	avrò risposto
CONDITIONAL	*CONDITIONAL PERFECT*
risponderei	avrei risposto
PRESENT SUBJUNCTIVE	*PERFECT SUBJUNCTIVE*
risponda	abbia risposto
IMPERFECT SUBJUNCTIVE	*PLUPERFECT SUBJUNCTIVE*
rispondessi	avessi risposto

Ha risposto subito alla mia proposta.	*He replied* immediately to my proposal.
Risposi per iscritto.	*I replied* in writing.
Gianna *rispose* con un cenno del capo.	Gianna *replied* with a nod of the head.
Io non *rispondo* delle azioni di mio fratello.	I cannot *be held responsible* for the actions of my brother.
Questo motore non *risponde*.	This engine *is* not *responding*.
Nascose la sua identità.	*He hid* his identity.
Dove è andato a *nascondersi*?	Where *has* he gone and *hidden*?
La descrizione nel dépliant non *corrispondeva* alla realtà.	The description in the brochure *did* not *correspond* to reality/give a true picture.

GERUND	PAST PARTICIPLE
rompendo	**rotto**

PRESENT	PERFECT
rompo	ho rotto

PRESENT CONTINUOUS	IMPERFECT CONTINUOUS
sto rompendo	stavo rompendo

IMPERFECT	PAST DEFINITE
rompevo	**ruppi**
	rompesti
	ruppe
	rompemmo
	rompeste
	ruppero

Similar verbs

corrompere	corrupt
interrompere	interrupt
irrompere	rush in upon
prorompere	burst out
*rompersi	break up

Note   The main irregular features of the verb are

  • the past definite tense
  • the past participle

IMPERATIVE
rompi (tu)   rompiamo (noi)   rompete (voi)   rompa (Lei)

PLUPERFECT avevo rotto	**PAST ANTERIOR** ebbi rotto
FUTURE romperò	**FUTURE PERFECT** avrò rotto
CONDITIONAL romperei	**CONDITIONAL PERFECT** avrei rotto
PRESENT SUBJUNCTIVE rompa	**PERFECT SUBJUNCTIVE** abbia rotto
IMPERFECT SUBJUNCTIVE rompessi	**PLUPERFECT SUBJUNCTIVE** avessi rotto

---

Ho *rotto* un vaso ieri.	*I broke* a vase yesterday.
Hai *rotto* la tua promessa!	*You have broken* your promise!
Vorrei *romperla* con quel ragazzo.	I want *to break up* with that boy.
La nave *si ruppe* sulle rocce.	The ship *broke up* on the rocks.
Hai *corrotto* tutto!	*You have corrupted* everything!
Interruppe la nostra conversazione.	*He interrupted* our conversation.
Ho *interrotto* il viaggio a Firenze.	*I broke* my journey in Florence.
La corrente è stata *interrotta* per un'ora.	The electricity supply was *cut off* for an hour.
I ladri *irruppero* nella casa.	The thieves *broke into* the house.
La folla *irruppe* nello stadio.	The crowd *broke into* the stadium.

GERUND	**PAST PARTICIPLE**
salendo	salito

PRESENT	**PERFECT**
salgo	ho salito/sono salito/a
sali	
sale	
saliamo	
salite	
salgono	

PRESENT CONTINUOUS	**IMPERFECT CONTINUOUS**
sto salendo	stavo salendo

IMPERFECT	**PAST DEFINITE**
salivo	salii

Similar verb

† assalire   assail

Note   The main irregular features of the verb are

      • the present indicative and subjunctive tenses
      • it takes **avere** when used transitively and **essere** when used
      intransitively

IMPERATIVE
sali (tu)   saliamo (noi)   salite (voi)   **salga** (Lei)

PLUPERFECT	**PAST ANTERIOR**
avevo salito/ero salito/a	ebbi salito/fui salito/a

FUTURE	**FUTURE PERFECT**
salirò	avrò salito/sarò salito/a

CONDITIONAL	**CONDITIONAL PERFECT**
salirei	avrei salito/sarei salito/a

PRESENT SUBJUNCTIVE   **PERFECT SUBJUNCTIVE**
salga   abbia salito/sia salito/a
salga
salga
saliamo
saliate
salgano

IMPERFECT SUBJUNCTIVE   **PLUPERFECT SUBJUNCTIVE**
salissi   avessi salito/fossi salito/a

– *Saliamo* fino a quel punto lì ?   – *Shall we go up* to that point there?

– Io non *salgo* più !   – I'*m* not *going up* any further.

– Che peccato che tu non *salga* lassù – c'è un panorama bellissimo da quel punto.   – What a shame that *you are* not *going up* there – there is a beautiful view from that point.

Fu *assalita* dai dubbi.   She was *attacked* by doubts.

Fummo *assaliti* dal temporale.   We *were caught* in the storm.

GERUND	PAST PARTICIPLE
sapendo	saputo

PRESENT	PERFECT
so	ho saputo
sai	
sa	
sappiamo	
sapete	
sanno	

PRESENT CONTINUOUS	IMPERFECT CONTINUOUS
sto sapendo	stavo sapendo

IMPERFECT	PAST DEFINITE
sapevo	**seppi**
	sapesti
	seppe
	sapemmo
	sapeste
	seppero

Notes The verb **sapere** is frequently used as a modal verb. It is important to distinguish between **potere** [➤65] and **sapere,** both of which can translate the English word 'can'. The verb **sapere** denotes skill rather than physical capability.

It is also important to distinguish between the verbs **conoscere** [➤34] and **sapere**, which can both be translated as 'to know' in English. **Conoscere** means to know a person or a place, whereas **sapere** means to know a fact or to know how to do something.

The main irregular features of the verb **sapere** are

• the present indicative and subjunctive tenses
• the past definite tense
• the future stem

IMPERATIVE
sappi (tu)   **sappiamo** (noi)   **sappiate** (voi)   **sappia** (Lei)

PLUPERFECT avevo saputo	*PAST ANTERIOR* ebbi saputo
FUTURE **saprò**	*FUTURE PERFECT* avrò saputo
CONDITIONAL **saprei**	*CONDITIONAL PERFECT* avrei saputo
PRESENT SUBJUNCTIVE **sappia** **sappia** **sappia** **sappiamo** **sappiate** **sappiano**	*PERFECT SUBJUNCTIVE* abbia saputo
IMPERFECT SUBJUNCTIVE sapessi	*PLUPERFECT SUBJUNCTIVE* avessi saputo

---

– *So* suonare il flauto adesso.
– Non *saprei* da dove cominciare!
– Conosci la mia maestra?
– No, non la conosco, ma *so* dove abita.
– Pare che sappia *suonare* molto bene.

– *I know* how to play the flute now.
– *I would*n't *know* where to begin!
– Do you know my teacher?
– No, I don't know her, but *I know* where she lives.
– It seems that she *knows* how to play very well.

205

GERUND	*PAST PARTICIPLE*
scendendo	**sceso**

PRESENT	*PERFECT*
scendo	ho sono sceso/a

PRESENT CONTINUOUS	*IMPERFECT CONTINUOUS*
sto scendendo	stavo scendendo

IMPERFECT	*PAST DEFINITE*
scendevo	**scesi**
	scendesti
	scese
	scendemmo
	scendeste
	scesero

Similar verbs

† **accondiscendere**	condescend
† **ascendere**	ascend
† **discendere**	descend

† Like **scendere,** these verbs can take either **avere** or **essere**, depending on whether they are used transitively or intransitively.

Note   The main irregular features of the verb are

- the past definite tense
- the past participle

Sono sceso/a.	*I went downstairs.*
Scese correndo le scale.	*He came running downstairs.*
Sono scesi dal tram.	*They got off the tram/trolleybus.*
La montagna scende verso il mare.	The mountain *sloped down* towards the sea.

IMPERATIVE
scendi (tu)   scendiamo (noi)   scendete (voi)   scenda (Lei)

PLUPERFECT avevo sceso/ero sceso/a	*PAST ANTERIOR* ebbi sceso/fui sceso/a
FUTURE scenderò	*FUTURE PERFECT* avrò sceso/sarò sceso/a
CONDITIONAL scenderei	*CONDITIONAL PERFECT* avrei sceso/sarei sceso/a
PRESENT SUBJUNCTIVE scenda	*PERFECT SUBJUNCTIVE* abbia sceso/sia sceso/a
IMPERFECT SUBJUNCTIVE scendessi	*PLUPERFECT SUBJUNCTIVE* avessi sceso/fossi sceso/a

---

La temperatura *è scesa* oggi.	The temperature *has gone down* today.
Non *scendo* a parlare con gente simile.	I won't *stoop* to speak to people like that.
I capelli le *scendevano* alle spalle.	Her hair *fell over* her shoulders.
***Accondiscese* a una riduzione di prezzo.**	*He agreed* to a reduction in price.
***Ascese* al trono.**	*He/she/you ascended* to the throne.
Le spese *ascendono* a dieci mille lire.	The expenses *amount* to 10,000 lire.
***Discesi* le scale.**	*I went* downstairs.
Il fiume *discende* verso il mare.	The river *flows down* to the sea.

GERUND	**PAST PARTICIPLE**
scorgendo	**scorto**

PRESENT	**PERFECT**
scorgo	ho scorto

PRESENT CONTINUOUS	**IMPERFECT CONTINUOUS**
sto scorgendo	stavo scorgendo

IMPERFECT	**PAST DEFINITE**
scorgevo	**scorsi**
	scorgesti
	scorse
	scorgemmo
	scorgeste
	scorsero

Similar verbs

*accorgersi	perceive, notice
porgere	hand, give, hold out
*sorgere	arise
*sporgere	project, stick out, jut out
*sporgersi	lean out
*risorgere	rise again, revive

Note   The main irregular features of the verb are

- the past definite tense
- the past participle

Non *scorgevo* molta differenza tra le due pitture.	*I did* not *notice* much difference between the two paintings.
Se ne andò senza farsi *scorgere*.	He went away without *being noticed*.
Non vuole farsi *scorgere* da lui.	S/he does not want him *to notice* him/her.

IMPERATIVE
scorgi (tu)   scorgiamo (noi)   scorgete (voi)   scorga (Lei)

PLUPERFECT	**PAST ANTERIOR**
avevo scorto	ebbi scorto
FUTURE	**FUTURE PERFECT**
scorgerò	avrò scorto
CONDITIONAL	**CONDITIONAL PERFECT**
scorgerei	avrei scorto
PRESENT SUBJUNCTIVE	**PERFECT SUBJUNCTIVE**
scorga	abbia scorto
IMPERFECT SUBJUNCTIVE	**PLUPERFECT SUBJUNCTIVE**
scorgessi	avessi scorto

Non me ne sono nemmeno accorto!	I *didn't* even *notice*!
Non si era *accorta* che pioveva.	She *didn't notice* it was raining.
Poi *sorse* una grande discussione.	Then a great discussion *arose*.
Le montagne *sorgono* davanti a me.	The mountains *are looming* in front of me.
Ho visto *sorgere* il sole.	I saw the sun *rise*.
La nebbia *sorse* dal lago.	The fog *rose* from the lake.
Le sue speranze *risorsero*.	His hopes *revived*.
Vi *porgo* i miei più distinti saluti.	Yours sincerely.
È pericoloso *sporgersi* dal finestrino.	It is dangerous *to lean out* of the window.

GERUND	PAST PARTICIPLE
scrivendo	**scritto**

PRESENT	PERFECT
scrivo	ho scritto

PRESENT CONTINUOUS	IMPERFECT CONTINUOUS
sto scrivendo	stavo scrivendo

IMPERFECT	PAST DEFINITE
scrivevo	**scrissi**
	scrivesti
	scrisse
	scrivemmo
	scriveste
	scrissero

Similar verbs

descrivere	describe
iscrivere	enrol/enroll, register
***iscriversi**	enrol/enroll (oneself)

Note The main irregular features of the verb are

- the past definite tense
- the past participle

IMPERATIVE
scrivi (tu)   scriviamo (noi)   scrivete (voi)   scriva (Lei)

PLUPERFECT	*PAST ANTERIOR*
avevo scritto	ebbi scritto

FUTURE	*FUTURE PERFECT*
scriverò	avrò scritto

CONDITIONAL	*CONDITIONAL PERFECT*
scriverei	avrei scritto

PRESENT SUBJUNCTIVE	*PERFECT SUBJUNCTIVE*
scriva	abbia scritto

IMPERFECT SUBJUNCTIVE	*PLUPERFECT SUBJUNCTIVE*
scrivessi	avessi scritto

Come si *scrive* questa parola?	How *do you spell* this word?
Sa *scrivere* la musica.	He knows how *to write* music.
Gli *ho scritto* due righe.	I *wrote* him a note (two lines).
Scrisse a casa ogni due settimane.	He *wrote* home every 2 weeks.
Ti *iscrivo* al club?	Shall I *enrol/enroll* you (as a member) in the club?
Mi sono *iscritto* all'università.	I have *registered/matriculated* with the university.
Descrisse la scena in montagna.	He *described* the scene in the mountains.
Vorrei *descrivere* un'ampia curva.	I would like *to describe* a wide curve.

GERUND	PAST PARTICIPLE
scuotendo	**scosso**

PRESENT	PERFECT
scuoto	ho scosso
scuoti	
scuote	
scuotiamo	
scuotete	
scuotono	

PRESENT CONTINUOUS	IMPERFECT CONTINUOUS
sto scuotendo	stavo scuotendo

IMPERFECT	PAST DEFINITE
scuotevo	**scossi**
	scuotesti
	scosse
	scuotemmo
	scuoteste
	scossero

Similar verbs

riscuotere	draw, collect, cash
percuotere	beat
ripercuotere	beat again
***ripercuotersi**	riverberate, influence

Note   The main irregular features of the verb are

- the past definite tense
- the past participle

IMPERATIVE

scuoti (tu)   scuotiamo (noi)   scuotete (voi)   scuota (Lei)

PLUPERFECT	*PAST ANTERIOR*
avevo scosso	ebbi scosso
FUTURE	*FUTURE PERFECT*
scuoterò	avrò scosso
CONDITIONAL	*CONDITIONAL PERFECT*
scuoterei	avrei scosso
PRESENT SUBJUNCTIVE	*PERFECT SUBJUNCTIVE*
scuota	abbia scosso
IMPERFECT SUBJUNCTIVE	*PLUPERFECT SUBJUNCTIVE*
scuotessi	avessi scosso

Scosse l'albero.	*He shook* the tree.
Scuote la testa.	*He shook* his head.
Fu *scossa* dalla notizia.	She was *shaken* by the news.
Ho riscosso l'assegno.	*I cashed* the cheque/check.
La sua influenza si *ripercosse* su tutti i colleghi.	His influence *is to be found* on all his colleagues.
Lo *percosse* a morte.	*He struck* him dead.

GERUND	PAST PARTICIPLE
solendo	**solito**

PRESENT	PERFECT
soglio	sono solito/a
suoli	
suole	
sogliamo	
solete	
sogliono	

PRESENT CONTINUOUS	IMPERFECT CONTINUOUS
sto solendo	stavo solendo

IMPERFECT	PAST DEFINITE
solevo	solei

Note   The main irregular features of the verb are

- the present indicative
- the past participle

IMPERATIVE
soli (tu)   soliamo (noi)   solete (voi)   **soglia** (Lei)

PLUPERFECT ero solito/a	**PAST ANTERIOR** fui solito/a
FUTURE solerò	**FUTURE PERFECT** avrò solito/a
CONDITIONAL solerei	**CONDITIONAL PERFECT** sarei solito/a
PRESENT SUBJUNCTIVE sola	**PERFECT SUBJUNCTIVE** sia solito/a
IMPERFECT SUBJUNCTIVE solessi	**PLUPERFECT SUBJUNCTIVE** fossi solito/a

Soleva alzarsi tardi.	*He used* to get up late.
Oggi lavora di più di quanto *soleva* fare due anni fa.	He works today more than *he used* to 2 years ago.
Suole alzarsi di buon'ora.	He usually gets up early.

GERUND	**PAST PARTICIPLE**
spargendo	**sparso**

PRESENT	**PERFECT**
spargo	ho sparso

PRESENT CONTINUOUS	**IMPERFECT CONTINUOUS**
sto spargendo	stavo spargendo

IMPERFECT	**PAST DEFINITE**
spargevo	**sparsi**
	spargesti
	sparse
	spargemmo
	spargeste
	sparsero

Similar verbs

aspergere	sprinkle
***emergere**	emerge
immergere	immerse
sommergere	submerge

Note   The main irregular features of the verb are

- the past definite tense
- the past participle

IMPERATIVE
spargi (tu)   spargiamo (noi)   spargete (voi)   sparga (Lei)

PLUPERFECT
avevo sparso

PAST ANTERIOR
ebbi sparso

FUTURE
spargerò

FUTURE PERFECT
avrò sparso

CONDITIONAL
spargerei

CONDITIONAL PERFECT
avrei sparso

PRESENT SUBJUNCTIVE
sparga

PERFECT SUBJUNCTIVE
abbia sparso

IMPERFECT SUBJUNCTIVE
spargessi

PLUPERFECT SUBJUNCTIVE
avessi sparso

Sparse fiori sulla tomba.	*He scattered* flowers on the grave.
Ho sparso zucchero sulla torta.	*I sprinkled* sugar on the cake.
Il lume *spargeva* una luce fioca.	The lamp *shed* a dim light.
Sparge una notizia a quattro venti!	He always tells everyone!
Il prete *aspergerà* l'acqua sul bambino.	The priest *will sprinkle* water on the baby.
Le onde avevano *sommerso* la barca.	The waves had *submerged* the boat.
L'*ho immerso* in acqua.	*I immersed* it in water.
Una sirena *è emersa* dall'acqua.	A mermaid *emerged* from the water.

85 spegnere — switch off, extinguish

GERUND	PAST PARTICIPLE
spegnendo	**spento**

PRESENT	PERFECT
spengo	ho spento
spegni	
spegne	
spegniamo	
spegnete	
spengono	

PRESENT CONTINUOUS	IMPERFECT CONTINUOUS
sto spegnendo	stavo spegnendo

IMPERFECT	PAST DEFINITE
spegnevo	**spensi**
	spegnesti
	spense
	spegnemmo
	spegneste
	spensero

Note The main irregular features of the verb are

- the present indicative and subjunctive tenses
- the past definite tense
- the past participle

IMPERATIVE
spegni (tu)   spegniamo (noi)   spegnete (voi)   **spenga** (Lei)

PLUPERFECT
avevo spento

PAST ANTERIOR
ebbi spento

FUTURE
spegnerò

FUTURE PERFECT
avrò spento

CONDITIONAL
spegnerei

CONDITIONAL PERFECT
avrei spento

PRESENT SUBJUNCTIVE
spenga
spenga
spenga
spegniamo
spegniate
spengano

PERFECT SUBJUNCTIVE
abbia spento

IMPERFECT SUBJUNCTIVE
spegnessi

PLUPERFECT SUBJUNCTIVE
avessi spento

Gianna *spense* la luce nella sala.
Spenta la luce, cominciò ad avere paura.
«Ho paura che il fantasma *spenga* ogni luce nella casa», disse.

Gianna *switched off* the lights in the room.
When the light *went off*, she began to be afraid.
"I am afraid that the ghost *will switch off* every light in the house," she said.

GERUND	PAST PARTICIPLE
spingendo	**spinto**

PRESENT	PERFECT
spingo	ho spinto

PRESENT CONTINUOUS	IMPERFECT CONTINUOUS
sto spingendo	stavo spingendo

IMPERFECT	PAST DEFINITE
spingevo	**spinsi**
	spingesti
	spinse
	spingemmo
	spingeste
	spinsero

Similar verbs

dipingere	paint
distinguere	distinguish
fingere	pretend
respingere	push back
sospingere	push, drive

Note   The main irregular features of the verb are

• the past definite tense
• the past participle

IMPERATIVE
spingi (tu)   spingiamo (noi)   spingete (voi)   spinga (Lei)

PLUPERFECT	*PAST ANTERIOR*
avevo spinto	ebbi spinto

FUTURE	*FUTURE PERFECT*
spingerò	avrò spinto

CONDITIONAL	*CONDITIONAL PERFECT*
spingerei	avrei spinto

PRESENT SUBJUNCTIVE	*PERFECT SUBJUNCTIVE*
spinga	abbia spinto

IMPERFECT SUBJUNCTIVE	*PLUPERFECT SUBJUNCTIVE*
spingessi	avessi spinto

Spingete!	*Push!*
Che cosa ti *ha spinto* a partire così presto?	What *has driven* you to leave so early?
Mio padre mi *spinge* a studiare di più.	My father *is urging* me to study harder.
***Spinse* Luigi dentro.**	*He pushed* Luigi inside.
***Spinse* l'amore fino al ridicolo.**	*She carried her* love to ridiculous extremes.
***Hai spinto* quello scherzo oltre i limiti.**	*You have pushed* that joke too far.
***Respinsero* la folla.**	*They pushed back* the crowd.
La fame la *sospinse* a rubare.	Hunger *drove* her to steal.

GERUND	PAST PARTICIPLE
stando	stato

PRESENT	PERFECT
sto	sono stato/a
stai	
sta	
stiamo	
state	
stanno	

PRESENT CONTINUOUS	IMPERFECT CONTINUOUS
sto	stavo

IMPERFECT	PAST DEFINITE
stavo	**stetti**
	stesti
	stette
	stemmo
	steste
	stettero

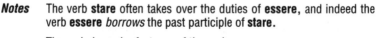

Notes   The verb **stare** often takes over the duties of **essere,** and indeed the verb **essere** *borrows* the past participle of **stare.**

The main irregular features of the verb are

- the present indicative and subjunctive tenses
- the imperfect subjunctive tense
- the past definite tense
- the future stem

IMPERATIVE
sta' (tu)   stiamo (noi)   state (voi)   **stia** (Lei)

PLUPERFECT	*PAST ANTERIOR*
ero stato	fui stato/a
FUTURE	*FUTURE PERFECT*
starò	sarò stato/a
CONDITIONAL	*CONDITIONAL PERFECT*
starei	sarei stato/a
PRESENT SUBJUNCTIVE	*PERFECT SUBJUNCTIVE*
stia	sia stato/a
stia	
stia	
stiamo	
stiate	
stiano	
IMPERFECT SUBJUNCTIVE	*PLUPERFECT SUBJUNCTIVE*
stessi	fossi stato/a
stessi	
stesse	
stessimo	
steste	
stessero	

– **Come *sta* oggi?**	– How *are you* today?
– *Sto* **un po' meglio, grazie.**	– *I am* a little better, thank you.
– **Fatto *sta* che è uscita quando doveva *stare* a casa.**	– The fact *remains* you (fem.) went out when you should have *stayed* at home.
– *Stia* **tranquillo, *stavo* per tornare quando mi ha parlato.**	– Don't worry, *I was* about to go home when you spoke to me.

GERUND stringendo	**PAST PARTICIPLE** **stretto**

PRESENT stringo	**PERFECT** ho stretto

PRESENT CONTINUOUS sto stringendo	**IMPERFECT CONTINUOUS** stavo stringendo

IMPERFECT stringevo	**PAST DEFINITE** **strinsi** stringesti **strinse** stringemmo stringeste **strinsero**

Similar verbs

costringere   force
restringere   narrow, tighten

Note   The main irregular features of the verb are

• the past definite tense
• the past participle

IMPERATIVE
stringi (tu)   stringiamo (noi)   stringete (voi)   stringa (Lei)

PLUPERFECT
avevo stretto

PAST ANTERIOR
ebbi stretto

FUTURE
stringerò

FUTURE PERFECT
avrò stretto

CONDITIONAL
stringerei

CONDITIONAL PERFECT
avrei stretto

PRESENT SUBJUNCTIVE
stringa

PERFECT SUBJUNCTIVE
abbia stretto

IMPERFECT SUBJUNCTIVE
stringessi

PLUPERFECT SUBJUNCTIVE
avessi stretto

Mi *strinse* la mano.	*He shook* my hand.
Strinsi mia figlia tra le braccia.	*I hugged* my daughter.
Ha stretto la moneta in mano.	*He kept a tight grip* of the coin in his hand.
Devo *stringere* la cinghia.	I must *tighten* my belt.
Questa vista mi *stringe* il cuore.	This sight *tears at* my heart strings.
Mi *ha costretto* a venire stasera.	*He made* me come this evening.
Ho fatto *restringere* il vestito.	I have had the dress *taken in*.

GERUND struggendo	*PAST PARTICIPLE* **strutto**

PRESENT struggo	*PERFECT* ho strutto

PRESENT CONTINUOUS sto struggendo	*IMPERFECT CONTINUOUS* stavo struggendo

IMPERFECT struggevo	*PAST DEFINITE* **strussi** struggesti **strusse** struggemmo struggeste **strussero**

Similar verb

distruggere   destroy

Note   The main irregular features of the verb are

- the past definite tense
- the past participle

IMPERATIVE
struggi (tu)   struggiamo (noi)   struggete (voi)   strugga (Lei)

PLUPERFECT	*PAST ANTERIOR*
avevo strutto	ebbi strutto
FUTURE	*FUTURE PERFECT*
struggerò	avrò strutto
CONDITIONAL	*CONDITIONAL PERFECT*
struggerei	avrei strutto
PRESENT SUBJUNCTIVE	*PERFECT SUBJUNCTIVE*
strugga	abbia strutto
IMPERFECT SUBJUNCTIVE	*PLUPERFECT SUBJUNCTIVE*
struggessi	avessi strutto

***Strussi* la cera.**	*I melted* the wax.
La malattia lo *strugge*.	He *is wasting away* because of the illness/sickness.
***Distrussero* la casa.**	*They destroyed* the house.
Fu *distrutto* dal dolore alla gamba.	He was *overcome* with the pain in his leg.
Il vino l'*ha distrutto*.	Wine has been his ruin.

GERUND	**PAST PARTICIPLE**
tacendo	taciuto

PRESENT	**PERFECT**
taccio	ho taciuto
taci	
tace	
taciamo	
tacete	
tacciono	

PRESENT CONTINUOUS	**IMPERFECT CONTINUOUS**
sto tacendo	stavo tacendo

IMPERFECT	**PAST DEFINITE**
tacevo	**tacqui**
	tacesti
	tacque
	tacemmo
	taceste
	tacquero

Note   The main irregular features of the verb are

- the present indicative and subjunctive tenses
- the past definite tense
- the additional **i** in the past participle

IMPERATIVE
taci (tu)   taciamo (noi)   tacete (voi)   **taccia** (Lei)

PLUPERFECT avevo taciuto	*PAST ANTERIOR* ebbi taciuto
FUTURE tacerò	*FUTURE PERFECT* avrò taciuto
CONDITIONAL tacerei	*CONDITIONAL PERFECT* avrei taciuto
PRESENT SUBJUNCTIVE **taccia** **taccia** **taccia** taciamo taciate **tacciano**	*PERFECT SUBJUNCTIVE* abbia taciuto
IMPERFECT SUBJUNCTIVE tacessi	*PLUPERFECT SUBJUNCTIVE* avessi taciuto

---

Il padre *tacque*. **I ragazzi non *tacquero*, però.**	The father *fell silent*. The children *were* not *silent*, however.
«*Tacete*», disse la mamma.	"*Be quiet*," said their mother.

GERUND	*PAST PARTICIPLE*
tendendo	**teso**

PRESENT	*PERFECT*
tendo	ho teso

PRESENT CONTINUOUS	*IMPERFECT CONTINUOUS*
sto tendendo	stavo tendendo

IMPERFECT	*PAST DEFINITE*
tendevo	**tesi**
	tendesti
	tese
	tendemmo
	tendeste
	tesero

Similar verbs

attendere	wait
contendere	contend
distendere	stretch
estendere	extend
intendere	intend, understand
pretendere	claim
sottintendere	hint at
stendere	spread, stretch out

Note   The main irregular features of the verb are

• the past definite tense
• the past participle

Mi *tese* la mano.	He *stretched out* his hand.
Il cane *ha teso* gli orecchi.	The dog *pricked up* its ears.
***Ho teso* la corda.**	*I pulled* the rope tight.
***Ha teso* le corde del violino.**	He *tightened* the strings of the violin.

IMPERATIVE
tendi (tu)   tendiamo (noi)   tendete (voi)   tenda (Lei)

PLUPERFECT	*PAST ANTERIOR*
avevo teso	ebbi teso

FUTURE	*FUTURE PERFECT*
tenderò	avrò teso

CONDITIONAL	*CONDITIONAL PERFECT*
tenderei	avrei teso

PRESENT SUBJUNCTIVE	*PERFECT SUBJUNCTIVE*
tenda	abbia teso

IMPERFECT SUBJUNCTIVE	*PLUPERFECT SUBJUNCTIVE*
tendessi	avessi teso

Tende ad ingrassare.	*She tends to get fat.*
Che colore è? *Tende* al rosso.	*What colour/color is it? A reddish colour/color.*
Pretende di essere un grande artista.	*He pretends to be a great artist.*
Pretese di aver ragione.	*He claimed to be right.*
Attendiamo una pronta risposta.	*We are waiting for a prompt reply.*
Nessuno gli *contese* i suoi diritti.	No one *contested* his rights.
Distesi la mano per aiutare la ragazza.	*I stretched out my hand to help the girl.*
Che cosa *intendi* fare?	What *do you intend* doing?
Sottintende la verità.	*He is hinting at the truth.*
Giuliana *stese* il bucato sull'erba.	Giuliana *laid out* the washing on the grass.
Mi *ha steso* la mano.	*He streched out his hand to me.*

GERUND	PAST PARTICIPLE
tenendo	tenuto

PRESENT	PERFECT
tengo	ho tenuto
tieni	
tiene	
teniamo	
tenete	
tengono	

PRESENT CONTINUOUS	IMPERFECT CONTINUOUS
sto tenendo	stavo tenendo

IMPERFECT	PAST DEFINITE
tenevo	**tenni**
	tenesti
	tenne
	tenemmo
	teneste
	tennero

Similar verbs

appartenere	belong	***astenersi**	abstain
contenere	contain	**detenere**	detain, stop
mantenere	maintain	**ottenere**	obtain
ritenere	retain	**sostenere**	support
trattenere	restrain, detain		

Note   The main irregular features of the verb are

- the present indicative and subjunctive tenses
- the past definite tense
- the future stem

– **Non riesco a *tenerlo* più. *Tieni.***	– I can't *hold* it any longer. *Here you are.*
– **Lo *terrò* soltanto due minuti !**	– *I'll* only *hold* it for two minutes.

IMPERATIVE
tieni (tu)   teniamo (noi)   tenete (voi)   **tenga** (Lei)

PLUPERFECT	*PAST ANTERIOR*
avevo tenuto	ebbi tenuto

FUTURE	*FUTURE PERFECT*
terrò	avrò tenuto

CONDITIONAL	*CONDITIONAL PERFECT*
terrei	avrei tenuto

PRESENT SUBJUNCTIVE	*PERFECT SUBJUNCTIVE*
tenga	abbia tenuto
tenga	
tenga	
teniamo	
teniate	
tengano	

IMPERFECT SUBJUNCTIVE	*PLUPERFECT SUBJUNCTIVE*
tenessi	avessi tenuto

– A chi *appartiene* quel cane?	– Who does that dog *belong* to?
– L'ho *ottenuto* l'anno scorso.	– *I got* it last year.
Questa bevanda *contiene* l'alcool.	This drink *contains* alcohol.
Dovrei *astenermi* dall'alcool.	I should *abstain* from drinking alcohol.
Mantengo sempre buone relazioni con Giovanni.	*I* always *maintain* a good relationship with Giovanni.
Il muro è *sostenuto* da lunghi pali.	The wall is *supported* by long poles.
Sostenne la sua innocenza.	He *maintained* his innocence.
Fu *trattenuto* a scuola.	He was *kept in* at school.

93 tingere — dye, tint

GERUND tingendo	**PAST PARTICIPLE** **tinto**

PRESENT tingo	**PERFECT** ho tinto
PRESENT CONTINUOUS sto tingendo	**IMPERFECT CONTINUOUS** stavo tingendo
IMPERFECT tingevo	**PAST DEFINITE** **tinsi** tingesti **tinse** tingemmo tingeste **tinsero**

Similar verbs

attingere   draw up, draw out
dipingere   paint, portray

Note   The main irregular features of the verb are

- the past definite tense
- the past participle

IMPERATIVE
tingi (tu)   tingiamo (noi)   tingete (voi)   tinga (Lei)

PLUPERFECT avevo tinto	**PAST ANTERIOR** ebbi tinto
FUTURE tingerò	**FUTURE PERFECT** avrò tinto
CONDITIONAL tingerei	**CONDITIONAL PERFECT** avrei tinto
PRESENT SUBJUNCTIVE tinga	**PERFECT SUBJUNCTIVE** abbia tinto
IMPERFECT SUBJUNCTIVE tingessi	**PLUPERFECT SUBJUNCTIVE** avessi tinto

---

– *Hai tinto* i capelli?	– *Have you dyed* your hair?
– No, ma *ho tinto* questo vestito di nero!	– No, but *I have dyed* this dress black.
Il sole *tingeva* le montagne di rosa.	The sun *tinged* the mountains with a rosy glow.
Attinse l'acqua dal pozzo.	*He drew out* water from the well.
Ha dipinto il ritratto ad olio.	*He painted* the picture in oils.

GERUND torcendo	**PAST PARTICIPLE** **torto**

PRESENT torco	**PERFECT** ho torto

PRESENT CONTINUOUS sto torcendo	**IMPERFECT CONTINUOUS** stavo torcendo

IMPERFECT torcevo	**PAST DEFINITE** **torsi** torcesti **torse** torcemmo torceste **torsero**

Similar verbs

contorcere	contort, distort
*contorcersi	writhe, twist
storcere	twist, wrench
*torcersi	twist, writhe

Note   The main irregular features of the verb are

- the past definite tense
- the past participle

IMPERATIVE
torci (tu)   torciamo (noi)   torcete (voi)   torca (Lei)

PLUPERFECT
avevo torto

PAST ANTERIOR
ebbi torto

FUTURE
torcerò

FUTURE PERFECT
avrò torto

CONDITIONAL
torcerei

CONDITIONAL PERFECT
avrei torto

PRESENT SUBJUNCTIVE
torca

PERFECT SUBJUNCTIVE
abbia torto

IMPERFECT SUBJUNCTIVE
torcessi

PLUPERFECT SUBJUNCTIVE
avessi torto

Vorrei *torcere* il collo a quel ragazzo.	I'd like *to wring* that boy's neck!
***Torse* i panni.**	He *wrung out* the washing.
***Torceva* il naso.**	He *was turning up* his nose.
Anna *ha torto* i fili.	Anna *twisted* the threads.
Si *torceva* dal dolore.	He *was writhing* in pain.

translate

GERUND	PAST PARTICIPLE
traducendo	**tradotto**

PRESENT	PERFECT
traduco	ho tradotto
traduci	
traduce	
traduciamo	
traducete	
traducono	

PRESENT CONTINUOUS	IMPERFECT CONTINUOUS
sto traducendo	stavo traducendo

IMPERFECT	PAST DEFINITE
traducevo	**tradussi**
	traducesti
	tradusse
	traducemmo
	traduceste
	tradussero

Similar verbs

addurre	convey	**introdurre**	introduce
condurre	conduct, lead, drive	**produrre**	produce
		ridurre	reduce
dedurre	deduce	**riprodurre**	reproduce
indurre	induce, induct	**sedurre**	seduce

Note The main irregular features of the verb are

- the irregular present tense stem
- the irregular future stem
- the past definite tense
- the past participle

Abbiamo tradotto quel libro.   *We translated* that book.

IMPERATIVE
traduci (tu)   traduciamo (noi)   traducete (voi)   traduca (Lei)

PLUPERFECT avevo tradotto	**PAST ANTERIOR** ebbi tradotto
FUTURE **tradurrò**	**FUTURE PERFECT** avrò tradotto
CONDITIONAL **tradurrei**	**CONDITIONAL PERFECT** avrei tradotto
PRESENT SUBJUNCTIVE traduca	**PERFECT SUBJUNCTIVE** abbia tradotto
IMPERFECT SUBJUNCTIVE traducessi	**PLUPERFECT SUBJUNCTIVE** avessi tradotto

---

Dubito che *abbia tradotto* l'opera.	I doubt whether *he translated* the work.
Mi *condusse* al teatro.	*He took* me to the theatre/theater.
***Condussero* una vita miserabile.**	*They led* a miserable life.
Tutte le strade *conducono* a Roma.	All roads *lead* to Rome.
Mi *introdusse* allo studio della lettura italiana.	*He introduced* me to the study of Italian literature.
Quest'albero non *ha prodotto* mai frutta.	This tree *has* never *produced* fruit.
***Ridusse* la velocità all'angolo della strada.**	*He reduced* his speed at the corner of the road.
Fu *ridotto* a mendicare.	He was *reduced* to begging.

GERUND	PAST PARTICIPLE
traendo	**tratto**

PRESENT	PERFECT
traggo	ho tratto
trai	
trae	
traiamo	
traete	
traggono	

PRESENT CONTINUOUS	IMPERFECT CONTINUOUS
sto traendo	stavo traendo

IMPERFECT	PAST DEFINITE
traevo	**trassi**
	traesti
	trasse
	traemmo
	traeste
	trassero

Similar verbs

attrarre	attract
contrarre	contract
distrarre	distract
estrarre	extract
sottrare	subtract
***sottrarsi**	avoid

Note   The main irregular features of these verbs are

- the present indicative and subjunctive tenses
- the future stem
- the past definite tense
- the past participle

IMPERATIVE
trai (tu)   traiamo (noi)   traete (voi)   **tragga** (Lei)

PLUPERFECT avevo tratto	**PAST ANTERIOR** ebbi tratto
FUTURE **trarrò**	**FUTURE PERFECT** avrò tratto
CONDITIONAL **trarrei**	**CONDITIONAL PERFECT** avrei tratto
PRESENT SUBJUNCTIVE **tragga** **tragga** **tragga** traiamo traiate **traggano**	**PERFECT SUBJUNCTIVE** abbia tratto
IMPERFECT SUBJUNCTIVE traessi	**PLUPERFECT SUBJUNCTIVE** avessi tratto

---

Non ne *traggo* nessun piacere.	I *don*'t *get* any pleasure from it.
***Trasse* origine da una nobile famiglia.**	He *traced* his origins from a noble family.
La minima cosa lo *distraeva*.	The slightest thing *distracted* him.
Mi sento *attratto* verso quella ragazza.	I feel *attracted* to that girl.
***Sottrai* quattro da dieci.**	Subtract 4 from 10.
Lo *sottrassero* alla morte.	They *rescued* him from death.
Luigi si *sottrasse* al proprio dovere.	Luigi *avoided* doing his duty.
***Contrasse* una malattia dolorosa.**	He *contracted* a painful illness/sickness.

GERUND	**PAST PARTICIPLE**
uccidendo	**ucciso**

PRESENT	**PERFECT**
uccido	ho ucciso

PRESENT CONTINUOUS	**IMPERFECT CONTINUOUS**
sto uccidendo	stavo uccidendo

IMPERFECT	**PAST DEFINITE**
uccidevo	**uccisi**
	uccidesti
	uccise
	uccidemmo
	uccideste
	uccisero

Similar verb

*uccidersi   kill oneself, commit suicide

Note   The main irregular features of this verb are:

- the past definite tense
- the past participle

IMPERATIVE
uccidi (tu)   uccidiamo (noi)   uccidete (voi)   uccida (Lei)

PLUPERFECT avevo ucciso	**PAST ANTERIOR** ebbi ucciso
FUTURE ucciderò	**FUTURE PERFECT** avrò ucciso
CONDITIONAL ucciderei	**CONDITIONAL PERFECT** avrei ucciso
PRESENT SUBJUNCTIVE uccida	**PERFECT SUBJUNCTIVE** abbia ucciso
IMPERFECT SUBJUNCTIVE uccidessi	**PLUPERFECT SUBJUNCTIVE** avessi ucciso

Ha ucciso un lupo.	*He killed* a wolf.
Uccise l'uomo, sparandogli alla testa.	*He shot* the man through the head.
Fu ucciso.	He was *killed.*
Si uccise per disperazione.	*He killed himself* out of despair.

GERUND	*PAST PARTICIPLE*
udendo	udito

PRESENT	*PERFECT*
odo	ho udito
odi	
ode	
udiamo	
udite	
odono	

PRESENT CONTINUOUS	*IMPERFECT CONTINUOUS*
sto udendo	stavo udendo

IMPERFECT	*PAST DEFINITE*
udivo	udii

Note The main irregular features of the verb are

  • the present indicative and subjunctive tenses

IMPERATIVE
odi (tu) udiamo (noi) udite (voi) **oda** (Lei)

PLUPERFECT	**PAST ANTERIOR**
avevo udito	ebbi udito
FUTURE	**FUTURE PERFECT**
udirò	avrò udito
CONDITIONAL	**CONDITIONAL PERFECT**
udirei	avrei udito
PRESENT SUBJUNCTIVE	**PERFECT SUBJUNCTIVE**
oda	abbia udito
oda	
oda	
udiamo	
udiate	
odano	
IMPERFECT SUBJUNCTIVE	**PLUPERFECT SUBJUNCTIVE**
udissi	avessi udito

– L'*hai* mai *udito* cantare?	– *Have you* ever *heard* him sing?
– **Non ancora, ma l'***udirò* **forse domani.**	– *Not yet, but I shall* perhaps *hear* him tomorrow.
Spero che Dio *oda* **le mie preghiere!**	I hope God *will listen to* my prayers.

GERUND uscendo	**PAST PARTICIPLE** uscito

PRESENT **esco** **esci** **esce** usciamo uscite **escono**	**PERFECT** sono uscito/a

PRESENT CONTINUOUS sto uscendo	**IMPERFECT CONTINUOUS** stavo uscendo

IMPERFECT uscivo	**PAST DEFINITE** uscii

Similar verb

*riuscire   succeed

Note   The main irregular features of the verb are

• the present indicative and subjunctive tenses

IMPERATIVE
esci (tu)   usciamo (noi)   uscite (voi)   **esca** (Lei)

PLUPERFECT ero uscito	**PAST ANTERIOR** fui uscito/a
FUTURE uscirò	**FUTURE PERFECT** sarò uscito/a
CONDITIONAL uscirei	**CONDITIONAL PERFECT** sarei uscito/a

PRESENT SUBJUNCTIVE
esca
esca
esca
usciamo
usciate
escano

PERFECT SUBJUNCTIVE
sia uscito/a

IMPERFECT SUBJUNCTIVE
uscissi

PLUPERFECT SUBJUNCTIVE
fossi uscito/a

– A che ora *usciamo* stasera?	– What time *are we going out* tonight?
– Beh, io *esco* alle sette, ma Mario non *esce* fino alle sette e mezzo.	– Well, *I'm going out* at 7:00, but Mario *is* not *going out* till 7:30.
– E Carlo?	– And what about Carlo?
– Non credo che *esca* stasera.	– I don't think *he's going out* tonight.
– Non *sei riuscito* a telefonargli?	– *Did you* not *manage* to call him?
– Sì, ci *sono riuscito*, ma *era uscito* con Antonia.	– Yes I *did manage to*, but *he had gone out* with Antonia.

GERUND	PAST PARTICIPLE
valendo	**valso**

PRESENT	PERFECT
valgo	sono valso/a
vali	
vale	
valiamo	
valete	
valgono	

PRESENT CONTINUOUS	IMPERFECT CONTINUOUS
sto valendo	stavo valendo

IMPERFECT	PAST DEFINITE
valevo	**valsi**
	valesti
	valse
	valemmo
	valeste
	valsero

Similar verb

*prevalere   prevail

Note   The main irregular features of the verb are

- the present indicative and subjunctive tenses
- the past definite tense
- the past participle
- the future stem

IMPERATIVE
vali (tu)   valiamo (noi)   valete (voi)   **valga** (Lei)

PLUPERFECT ero valso/a	*PAST ANTERIOR* fui valso/a
FUTURE **varrò**	*FUTURE PERFECT* sarò valso/a
CONDITIONAL **varrei**	*CONDITIONAL PERFECT* sarei valso/a
PRESENT SUBJUNCTIVE **valga** **valga** **valga** valiamo valiate **valgano**	*PERFECT SUBJUNCTIVE* sia valso/a
IMPERFECT SUBJUNCTIVE valessi	*PLUPERFECT SUBJUNCTIVE* fossi valso/a

– **Quanto *valgono* queste due statue ?**	– How much *are* these 2 statues *worth*?
– **Non credo che *valgano* molto.**	– I do not think *they are worth* a lot.
– **Quella più grande *vale* forse mezza milione.**	– The larger one is perhaps *worth* half a million lire.
Questo biglietto *vale* per 24 ore.	This ticket *is valid* for 24 hours.
Fu molto difficile, ma *valeva* la pena.	It was very difficult, but it *was worth*while.
Quello che dici non *vale* niente in questo caso.	What you are saying *counts for* nothing in this case.

GERUND	PAST PARTICIPLE
vedendo	**visto**/veduto

PRESENT	PERFECT
vedo	ho visto

PRESENT CONTINUOUS	IMPERFECT CONTINUOUS
sto vedendo	stavo vedendo

IMPERFECT	PAST DEFINITE
vedevo	**vidi**
	vedesti
	vide
	vedemmo
	vedeste
	videro

Similar verbs

*avvedersi	perceive
prevedere	foresee
provvedere	provide
rivedere	see again
travedere	be wrong

Note The main irregular features of the verb are

• the past definite tense
• the past participle (although the regular past participle is also accepted)
• the future stem

IMPERATIVE
vedi (tu)   vediamo (noi)   vedete (voi)   veda (Lei)

PLUPERFECT avevo visto	*PAST ANTERIOR* ebbi visto
FUTURE **vedrò**	*FUTURE PERFECT* avrò visto
CONDITIONAL **vedrei**	*CONDITIONAL PERFECT* avrei visto
PRESENT SUBJUNCTIVE veda	*PERFECT SUBJUNCTIVE* abbia visto
IMPERFECT SUBJUNCTIVE vedessi	*PLUPERFECT SUBJUNCTIVE* avessi visto

---

– *Vedi* quell'uomo laggiù?	– *Do you see* that man down there?
– Sì, l'*ho visto* anche ieri. Chi è?	– Yes, *I saw* him yesterday as well. Who is he?
– Non lo so. Mai *visto* prima!	– I don't know, *I have* never *seen* him before today.
– Credi che lui mi abbia *visto*?	– Do you think *he has seen* me?
Tu *travedi*, se credi che lui sia colpevole.	You *are making a mistake* if you think he is guilty.
Non l'ho mai più *rivista*.	*I* never *saw* her *again*.
Non potevi *prevederlo*.	You could not have *foreseen* it.
Ti ferì senza *avvedersene*.	He hurt your feelings without *realizing*.
L'ho sempre *provveduto* di tutto.	*I have* always *provided* him with everything.

GERUND	PAST PARTICIPLE
venendo	**venuto**

PRESENT	PERFECT
vengo	sono venuto/a
vieni	
viene	
veniamo	
venite	
vengono	

PRESENT CONTINUOUS	IMPERFECT CONTINUOUS
sto venendo	stavo venendo

IMPERFECT	PAST DEFINITE
venivo	**venni**
	venisti
	venne
	venimmo
	veniste
	vennero

Similar verbs

*avvenire	happen	***provenire**	proceed from,
*convenire	agree, gather		come from
	together	**†rinvenire**	find, discover,
*divenire	become		recover
*intervenire	intervene	***sopravvenire**	arrive, happen
*pervenire	reach, arrive	***sovvenire**	aid
		*svenire	faint

Note   The main irregular features of the verb are

- the present indicative and subjunctive tenses
- the past definite tense
- the past participle
- the future stem

IMPERATIVE
vieni (tu)   veniamo (noi)   venite (voi)   **venga** (Lei)

PLUPERFECT
ero venuto/a

PAST ANTERIOR
fui venuto/a

FUTURE
verrò

FUTURE PERFECT
sarò venuto/a

CONDITIONAL
verrei

CONDITIONAL PERFECT
sarei venuto/a

PRESENT SUBJUNCTIVE
venga
venga
venga
veniamo
veniate
vengano

PERFECT SUBJUNCTIVE
sia venuto/a

IMPERFECT SUBJUNCTIVE
venissi

PLUPERFECT SUBJUNCTIVE
fossi venuto/a

Digli che *venga* subito.	Tell him *to come* at once.
Ha detto che *verrà* domani.	He said *he will come* tomorrow.
Avevo paura che non *venisse* oggi.	I was afraid that *he might* not *come* today.
Ci *conviene* partire subito.	*We had better* leave immediately.
Il prezzo è *convenuto*.	The price *is agreed upon*.
Non credo che *provenga* da una buona famiglia.	I don't think *he comes* from a good family.
***Svenne* per la fame.**	*He fainted* from hunger.
Antonella *ha rinvenuto* un libro raro.	Antonella *found* a rare book.
La ragazza è *rinvenuta* adesso.	The girl *has* now *come to*.

GERUND	**PAST PARTICIPLE**
vincendo	**vinto**

PRESENT	**PERFECT**
vinco	ho vinto

PRESENT CONTINUOUS	**IMPERFECT CONTINUOUS**
sto vincendo	stavo vincendo

IMPERFECT	**PAST DEFINITE**
vincevo	**vinsi**
	vincesti
	vinse
	vincemmo
	vinceste
	vinsero

Similar verbs

avvincere	bind, to tie up
convincere	convince

Note   The main irregular features of the verb are

- the past definite tense
- the past participle

IMPERATIVE
vinci (tu)   vinciamo (noi)   vincete (voi)   vinca (Lei)

PLUPERFECT avevo vinto	**PAST ANTERIOR** ebbi vinto
FUTURE vincerò	**FUTURE PERFECT** avrò vinto
CONDITIONAL vincerei	**CONDITIONAL PERFECT** avrei vinto
PRESENT SUBJUNCTIVE vinca	**PERFECT SUBJUNCTIVE** abbia vinto
IMPERFECT SUBJUNCTIVE vincessi	**PLUPERFECT SUBJUNCTIVE** avessi vinto

---

La sua bellezza mi *vinse*.	I *was won over* by her beauty.
Hai vinto un premio?	*Did you win* a prize?
Il partito *ha vinto*.	The (political) party *has won*.
Vinsi di stretta misura.	I *won* by a short margin.
Il ladro *avvinse* l'uomo.	The robber *tied up* the man.
Mi sono lasciato *vincere* dalla tentazione.	I *yielded* to temptation.
Fu vinto dall'ira.	He was overcome by rage.
L'*hai convinto*?	*Did you convince* him?

GERUND	**PAST PARTICIPLE**
vivendo	**vissuto**

PRESENT	**PERFECT**
vivo	ho vissuto/sono vissuto/a

PRESENT CONTINUOUS	**IMPERFECT CONTINUOUS**
sto vivendo	stavo vivendo

IMPERFECT	**PAST DEFINITE**
vivevo	**vissi**
	vivesti
	visse
	vivemmo
	viveste
	vissero

Similar verbs

† rivivere	live again, revive
† sopravvivere	survive

These verbs, like **vivere** take **avere** when used transitively and **essere** when used intransitively.

Note   The main irregular features of the verb are

- the past definite tense
- the past participle

IMPERATIVE
vivi (tu) viviamo (noi) vivete (voi) viva (Lei)

PLUPERFECT
avevo vissuto/ero vissuto/a

PAST ANTERIOR
ebbi vissuto/fui vissuto/a

FUTURE
viverò

FUTURE PERFECT
avrò vissuto/sarò vissuto/a

CONDITIONAL
viverei

CONDITIONAL PERFECT
avrei vissuto/sarei vissuto/a

PRESENT SUBJUNCTIVE
viva

PERFECT SUBJUNCTIVE
abbia vissuto/sia vissuto/a

IMPERFECT SUBJUNCTIVE
vivessi

PLUPERFECT SUBJUNCTIVE
avessi vissuto/fossi vissuto/a

Vive in città da tre anni.	*He has been living* in town for 3 years.
Visse bene del proprio lavoro.	*He lived* well from his own work.
Hai di che *vivere*?	Do you have enough *to live on*?
Antonio sa *vivere*.	Antonio knows how *to live*!
Come si *vive* così si muore.	As *we live* so shall we die. *(Proverb)*
Vorrei *rivivere* quei momenti.	I would like *to relive* those moments.
Mi sento *rivivere*.	I feel like a new person.

GERUND	*PAST PARTICIPLE*
volendo	voluto

PRESENT	*PERFECT*
voglio	ho voluto/sono voluto/a
vuoi	
vuole	
vogliamo	
volete	
vogliono	

PRESENT CONTINUOUS	*IMPERFECT CONTINUOUS*
sto volendo	stavo volendo

IMPERFECT	*PAST DEFINITE*
volevo	**volli**
	volesti
	volle
	volemmo
	voleste
	vollero

Notes   The verb **volere** is frequently used as a modal verb, before the infinitive of another verb. It takes **avere** or **essere** according to which one the dependent infinitive takes, although, in speech, **avere** is more common when wishing/wanting is stressed.

The main irregular features of the verb are

• the present indicative and subjunctive tenses
• the past definite tense
• the future stem

IMPERATIVE
vogli (tu)   vogliamo (noi)   **vogliate** (voi)   **voglia** (Lei)

PLUPERFECT avevo voluto/ero voluto/a	**PAST ANTERIOR** ebbi voluto/fui voluto/a
FUTURE vorrò	**FUTURE PERFECT** avrò voluto/sarò voluto/a
CONDITIONAL vorrei	**CONDITIONAL PERFECT** avrei voluto/sarei voluto/a
PRESENT SUBJUNCTIVE voglia voglia voglia vogliamo vogliate vogliano	**PERFECT SUBJUNCTIVE** abbia voluto/sia voluto/a
IMPERFECT SUBJUNCTIVE volessi	**PLUPERFECT SUBJUNCTIVE** avessi voluto/fossi voluto/a

---

Non capisco ciò che *vuoi* dire.	I don't understand what you mean.
***Voglio* rimanere qui in Italia.**	*I want* to stay in Italy.
Non *vorrei* sentire più di quell'affare.	*I would like* to hear no more about that matter.
Ci *vuole* almeno un'ora per andare da Anna.	*It takes* at least an hour to get to Anna's house.
***Vorresti* accompagnarmi?**	*Would you like* to come with me?
***Avevo voluto* mangiare in quel ristorante.**	*I had wanted* to eat in that restaurant.

GERUND	*PAST PARTICIPLE*
volgendo	**volto**

PRESENT	*PERFECT*
volgo	ho volto

PRESENT CONTINUOUS	*IMPERFECT CONTINUOUS*
sto volgendo	stavo volgendo

IMPERFECT	*PAST DEFINITE*
volgevo	**volsi**
	volgesti
	volse
	volgemmo
	volgeste
	volsero

Similar verbs

avvolgere	wrap up
coinvolgere	involve
involgere	wrap
ravvolgere	wrap up
rivolgere	turn
sconvolgere	overturn
svolgere	unfold

Note   The main irregular features of the verb are

- the past definite tense
- the past participle

IMPERATIVE
volgi (tu)   volgiamo (noi)   volgete (voi)   volga (Lei)

PLUPERFECT
avevo volto

PAST ANTERIOR
ebbi volto

FUTURE
volgerò

FUTURE PERFECT
avrò volto

CONDITIONAL
volgerei

CONDITIONAL PERFECT
avrei volto

PRESENT SUBJUNCTIVE
volga

PERFECT SUBJUNCTIVE
abbia volto

IMPERFECT SUBJUNCTIVE
volgessi

PLUPERFECT SUBJUNCTIVE
avessi volto

Volgeva le pagine del libro. — *He turned the pages of the book.*

Volse i passi verso la casa. — *He turned his steps towards home.*

Volsi la scenetta al proprio vantaggio. — *I turned the scene to my advantage.*

Volgo la vicenda nella mente. — *I am turning over the event in my mind.*

Il tempo volge al brutto. — *The weather is making a turn for the worst.*

Avvolse il regalo nella carta. — *He wrapped up the present in paper.*

Ho ravvolto il libro nella carta. — *I have wrapped the book in paper.*

Sconvolsero i suoi piani. — *They disturbed his plans.*

C

SUBJECT INDEX

SUBJECT INDEX

The references given here relate to the relevant section in *The verb system in Italian.*

D
VERB INDEX

Verb index

An **[M]** beside a verb indicates that it is one of the Model Verbs.

An * before a verb indicates that this verb takes **essere**.

A † before a verb indicates that this verb can take **essere** or **avere**, usually this means it takes **essere** when intransitive and **avere** when transitive.

If the verb is usually used impersonally, this is indicated by *(Imp.)*

The number beside the verb indicates the model verb pattern(s) which it follows.

A

abbagliare *(tr)*	dazzle 13
abbaiare *(intr)*	bark 13
abbandonare *(tr)*	abandon, desert, give up 3
abbassare *(tr)*	depress, turn down (light/window) 3
abbattere *(tr)*	knock over 4
***abbattersi su**	hit upon 4, 7
abbondare *(intr)*	abound 3
abbordare *(tr)*	accost 3
abbottonare *(tr)*	button 3
abbozzare *(tr)*	draft, sketch 3
abbracciare *(tr)*	cuddle, embrace 12
***abbronzarsi** *(intr/refl)*	tan, brown in sun 7
abitare *(tr)*	live, dwell 3
abituare *(tr)*	accustom 3
***abituarsi a** *(intr/refl)*	become accustomed to, get used to 7
abolire *(tr)*	abolish 6
abortire *(tr/intr)*	miscarry 6
***abortire** *(intr)*	fail, come to nothing 6
***accadere** *(intr)*	occur, happen, turn out, transpire *(Imp.)* 28
accalcarsi *(intr/refl)*	huddle 7, 11
accarezzare *(tr)*	caress, stroke 3
accecare *(tr)*	blind 11
***accedere** *(intr)*	access, approach, comply with 33
accelerare *(tr/intr)*	speed up, accelerate 3

accendere *(tr)*	ignite, turn on, light, strike (match) 17 **[M]**
*accendersi *(intr)*	go on (of lighting), light up 17, 7
accennare a *(intr)*	refer to, mention 3
accennare di sì *(intr)*	nod 3
accentuare *(tr)*	emphasize 3
accertare *(tr)*	assess 3
accettare di *(tr)*	accept 3
acchiappare *(tr)*	catch 3
*accoccolarsi *(intr/refl)*	squat, crouch 7
accomodare *(tr)*	arrange 3
accompagnare *(tr)*	accompany, take (for a walk) 3
*accondiscendere a *(intr)*	deign to 79
acconsentire a *(intr)*	accept, agree to 5
*accontentarsi di *(intr/refl)*	make do with 7
accoppiare *(tr)*	couple 13
*accoppiarsi *(intr/refl)*	mate 13, 7
accorciare *(tr)*	shorten 12
*accorciarsi *(intr/refl)*	become shorter, draw in 12, 7
accordare *(tr)*	grant, concede, tune, string (instrument) 3
*accordarsi *(intr/refl)*	agree 7
*accorgersi di *(intr/refl)*	notice, take note 80, 7
accumulare *(tr)*	accumulate, hoard 3
accusare di *(tr)*	accuse (of), charge (criminal) 3
accusare ricevuta di	acknowledge receipt of 3
acquistare *(tr)*	acquire, get 3
adattare *(tr)*	adapt 3
adattare a *(intr)*	adapt to 3
addebitare *(tr)*	charge to account, debit 3
addizionare *(tr)*	count up 3
addolcire *(tr)*	sweeten 6
*addormentarsi *(intr/refl)*	fall asleep 7
adempire *(tr)*	implement, perform (a function) 6
aderire a *(intr)*	adhere to 6
adorare *(tr)*	adore, worship 3
adottare *(tr)*	adopt 3
aerare *(tr)*	air a room 3
affascinare *(tr)*	charm, fascinate 3
affermare *(tr)*	affirm, assert 3
afferrare *(tr)*	grasp, snatch, tackle 3
afferrare strettamente *(tr)*	grip 3
affettare *(tr)*	affect, feign, simulate 3
*affezionarsi a *(intr/refl)*	become fond of, take a liking to 7
affidare *(tr)*	entrust 3
*affidarsi a *(intr/refl)*	rely on, trust in 7
affiggere *(tr)*	stick, attach 18 **[M]**

affilare *(tr)*	sharpen 3
affittare *(tr)*	hire, rent house, lease out 3
affliggere *(tr)*	afflict 19 **[M]**
†affogare *(tr/intr)*	drown 2, 11
affollare *(intr)*	crowd 3
affrettare *(tr)*	hurry 3
***affrettarsi a** *(intr/refl)*	hurry (to) 7
affrontare *(tr)*	confront, stand up to, face 3
agganciare *(tr)*	hook 12
aggiogare *(tr)*	yoke 11
aggiornare *(tr)*	adjourn, postpone, write up (diary) 3
***aggiornarsi** *(intr/refl)*	to get up to date 7
aggiungere *(tr)*	add, say further, append, add 52
aggiustare *(tr)*	adjust, patch 3
agire *(intr)*	act, do 6
agire per *(intr)*	act for 6
agire seguendo i consigli	act on advice 6
agire su	act on, work on 6
agitare *(tr)*	ruffle, stir, shake, stir, move 3
***agitarsi** *(intr/refl)*	bustle 7
aiutare *(tr)*	aid, assist, help 3
albeggiare *(intr)*	dawn 12
alienare *(tr)*	alienate 3
alimentare *(tr)*	feed 3
allacciare *(tr)*	fasten (seatbelt) 12
allargare *(tr)*	broaden, enlarge, widen 11
allarmare *(tr)*	alarm 3
allattare *(tr)*	nurse (baby), suckle 3
alleggerire *(tr)*	lighten 6
***allenarsi** *(intr/refl)*	exercize 7
allentare *(tr)*	slacken 3
allevare *(tr)*	raise, rear 3
alleviare *(tr)*	alleviate, relieve (pain, anxiety) 13
allineare *(tr)*	align 3
***allinearsi** *(intr/refl)*	line up 7
alloggiare *(tr)*	house 12
alloggiare in *(intr)*	stay (as guest) 12
allontanare *(tr)*	push away 3
***allontanarsi da** *(intr/refl)*	get away from 7
alludere a *(intr)*	allude at, hint at 20 **[M]**
allungare *(tr)*	draw out, become longer, stretch out 11
alterare *(tr)*	alter 3
alternare *(tr)*	alternate 3
alzare *(tr)*	elevate, put up (price), raise, lift 3
alzare *(tr)* **la voce**	speak up 3

alzare gli occhi *(tr)*	look up 3
*alzarsi *(intr/refl)*	get up, stand, rise to feet 7
amalgamare *(tr)*	amalgamate 3
amare *(tr)*	love 3
ammaccare *(tr)*	bruise 11
*ammalarsi *(intr/refl)*	become ill, fall ill 7
ammettere di *(tr)*	admit, grant to be true, allow 54
ammiccare a qlcu. *(intr)*	wink 11
amministrare *(tr)*	administer, run, manage 3
ammirare *(tr)*	admire 3
ammobiliare *(tr)*	furnish, equip 13
†ammontare a (intr/tr)	number, amount to 3
ammorbidire *(tr)*	soften 6
ammucchiare *(tr)*	heap, pile up 13
*ammucchiarsi *(intr/refl)*	pile up 13, 7
ammuffire *(intr)*	go moldy 6
amplificare *(tr)*	amplify 11
amputare *(tr)*	amputate 3
analizzare *(tr)*	analyze 3
ancorare *(tr)*	anchor, moor 3
*andare *(intr)*	go, ride (in car) 21 **[M]**
*andare a fare le spese *(intr)*	shop 21
*andare a prendere *(intr)*	go for (e.g. doctor), fetch 21
*andare a trovare *(tr)*	call on, visit 21
*andare a vapore *(intr)*	steam, move by steam 21
*andare avanti *(intr)*	get on, be fast (clock) 21
*andare bene *(intr)*	fit, be right size, match in color/colour 21
*andare bene a *(intr)*	suit 21
*andare d'accordo con *(intr)*	get along with 21
*andare da *(intr)*	see (doctor) 21
*andare in autobus *(intr)*	bus 21
*andare in bicicletta *(intr)*	bike 21
*andare in fretta *(intr)*	speed 21
*andare in pensione *(intr)*	retire 21
*andare meglio *(intr)*	get better 21
*andare pazzo per *(intr)*	rave about 21
*andarsene (refl/intr)	go away, clear off 21
anestetizzare *(tr)*	anaesthetize 3
animare *(tr)*	animate, brighten up 3
annegare *(tr)*	drown 11
†annerire *(tr)*	blacken 6
annettere *(tr)*	annex a country 22 **[M]**
annichilire *(tr)*	annihilate 6
annodare *(tr)*	knot (rope) 3
annoiare *(tr)*	bore 13
*annoiarsi *(intr/refl)*	be bored 13, 7

annullare *(tr)*	annul, write off, accept loss of 3
*annullarsi *(intr/refl)*	cancel out 7
annunziare *(tr)*	announce 13
*annuvolarsi *(intr/refl)*	cloud over 7
ansimare *(intr)*	pant 3
anticipare *(tr)*	advance payment, anticipate 3
appannarsi *(intr/refl)*	become misty 7
apparecchiare *(tr)*	lay (table) 13
*apparire *(intr)*	appear, make an appearance 23 **[M]**
appartenere *(intr)*	belong 92
*appassire *(intr)*	wilt, dry up 6
*appellarsi a *(intr/refl)*	appeal to the law 7
appendere *(tr)*	hang, suspend 17
appianare *(tr)*	even out 3
appiattire *(tr)*	flatten 6
applaudire *(intr)*	applaud, clap 6
applicare *(tr)*	apply, use 11
applicare *(tr)* le manette a	handcuff 11
*appoggiarsi *(intr/refl)*	lean up against (back) 12, 7
apprendere a *(tr)*	learn (to) 66
*apprestarsi a *(intr/refl)*	get ready to 7
apprezzare *(tr)*	appreciate the value , prize 3
*approfittare di *(intr)*	take advantage of 3
approfondire *(tr)*	deepen 6
appropriare*(tr)*	appropriate 13
*appropriarsi indebitamente di *(intr/refl)*	embezzle 13, 7
approssimare *(tr)*	approximate 3
approvare *(tr)*	approve, endorse, pass (a law) 3
aprire *(tr)*	open 24 **[M]**
aprire con chiave *(tr)*	unlock 24
arare *(tr)*	plough 3
arbitrare *(tr)*	arbitrate, umpire, referee, file (IT) 3
ardere *(tr)*	blaze 47
armare *(tr)*	arm 3
armonizzare *(intr)*	harmonize, match 3
aromatizzare *(tr)*	flavour/flavor 3
*arrabbiarsi con *(intr/refl)*	be/get angry, lose one's temper with 13, 7
arrampicare *(tr)*	climb 11
*arrendersi *(intr/refl)*	capitulate 71, 7
arrestare *(tr)*	arrest, stem, check, stop 3
†arricchire (intr/tr)	enrich, grow rich 6
arricciare *(tr)*	curl 12
arrischiare *(tr)*	chance, gamble 13
*arrivare a *(intr)*	arrive at, get to 2

*arrossire *(intr)*	blush 6
arrostire *(tr)*	roast 6
arrotondare *(tr)*	approximate, round up (figures) 3
*arrugginirsi *(intr/refl)*	rust 6, 7
arruolare *(tr)*	enrol in 3
*arruolarsi *(intr/refl)*	join up army 7
*ascendere *(intr)*	ascend 79
asciugare *(tr)*	dry, wipe, wipe up 11
ascoltare *(tr)*	listen, listen to 3
aspettare *(tr)*	expect, hold (telephone), wait 3
*aspettarsi di *(intr/refl)*	anticipate, expect 7
aspirare a *(intr)*	aspire to 3
assalire *(tr)*	attack, besiege 77
assassinare *(tr)*	assassinate, murder 3
assegnare *(tr)*	allocate, assign, award 3
*assentarsi da *(intr/refl)*	absent oneself, be absent 7
assicurare *(tr)*	assure, ensure, insure, secure 3
assimilare *(tr)*	assimilate 3
assistere *(tr)*	to assist 25 **[M]**
assistere a *(intr)*	be present, stand by, observe, attend 25
associare *(tr)*	associate 12
assolvere *(tr)*	absolve, acquit 74
assomigliare a *(intr)*	resemble 13
*assopirsi *(intr/refl)*	nod off, doze off 6, 7
assorbire *(tr)*	absorb, soak up 6
assordare *(tr)*	deafen 3
assottigliare *(tr)*	taper, thin down 13
assumere *(tr)*	assume, engage (an employee) 26 **[M]**
*assumersi *(intr/refl)*	undertake, assume (responsibility) 26, 7
*astenersi da *(intr/refl)*	abstain, refrain from 92, 7
astrarre *(tr)*	abstract 96
atomizzare *(tr)*	atomize 3
attaccare *(tr)*	attach, harness, hang up (telephone) 11
atterrire *(tr)*	terrorize 6
attestare *(tr)*	vouch 3
attirare/attrarre *(tr)*	attract, lure 3/96
attorcigliare *(tr)*	twist 13
attraversare *(tr)*	come across/over, go across/through 3
attraversare velocemente *(tr)*	shoot (rapids) 3
attribuire *(tr)*	credit with 6
attutire *(tr)*	deaden 6

†**aumentare** *(intr/tr)*	rise, add to, increase, raise (prices) 3
autorizzare a *(tr)*	authorize, licence s.one (to) 3
†**avanzare** *(intr/tr)*	progress, advance, move/put forward 3
avanzare a fatica *(intr)*	slog away 3
*****avanzarsi** *(intr/refl)*	advance, go forward 7
avere *(tr)*	have 27 **[M]**
avercela con *(tr)*	have it in for 27
avere bisogno di *(tr)*	need, require 27
avere caldo *(tr)*	feel hot 27
avere cura di *(tr)*	take care of 27
avere da *(tr)*	have to 27
avere disponibile *(tr)*	have available 27
avere fiducia in *(tr)*	trust 27
avere freddo *(tr)*	be/feel cold 27
avere il prurito *(tr)*	to itch, have an itch
avere in mente di *(tr)*	have in mind 27
avere l'aria di *(tr)*	look (like) 27
avere l'intenzione di *(tr)*	think, intend to, be going to 27
avere la diarrea *(tr)*	have diarrhoea 27
avere luogo *(tr)*	take place, happen 27
avere mal di mare *(tr)*	be seasick 27
avere paura di *(tr)*	be afraid, regret 27
avere qlc. in contrario a *(tr)*	object to 27
avere ragione *(tr)*	be right 27
avere tendenza ad *(tr)*	tend, be inclined to 27
avere torto *(tr)*	be wrong 27
avere un rapporto sessuale con *(tr)*	have intercourse with 27
avere un ruolo importante *(tr)*	star 27
avere uno strappo muscolare *(tr)*	have a pulled muscle 27
avere vergogna di *(tr)*	be ashamed of 27
avere voglia di *(tr)*	want 27
avvelenare *(tr)*	poison 3
*****avvenire** *(intr)*	happen *(Imp.)* 102
*****avventurarsi** *(intr/refl)*	venture 7
avvertire *(tr)*	warn, alert 5
*****avviarsi verso** *(intr/refl)*	make for, move towards 13, 7
avvicinare *(tr)*	approach 3
*****avvicinarsi a** *(intr)*	approach, close in 7
avvisare *(tr)*	advise, inform, notify 3
avvistare *(tr)*	sight 3
avvitare *(tr)*	screw 3
avvolgere *(tr)*	scroll, wrap 106
avvolgersi *(intr)*	coil up 106, 7
*****azzardarsi** *(intr/refl)*	dare (to) 7
*****azzuffarsi** *(intr/refl)*	brawl 7

B

baciare *(tr)*	kiss 13
badare *(intr)*	attend, pay attention 3
badare a *(intr)*	look after, mind 3
badare di *(intr)*	take care to 3
bagnare *(tr)*	bath, dampen, soak, wet 3
*bagnarsi *(intr/refl)*	bathe 7
balbettare *(tr)*	stammer 3
ballare *(tr)*	dance 3
barattare *(tr)*	barter 3
barcollare *(intr)*	stagger, totter 3
barricare *(tr)*	barricade 11
basare *(tr)*	base (an argument on) 3
*bastare *(intr)*	be enough, be sufficient *(Imp.)* 3
battere *(tr)*	beat, strike, hit, tap, whip 4
battere le palpebre *(tr)*	blink 4
battere violentemente *(tr)*	bang 4
battezzare *(tr)*	baptize 3
beccare *(tr)*	peck (chicken) 11
belare *(intr)*	bleat (animals) 3
bendare *(tr)*	bandage 3
benedire *(tr)*	bless 9
bere *(tr)*	drink 8 **[M]**
*biforcarsi *(intr/refl)*	fork (road), branch off 11, 7
bighellonare *(intr)*	saunter 3
bilanciare *(tr)*	balance, break even, even up 12
biodegradare *(tr)*	bio-degrade 6
bisbigliare *(tr)*	whisper 13
*bisognare *(intr)*	need *(Imp.)* 3
bloccare *(tr)*	block, stop 11
bocciare *(tr)*	fail someone in a test/an exam 12
boicottare *(tr)*	boycott 3
bollare *(tr)*	stamp 3
bollire *(tr)*	boil 5
bollire lentamente *(tr)*	simmer 5
bombardare *(tr)*	bomb, shell, bombard 3
brevettare *(tr)*	patent 3
brillare *(intr)*	shine, excel 3
brontolare *(intr)*	growl, grumble, nag 3
bruciare *(tr)*	burn 12
brulicare di *(intr)*	crawl with (insects) 11
bussare *(tr)*	knock 3
buttare via *(tr)*	throw away 3

C

cacciare *(tr)*	hunt, chase, drive away, cause to go 12
cacciare di frodo *(tr)*	poach 12
*cadere *(intr)*	fall (motion) 28 **[M]**

calare *(tr)*	lower 3
calare *(intr)*	set, go down 3
calciare *(tr)*	kick 12
calcolare *(tr)*	calculate, work out, plan 3
calmare *(tr)*	calm, allay, quieten 3
*calmarsi *(intr/refl)*	calm down 7
calunniare *(tr)*	slander 13
*calzarsi *(intr/refl)*	put shoes on 7
†cambiare *(tr)*	alter, change, exchange, turn 13
camminare *(intr)*	step, tread, walk 3
camminare a grandi passi *(intr)*	stride 3
†campare *(intr)*	earn (a living) 3
campeggiare *(intr)*	camp 12
cancellare *(tr)*	cancel, cross/rub out, delete (IT) 3
cantare *(intr/tr)*	sing 3
canterellare *(intr/tr)*	hum 3
capire *(tr)*	realize, understand 6
*capitare *(intr)*	occur, happen 3
capovolgere *(tr)*	turn upside down 106
caratterizzare *(tr)*	characterize 3
carezzare *(tr)*	pat 3
caricare *(tr)*	charge/wind up (battery/ watch), load, saddle 11
*cascare	fall 11
catalogare *(tr)*	catalogue/catalog 11
catturare *(tr)*	capture 3
causare *(tr)*	bring about, cause 3
cavalcare *(intr/tr)*	ride (horse) 11
cedere *(tr)* **a**	give in/up/way, surrender, yield 33
celebrare *(tr)*	celebrate 3
cenare *(intr)*	dine, have dinner 3
censurare *(tr)*	censor, censure 3
centralizzare *(tr)*	centralize 3
centrifugare *(tr)*	spin-dry 11
cercare *(tr)*	look/search for, seek 11
cercare di *(tr)*	try to 11
cercare errori *(tr)*	debug (IT) 11
certificare *(tr)*	certify 11
cessare di *(tr)*	stop, cease (doing sth.) 3
chiacchierare *(intr)*	chat, gossip 3
chiamare *(tr)*	call, term 3
chiamare con un cenno *(tr)*	beckon 3
*chiamarsi *(intr)*	be called 7
chiarificare *(tr)*	clarify 11
chiarire *(tr)*	clear, clear up 6
chiedere *(tr)*	beg, request, enquire 29 **[M]**
chiedere a qlcu. di *(tr)*	ask s.one to do 29

chiedere l'elemosina *(tr)*	beg as a beggar 29
chiedere notizie di qlcu. *(tr)*	ask after s.one 29
chiedere scusa a *(intr)*	apologize, beg forgiveness 29
*chinarsi *(intr/refl)*	bend, stoop, bow 7
chiudere *(tr)*	close, shut, zip up 30 **[M]**
chiudere a chiave *(tr)*	lock door/suitcase 30
chiudere con catenaccio *(tr)*	bolt down 30
cigolare *(intr)*	creak 3
cinguettare *(intr)*	twitter 3
cintare *(tr)*	fence 3
circolare *(tr)*	circulate, pass round 3
circondare con *(tr)*	encircle, enclose, surround 3
circondare con una siepe *(tr)*	hedge (round) 3
citare *(tr)*	quote 3
civettare *(intr)*	flirt 3
classificare *(tr)*	grade, rank, sort, label, classify 11
coabitare *(intr)*	cohabit 3
coesistere *(intr)*	coexist 25
cogliere *(tr)*	gather 31 **[M]**
coincidere *(intr)*	coincide 39
coinvolgere *(tr)*	involve in 106
colare *(intr/tr)*	leak, strain 3
collaborare *(tr)*	collaborate 3
collocare *(tr)*	place 11
colorare *(tr)*	colour/color in 3
colpire *(tr)*	impress, knock against, shock, smack, strike, hit 6
colpire a morte *(tr)*	shoot dead 6
colpire violentemente *(tr)*	bash 6
coltivare *(tr)*	farm, garden, rear (crops), till (soil) 3
comandare *(intr/tr)*	command, boss about, order 3
combattere *(tr)*	fight, wrestle 4
†cominciare a *(tr)*	begin, get started, initiate, begin, start, commence, take up (pastime) 12
commemorare *(tr)*	commemorate 3
commentare *(tr)*	comment 3
commerciare in *(intr)*	deal in, trade in 12
commettere *(tr)*	commit 54
commuovere *(tr)*	move, affect emotionally 15
commutare *(tr)*	commute 3
comp(e)rare *(tr)*	purchase, buy 1 **[M]**
*comparire *(intr)*	appear 6
compatire *(tr)*	pity 6
*compiacere *(intr)*	please 61
compiere/compire *(tr)*	finish, achieve 6

compilare *(tr)*	compile 3
completare *(tr)*	complete 3
complicare *(tr)*	complicate 11
complimentare *(tr)*	compliment 3
comporre *(tr)*	compose music 64
comporre un indice *(tr)*	index 64
comporre il numero *(tr)*	dial telephone number 64
*comportarsi *(intr/refl)*	behave (animals/humans) 7
comprare *(tr)*	buy, purchase 1 **[M]**
comprare il silenzio di qlcu. *(tr)*	bribe s.one 1
comprendere *(tr)*	include, understand 66
comprimere *(tr)*	compress 32 **[M]**
compromettere *(tr)*	compromise 54
computare *(tr)*	compute 3
comunicare *(intr/tr)*	communicate 11
comunicare per radio *(intr/tr)*	radio 11
concedere *(tr)* **a**	concede, grant 33 **[M]**
concentrare *(tr)*	concentrate 3
*concentrarsi in *(intr/refl)*	centre/center on 7
concepire *(tr)*	conceive 6
concludere *(tr)*	conclude 30
concretare *(tr)*	concrete 3
concupire *(tr)*	lust for 6
condannare *(tr)*	condemn 3
condannare qlcu. a *(tr)*	sentence s.one to 3
condensare *(tr)*	condense 3
condire *(tr)*	season (food) 6
condire con pepe *(tr)*	pepper 6
condividere *(tr)*	share 43
condividere *(tr)* **i sentimenti altrui**	sympathize 43
*condolersi *(intr/refl)*	condole with 44, 7
condurre *(tr)*	conduct, lead, be ahead 95
conferire *(tr)*	confer 6
confermare *(tr)*	confirm 3
confessare *(tr)*	confess 3
confezionare *(tr)*	tailor 3
conficcare *(tr)*	drive in (nail) 11
confidare in *(intr)*	confide in 3
confinare con *(intr)*	border on 3
confondere *(tr)*	bewilder, confuse, muddle up, puzzle 50
*conformarsi a *(intr/refl)*	comply with, conform to 7
confortare *(tr)*	comfort 3
confrontare *(tr)*	compare 3
confutare *(tr)*	refute 3
congedare *(tr)*	dismiss 38
*congedarsi *(intr/refl)*	take one's leave 38, 7

congiungere *(tr)*	graft onto 52
*congratularsi con *(intr/refl)*	congratulate 7
connettere *(tr)*	connect 54
conoscere *(tr)*	know person/place 34 **[M]**
conquistare *(tr)*	conquer, win 3
consegnare *(tr)*	deliver, hand in/over 3
conservare *(tr)*	conserve 3
considerare *(tr)*	regard, consider 3
consigliare a qlcu. di *(intr/tr)*	advise s.one to 13
consistere di *(intr)*	consist (of) 25
consolare *(tr)*	console 3
consolidare *(tr)*	consolidate 3
consultare *(tr)*	consult 3
consumare *(tr)*	consume, erode, spend, use up 3
contaminare *(tr)*	contaminate 3
contare *(tr)*	count, number 3
contare su *(intr)*	bank upon, reckon on 3
contemplare *(tr)*	survey, contemplate 3
contenere *(tr)*	contain, store 92
continuare a *(intr)*	carry on, keep going, go on 3
contorcere *(tr)*	twist, contort 94
contrabbandare *(tr)*	smuggle 38
contraddire *(tr)*	contradict 9
contrarre *(tr)*	contract 96
contrastare *(tr)*	contrast 3
contravvenire *(tr)*	contravene 102
contribuire *(tr)* a	contribute to 6
controllare *(tr)*	check verify, inspect, monitor, service 3
†convenire *(tr/intr)*	agree, gather together *(Imp.)* 102
conversare *(intr)*	converse with 3
convertire *(tr)*	convert 5
convincere a *(tr)*	convict, convince s.one (to) 103
convocare *(tr)*	summon 11
cooperare *(intr)*	co-operate 3
coordinare *(tr)*	coordinate 3
copiare *(tr)*	copy, write out 13
coprire *(tr)*	cap, cover 24
*coricarsi *(intr/refl)*	go to bed, lie down 7
coronare *(tr)*	crown 3
correggere *(tr)*	correct 70
†correre a *(tr/intr)*	run, race (to) 35 **[M]**
corrispondere *(intr)*	correspond with 75
corrodere *(tr)*	corrode 47
corrompere *(tr)*	corrupt 76
corrugare *(tr)*	wrinkle 11
corteggiare *(tr)*	court, woo 12

cospirare *(intr)*	conspire against 3
*costare *(intr)*	cost *(Imp.)* 3
costeggiare *(tr)*	skirt 12
costernare *(tr)*	dismay 3
costituire *(tr)*	constitute 6
costringere a *(tr)*	bully, compel (to), constrain, pin down 88
costruire *(tr)*	build, construct, erect 6
costruire un ponte su *(intr)*	bridge (a river) 6
covare *(tr)*	brood over, hatch 3
creare *(tr)*	create 3
credere di *(tr)*	believe 4
credere a/in *(intr)*	believe in 4
cremare *(tr)*	cremate 3
*crepare *(intr)*	break 3
†crescere *(tr/intr)*	grow, grow up 36 **[M]**
cristallizzare *(tr)*	crystalize 3
criticare *(tr)*	criticize 11
crocifiggere *(tr)*	crucify 18
crollare *(tr)*	collapse 3
cronometrare *(tr)*	time (race) 3
cucire *(tr)*	sew, stitch 5
cucire con graffette *(tr)*	staple 5
cultivare *(tr)*	cultivate 3
cuocere *(tr)*	cook 37 **[M]**
cuocere a stufato *(tr)*	braise 37
cuocere a vapore *(tr)*	steam, cook by steam 37
cuocere ai ferri *(tr)*	grill 37
cuocere al forno *(tr)*	bake 37
curare *(tr)*	care for, tend, nurse, look after, treat (patient), edit 3
curvare *(tr)*	bend, curve 3
*curvarsi *(intr)*	stoop 7

D

danneggiare *(tr)*	damage 12
dannare *(tr)*	damn 3
dare *(tr)*	give 38 **[M]**
dare (un esame) *(tr)*	sit (an examination) 38
dare (frutti) *(tr)*	bear (fruit) 38
dare il benvenuto a *(intr)*	welcome 38
dare a nolo *(tr)*	hire/rent out 38
dare alla luce *(tr)*	give birth 38
dare del Lei a qlcu. *(tr)*	use 'Lei' form 38
dare del tu a qlcu. *(tr)*	use 'tu' form 38
dare del voi a qlcu. *(tr)*	use 'voi' form 38
dare forma a *(tr)*	shape 38
dare il colpo di grazia a *(tr)*	finish off 38

dare su *(intr)*	open onto (doors) 38
dare sui nervi *(intr)*	get on the nerves of 38
dare un nome a *(tr)*	name 38
dare un pugno a *(tr)*	punch (with fist) 38
dare un'occhiata a *(tr)*	glance at 38
dare via *(tr)*	give away 38
*darsi a *(intr/refl)*	take to, adopt as habit 38, 7
*darsi delle arie *(intr/refl)*	show off, boast 38, 7
decidere di *(tr)*	decide (to), make up one's mind, settle 39 **[M]**
decidere su *(intr)*	decide upon 39
*decidersi a *(intr/refl)*	make up one's mind (to) 39, 7
decifrare *(tr)*	decode 3
declinare *(tr)*	disclaim (responsibility) 3
decollare *(tr)*	take off (plane) 3
decorare *(tr)*	decorate 3
*descrescere *(intr)*	decrease 36
decretare *(tr)*	decree 3
dedicare *(tr)*	dedicate, devote to 11
*dedicarsi a *(intr/refl)*	devote oneself to 11, 7
dedurre *(tr)*	deduce, deduct, infer 95
definire *(tr)*	define 6
defraudare *(tr)*	defraud 3
degradare *(tr)*	degrade 3
delegare *(tr)*	delegate 11
deliberare *(tr/intr)*	deliberate 3
delineare *(tr)*	outline, sketch out (plans) 3
deludere *(tr)*	disappoint, take in, delude, let down 30
demolire *(tr)*	demolish 6
denudare *(tr)*	bare 3
denunciare *(tr)*	denounce 12
*deperire *(intr)*	decay, waste away 6
depositare *(tr)*	deposit 3
depositare in una banca *(tr)*	bank (money) 3
deprimere *(tr)*	depress, make sad 32
*derivare da *(intr)*	be derived from, spring, result from 3
derubare *(tr)*	rob 3
descrivere *(tr)*	describe 81
desiderare *(tr)*	desire, long for, want, wish 3
designare *(tr)*	style, design 3
desumere *(tr)*	deduce, assume, infer assumere 26
deteriorare *(tr)*	deterioriate 3
determinare *(tr)*	determine 3
detestare *(tr)*	detest 3

dettare *(tr)*	dictate 3
devastare *(tr)*	devastate 3
deviare *(tr)*	deviate, divert, turn aside 13
diagnosticare *(tr)*	diagnose 11
dibattere *(tr)*	debate 4
dichiarare di *(tr)*	declare, state 3
difendere da *(tr)*	defend from 17
differenziare *(tr)*	differentiate 13
differire *(intr)*	differ 6
diffidare di *(intr)*	distrust 3
diffondere *(tr)*	broadcast 50
digerire *(tr)*	digest 6
digiunare *(intr)*	fast, not eat 3
diluire *(tr)*	dilute, water down 6
***dimagrire** *(intr)*	get thin, slim, eat less 6
dimenticare di *(tr)*	forget (to), leave behind 11 **[M]**
***dimenticarsi di** *(intr/refl)*	forget 11, 7
***dimettersi** *(intr/refl)*	resign 54, 7
†**diminuire** (intr/tr)	decrease, dwindle, diminish, lessen 6
dimostrare *(tr)*	demonstrate, show/prove (innocence) 3
***dipendere da** *(intr)*	depend on 17
dipingere *(tr)*	depict, paint 93
dire di *(tr)*	say, utter remark, tell (to), order 9 **[M]**
dirigere *(tr)*	conduct (music), control, direct, guide 40 **[M]**
***dirigersi verso** *(intr/refl)*	make one's way towards 40, 7
disapprovare *(tr)*	disapprove 3
disarmare *(tr)*	disarm 3
disciogliere *(tr)*	dissolve 31
discorrere di *(intr)*	discuss, talk about 35
discutere *(tr)*	argue, debate, discuss, dispute 41 **[M]**
discutere di *(intr)*	talk about 41
disdegnare *(tr)*	scorn 3
disegnare *(tr)*	draw (a picture) 3
diseredare *(tr)*	disinherit 3
disfare *(tr)*	undo, untie, unpack 10
***disfarsi di** *(intr/refl)*	dispose of 10, 7
disinfettare *(tr)*	disinfect 3
disintegrare *(tr)*	disintegrate 3
disorganizzare *(tr)*	disorganize 3
dispensare *(tr)*	exempt from 3
disperare *(intr)*	despair 3
disperdere *(intr)*	disperse 59

*dispiacere *(intr)*	be sorry (for), displease 61
disprezzare *(tr)*	scorn 3
*dissetarsi *(intr/refl)*	quench (one's thirst) 7
dissodare *(tr)*	dig up 3
dissolvere *(tr)*	dissolve 74
dissuadere *(tr)*	dissuade 60
distinguere *(tr)*	discern, distinguish, make out 42 **[M]**
distogliere *(tr)*	distract 31
distorcere *(tr)*	distort 94
distrarre *(tr)*	distract 96
distribuire *(tr)*	deal (cards), distribute, give out, hand out/round, share out 6
districare *(tr)*	disentangle 11
distruggere *(tr)*	destroy 89
disturbare *(tr)*	disturb, trouble, upset 3
disubbidire a *(intr)*	disobey 6
divagare *(intr)*	ramble on 11
*divenire *(intr)*	become 102
*diventare *(intr)*	become, turn into 3
*diventare grigio *(intr)*	go grey (hair) 3
*diventare peggio *(intr)*	get worse 3
divergere *(intr)*	diverge 84
divertire *(tr)*	amuse 5
*divertirsi a *(intr/refl)*	amuse/enjoy oneself, have fun (doing) 5, 7
dividere *(tr)*	divide, part, separate, split (cost) 43 **[M]**
dividere a metà *(tr)*	halve 43
divorare *(tr)*	devour 3
divorziare *(tr/intr)*	divorce, get divorced 13
*divorziarsi *(intr/refl)*	get divorced 13, 7
*dolere *(intr)*	ache, hurt 44 **[M]**
domandare *(tr)* qlco. a qlcu.	ask someone for something 3
domandare di *(intr)*	ask to 3
*domandarsi *(intr/refl)*	wonder, ask oneself 7
domare *(tr)*	tame 3
dominare *(tr)*	master 3
dominare dall'alto *(tr)*	overlook 3
donare *(tr)*	donate 3
dondolare *(tr)*	rock, swing 3
dormire *(intr)*	sleep 5 **[M]**
dormire troppo a lungo *(intr)*	oversleep 5
dosare *(tr)*	dose 3
†dovere *(intr)*	be supposed to, have to, owe 45 **[M]**
†dovere fare qlco. *(intr)*	be obliged to do sth. 45

drogare *(tr)*	dope, drug 11
***drogarsi** *(intr/refl)*	become addicted, take drugs 11, 7
dubitare *(tr)*	doubt 3
duplicare *(tr)*	duplicate 11
durare *(intr)*	go on, last 3

E

eccitare *(tr)*	excite, stir, work up (interest) 3
echeggiare *(intr)*	echo 12
editare *(tr)*	edit (IT) 3
educare *(tr)*	educate, train, bring up (children) 11
elaborare *(tr)*	process (data) 3
eleggere *(tr)*	elect 53
elencare *(tr)*	list 11
elettrificare *(tr)*	electrify 11
***elevarsi** *(intr/refl)*	soar (prices) 7
eliminare *(tr)*	delete, eliminate 3
emendare *(tr)*	amend 3
***emergere** *(intr)*	emerge from 84
emettere *(tr)*	send out, emit, utter, pass (sentence) 54
emettere *(tr)* **vapore**	steam, give out vapour/vapor 54
***emigrare** *(intr)*	emigrate, migrate 3
emulsionare *(tr)*	emulsify 3
***entrare in** *(intr)*	go/get in, come on (stage) 2 **[M]**
***entrare di nascosto in** *(intr)*	steal in 2
***entrare per caso in** *(intr)*	drop in 2
***entusiasmarsi per** *(intr/refl)*	be enthusiastic about 7
equipaggiare *(tr)*	equip 12
***equivalere** *(intr)*	amount to 100
ereditare *(tr)*	succeed, inherit 3
errare *(intr)*	wander, walk aimlessly 3
eruttare *(intr)*	erupt 3
esagerare *(tr)*	exaggerate 3
esalare *(intr)*	exhale 3
esaminare *(tr)*	study, examine carefully 3
esaurire *(tr)*	drain, exhaust, run out of 6
***esaurirsi** *(intr)*	break down (person) 6, 7
esclamare *(tr)*	exclaim 3
escludere *(tr)*	disqualify, except, exclude 30
eseguire *(tr)*	carry out, perform, execute 6
esercitare *(tr)*	drill (exercise) 3
esibire *(tr)*	exhibit 6
esigere *(tr)*	require 4, 25B
esiliare *(tr)*	banish 13
***esistere** *(intr)*	exist 25
esitare a *(intr)*	hesitate (to), pause 3

esonerare *(tr)*	exonerate 3
espellere *(tr)*	expel 46 **[M]**
*esplodere *(intr)*	explode 47 **[M]**
esplorare *(tr)*	explore 3
esportare *(tr)*	export 3
esprimere *(tr)*	say, express (opinion) 32
*essere *(intr)*	be 48 **[M]**
*essere afoso *(intr)*	be heavy/sultry 48
*essere a dieta *(tr)*	diet 48
*essere avanti *(intr)*	be fast (clock) 48
*essere contento *(intr)*	be pleased 48
*essere contro *(intr)*	be against 48
*essere d'accordo con *(intr)*	be in agreement, agree (with) 48
*essere di fronte a *(intr)*	face, be opposite 48
*essere disoccupato *(intr)*	to be unemployed 48
*essere diverso *(intr)*	be different 48
*essere dovuto a *(intr)*	be due to 48
*essere frequentato da spettri *(intr)*	to be haunted 48
*essere fuori *(intr)*	be out 48
*essere im/paziente *(intr)*	be im/patient 48
*essere imparentato *(intr)*	be related (family) 48
*essere in concorrenza con *(intr)*	to compete with 48
*essere in disaccordo *(intr)*	disagree 48
*essere in periodo di prosperità *(intr)*	be in a boom 48
*essere in ritardo *(intr)*	be delayed, be late 48
*essere indietro *(intr)*	be slow (clock) 48
*essere inguaiato *(intr)*	be stuck 48
*essere mite *(intr)*	be mild 48
*essere ne di *(intr)*	become of 48
*essere necessario *(intr)*	need, be necessary 48
*essere nuvoloso *(intr)*	be cloudy 48
*essere occupato *(intr)*	be busy 48
*essere per *(intr)*	be for, support 48
*essere pieno di	abound with, be full of 48
*essere promosso *(intr)*	go up (in school) 48
*essere responsabile per *(intr)*	be liable/responsible for 48
*essere ricco di *(intr)*	be abundant, abound in 48
*essere seduto *(intr)*	sit, be seated 48
*essere sonnambulo *(intr)*	walk in one's sleep 48
*essere stitico *(intr)*	be constipated 48
*essere sul punto di *(intr)*	be about to 48
*essere umido *(intr)*	be humid/damp 48
*essere valido *(intr)*	be valid 48
*estendersi *(intr/refl)*	expand, branch out 91, 7
evacuare *(tr)*	evacuate 3
*evadere *(intr)*	evade, escape 49 **[M]**

†evaporare *(tr/intr)*	evaporate, vaporize 3
evidenziare *(tr)*	highlight 13
evitare *(tr)*	avoid, bypass 3
evitare di fare qlco.	avoid doing something 3
evocare *(tr)*	evoke 11
*evolversi *(intr/refl)*	evolve, develop 4, 25B

F

fabbricare *(tr)*	manufacture 11
facilitare *(tr)*	facilitate 3
falciare *(tr)*	mow (grass) 12
*fallire *(intr)*	fail 6
falsificare *(tr)*	fake 11
farcire *(tr)*	stuff (turkey) 6
fare *(tr)*	do, make, add up to, study (subject), cause to be, serve, perform duties, take (photo/bath/shower) 10 **[M]**

fare a meno di *(intr)*	dispense with, do without 10
fare a pezzi *(tr)*	hack to pieces 10
fare amicizia con *(intr)*	make friends with 10
fare attenzione *(intr)*	pay attention, mind (warning) 10
fare bello *(intr)*	be nice/fine 10
fare brutto *(intr)*	be bad/awful 10
fare cadere *(tr)*	drop 10
fare caldo *(intr)*	be hot 10
fare colazione *(tr)*	have breakfast 10
fare da *(intr)*	act as 10
fare da spettatore *(intr)*	look on 10
fare del bene a *(intr)*	benefit, do good to 10
fare del pugilato *(intr)*	box (sport) 10
fare del suo meglio per *(tr)*	do one's best to 10
fare di tutto per *(tr)*	do everything possible to 10
fare dispetti a *(intr)*	tease 10
fare dispetto a *(intr)*	spite, annoy 10
fare entrare *(tr)*	show in (visitor) 10
fare esplodere *(tr)*	blast, set off explosion 10
fare fallire *(tr)*	bankrupt 10
fare fare a qlcu. *(intr)*	get s.one to do sth. 10
fare finta di *(intr)*	pretend 10
fare freddo *(intr)*	be cold 10
fare fresco *(intr)*	be cool/fresh 10
fare fronte a *(intr)*	cope (with) 10
fare giorno *(intr)*	get light 10
fare grazia della vita a qlcu. *(intr)*	spare (life) 10
fare i piatti *(tr)*	wash up 10
fare il jogging *(tr)*	jog 10
fare il nido *(tr)*	nest 10

fare il pieno *(tr)*	fill up (car) 10
fare impazzire *(tr)*	madden 10
fare inciampare *(tr)*	trip 10
fare l'autostop *(tr)*	hitch-hike 10
fare l'elemosina *(tr)*	give alms 10
fare l'interprete *(tr)*	act as interpreter 10
fare l'uovo *(tr)*	lay (egg) 10
fare la caricatura di *(intr)*	caricature 10
fare la carta di *(intr)*	chart 10
fare la coda *(tr)*	queue/wait in line 10
fare la conoscenza di *(intr)*	get to know 10
fare la cubatura *(intr)*	cube 10
fare la doccia *(tr)*	shower 10
fare la media di *(intr)*	average 10
fare la permanente *(tr)*	perm 10
fare la pubblicità a *(intr)*	publicize 10
fare le fusa *(tr)*	purr 10
fare le prove di *(intr)*	rehearse 10
fare male *(intr)*	ache 10
fare male a *(intr)*	harm 10
fare marcia indietro *(intr)*	back (car) 10
fare notte *(intr)*	get dark 10
fare pagare *(tr)*	charge (prices) 10
fare pareggio *(intr)*	draw in a match 10
fare parte di una giuria *(intr)*	sit on a jury 10
fare pervenire *(tr)*	send in, submit 10
fare piacere a *(intr)*	please 10
fare prigioniero	take prisoner 10
fare pubblicità *(intr)*	advertize 10
fare ricerche *(tr)*	research 10
fare risatine sciocche *(intr)*	giggle 10
fare saltare *(tr)*	blow up, explode 10
fare saltare *(tr)*	pop 10
fare scattare *(tr)*	clock in 10
fare sedere *(tr)*	seat, sit, cause to sit 10
fare segno a qlcu. *(intr)*	wave to s.one 10
fare soffrire a *(intr)*	pain 10
fare solletico a *(intr)*	tickle 10
fare tacere *(tr)*	silence 10
fare torto a *(intr)*	wrong 10
fare traslochi *(tr)*	remove (furniture) 10
fare tutto il possibile per *(intr)*	do everything possible to 10
fare un bilancio *(tr)*	budget 10
fare un brindisi *(tr)*	toast 10
fare un picnic *(tr)*	picnic 10
fare un salto mortale *(tr)*	somersault 10
fare una collezione di *(tr)*	collect (as a hobby) 10

fare una passeggiata *(tr)*	go for a walk 10
fare una trasfusione a *(tr)*	do a blood transfusion 10
fare uno spuntino *(tr)*	have a snack 10
fare vedere a *(intr)*	show 10
farla franca *(intr)*	get away with 10
farne di tutti i colori a *(intr)*	play up 10
*farsi operare *(intr/refl)*	have an operation 10, 7
*farsi prestare *(intr/refl)*	borrow 10, 7
*farsi vivo *(intr/refl)*	show up, turn up 10, 7
fasciare *(tr)*	swaddle (baby) 12
faticare *(intr)*	labour 11
fatturare *(tr)*	bill 3
favorire *(tr)*	favour/favor, treat well, further 6
ferire *(tr)*	injure, wound 6
fermare *(tr)*	stop, prevent 3
*fermarsi *(intr/refl)*	draw up, stop, stall (engine) 7
fermentare *(intr)*	ferment 3
ferrare *(tr)*	shoe (horse) 3
festeggiare *(tr/intr)*	celebrate, feast 12
ficcare *(tr)*	stick, push sth. pointed 11
*fidanzarsi *(intr/refl)*	get engaged 7
*fidarsi di *(intr/refl)*	trust 7
*figurarsi *(intr/refl)*	imagine 7
filare *(tr)*	spin (wool) 3
filtrare *(tr)*	filter, strain (wine) 3
filtrare attraverso *(intr)*	seep through 3
finanziare *(tr)*	finance 13
fingere di *(tr)*	pretend (to) 86
†finire di (intr/tr)	end, end up, finish 6 **[M]**
†finire per *(intr)*	end by, finish by 6
*fiorire *(intr)*	bloom, flower, flourish 6
firmare *(tr)*	sign (signature) 3
fischiare (intr/tr)	whistle 13 **[M]**
fissare *(tr)*	fix, gaze at, stare, stare at 3
fissare con caviglie *(tr)*	peg 3
fissare *(tr)* un appuntamento	make a date 3
fiutare rumorosamente *(tr)*	sniff 3
fondare *(tr)*	found 3
fondere *(tr)*	fuse, merge, melt 50 **[M]**
formare *(tr)*	fashion, form 3
formattare *(tr)*	format (IT) 3
fornire *(tr)*	fit out, provide, relay, stock, supply 6
fornire di personale *(tr)*	staff 6
forzare a *(tr)*	force, compel (to) 3
fotocopiare *(tr)*	photocopy, run off, duplicate 13
fotografare *(tr)*	photograph 3

frantumare *(tr)*	crush, smash, break 3
***frantumarsi** *(intr/refl)*	shiver 7
fratturare *(tr)*	fracture 3
fregare *(tr)*	rub, scrub 11
frenare *(tr)*	brake 3
***frenarsi** *(intr/refl)*	control oneself 7
frequentare *(tr)*	attend school, frequent 3
frequentare assiduamente *(tr)*	haunt 3
friggere *(tr)*	fry 19
frizzare *(tr)*	fizz 3
frustrare *(tr)*	foil, frustrate 3
†fuggire *(tr/intr)*	escape, run away, flee 5
fumare *(tr)*	smoke 3
funzionare *(intr)*	operate (of machine), work, function 3

G

galleggiare *(intr)*	float 12
garantire *(tr)*	guarantee 6
†gelare (intr/tr)	deepfreeze, freeze 3
gemere *(intr)*	groan, moan 4
generare *(tr)*	generate 3
germogliare *(intr)*	sprout 13
gettare *(tr)*	chuck, fling, pitch, throw, toss 3
***ghiacciare** *(intr)*	ice, chill, freeze 12
***giacere** *(intr)*	lie 51 **[M]**
giocare a *(intr)*	play, stake (gambling) 11
giocare a bocce *(intr)*	play bowls 11
girare *(intr)*	spin, move round, turn 3
girare intorno a *(intr)*	circle 3
girare un film *(tr)*	film, shoot a film/movie 3
***girarsi** *(intr/refl)*	turn around 7
giudicare da *(tr)*	judge by/on 11
giudicare male *(tr)*	misjudge 11
***giungere a** *(intr)*	arrive at, reach (a decision) 52 **[M]**
giurare di *(intr)*	swear (to) 3
giustificare *(tr)*	justify 11
gocciolare *(tr)*	drip 3
godere di *(intr)*	enjoy 4
†gonfiare (intr/tr)	inflate, swell 3
***gonfiarsi di** *(intr/refl)*	bulge with 7
gorgogliare *(intr)*	bubble 13
governare *(tr/intr)*	rule, govern 3
gracchiare *(intr)*	croak 13
graffiare *(tr)*	scratch 13
†grandinare *(intr)*	hail (weather) 3
grattare *(tr)*	scrape, scratch 3
grattugiare *(tr)*	grate (cheese) 12

gridare *(tr)*	shout, call out, cry out 3
grugnire *(intr)*	grunt 6
guadagnare *(tr)*	earn, gain 3
guardare *(tr)*	look, look at, watch 3
guardare furtivamente *(tr)*	peep 3
***guardarsi da** *(intr/refl)*	beware of 7
†**guarire** (intr/tr)	cure, heal, recover, get better 6
guastare *(tr)*	spoil (fruit) 3
guerreggiare *(tr)*	war 12
guidare *(tr)*	drive, lead, guide 3
gustare *(tr)*	savour, taste (food) 3

I

idealizzare *(tr)*	idealize 3
identificare *(tr)*	identify 11
ignorare *(tr)*	be unaware of, not know 3
illuminare *(tr)*	illuminate 3
illustrare *(tr)*	illustrate 3
imballare *(tr)*	pack, package 3
imbarazzare *(tr)*	embarrass 3
imbarcare *(tr)*	embark, ship 11
***imbarcarsi** *(intr/refl)*	board 11, 7
†**imbiancare** *(intr/tr)*	bleach, turn white 11
imbottigliare *(tr)*	bottle 13
imbucare *(tr)*	post 11
imburrare *(tr)*	butter 3
imitare *(tr)*	mime, imitate 3
immaginare di *(tr)*	imagine, think of 3
***immaginarsi** *(intr/refl)*	imagine 7
immergere *(tr)*	dip, steep (in liquid) 84
immigrare *(tr)*	immigrate 3
immunizzare *(tr)*	immunize 3
***impadronirsi di** *(intr/refl)*	seize 6, 7
***impallidire** *(intr)*	go white, turn pale 6
imparare a *(tr)*	learn (to) 6
***impazzire** *(intr)*	grow mad/crazy 6
impedire di *(tr)*	forbid, stop, hinder, prevent (from) 6
***impegnarsi a** *(intr/refl)*	commit oneself, undertake (to) 7
***impennarsi** *(intr/refl)*	rear up (horse) 7
impiegare *(tr)*	employ 11
imporre un'imposta su *(tr)*	excize 64
***importare** *(intr)*	care about, matter *(Imp.)* 3
importare *(tr)*	import 3
impressionare *(tr)*	strike, impress 3
imprigionare *(tr)*	imprison 3
inalare *(tr)*	inhale 3
inargentare *(tr)*	silver, coat with silver 3

inasprire *(tr)*	exasperate 6
incaricare *(tr)*	commission 11
incartare *(tr)*	wrap up (with paper) 3
incassare *(tr)*	cash 3
incatenare *(tr)*	chain (up) 3
incendiare *(tr)*	fire, set fire to 13
inchiodare *(tr)*	nail down 3
*inciampare *(intr)*	stumble 3
incidere su *(tr)*	engrave, incise, tape (onto) 39
incitare a *(intr)*	urge to 3
inclinare *(tr)*	incline 3
*inclinarsi *(intr/refl)*	lean 7
includere *(tr)*	comprise, count in, include 20
incollare *(tr)*	stick, glue 3
incolpare *(tr)*	blame 3
*incominciare *(intr)*	begin 12
†incontrare *(intr/tr)*	run/bump into, meet 3
*incontrarsi con *(intr/refl)*	meet 7
incoraggiare a *(tr)*	encourage (to) 12
incorniciare *(tr)*	frame (picture) 12
incorporare *(tr)*	incorporate 3
*incorrere in *(intr)*	incur 35
increspare *(tr)*	ruffle, wrinkle 3
*incrociarsi *(intr/refl)*	cross, intersect 12, 7
incuneare *(tr)*	wedge 3
incutere *(tr)*	strike, rouse 41
indagare su *(intr)*	investigate 11
†indebolire *(intr/tr)*	weaken 6
indicare *(tr)*	show, indicate 11
indicare a dito *(tr)*	point (with finger) 11
indirizzare *(tr)*	address/send a letter 3
*indirizzarsi *(intr/refl)*	apply 7
indossare *(tr)*	put on, wear (clothes) 3
indovinare *(tr)*	guess 3
*indugiarsi *(intr/refl)*	loiter 12, 7
indurire *(tr)*	harden, stiffen 6
*indurirsi *(intr/refl)*	harden 6, 7
infastidire *(tr)*	bother, worry s.one 6
infettare *(tr)*	infect 3
*infettarsi *(intr/refl)*	become infected 7
infiammare *(tr)*	inflame 3
infilare *(tr)*	thread 3
*infilarsi *(intr)*	slip on (clothes) 7
*infischiarsi *(intr/refl)*	care nothing (about sth.) 13, 7
influenzare *(tr)*	influence 3
influire su *(intr)*	influence, affect 6
informare *(tr)*	inform 3

*informarsi di/su *(intr/refl)*	get information about, ask about 7
ingannare *(tr)*	bluff, cheat, circumvent, deceive, mislead, trick 3
ingessare *(tr)*	plaster 3
inghiottire *(tr)*	swallow 6
*inginocchiarsi *(intr/refl)*	kneel down 13, 7
ingiuriare qlcu. *(tr)*	call s.one names 13
†ingrassare *(intr/tr)*	fatten, put on weight 3
iniettare *(tr)*	inject 3
inizializzare *(tr)*	boot (IT) 3
iniziare a *(tr)*	initiate (s.one) 13
innaffiare *(tr)*	water 13
innalzare *(tr)*	heighten 3
*innamorarsi di *(intr/refl)*	fall in love 7
*innervosirsi *(intr/refl)*	get nervous 6, 7
innestare la retromarcia *(tr)*	reverse (car) 3
inoculare *(tr)*	innoculate 3
inoltrare *(tr)*	send on (letters) 3
inoltrare una domanda	apply (for job) 3
inondare *(tr)*	flood, overflow 3
inquinare *(tr)*	pollute 3
insaponare *(tr)*	soap 3
insegnare a *(tr)*	teach (to) 3
inseguire *(tr)*	hound, pursue, track 5
inserire *(tr)*	write in, insert 6
insistere su *(intr)*	insist (on) 25
installare *(tr)*	install 3
insultare *(tr)*	be rude to, insult 3
integrare *(tr)*	integrate 3
intendere *(tr)*	mean, intend (to say) 91
*intendersi di *(intr/refl)*	know about, be an expert on 17, 7
intensificare *(tr)*	intensify 11
interdire *(tr)*	forbid 9
interessare *(tr)*	interest *(Imp.)* 3
*interessarsi (di/a) *(intr/refl)*	take an interest in, care 7
interferire *(intr)*	interfere 6
interpretare *(tr)*	interpret, read/play (a part) 3
interpretare male *(tr)*	misinterpret 3
interrogare *(tr)*	interrogate, question 11
interrompere *(tr)*	interrupt, switch off 76
*intervenire *(intr)*	intervene, chip in, cut off 102
intervistare *(tr)*	interview 3
intitolare *(tr)*	entitle 3
intraprendere *(tr)*	take on, undertake (journey) 66
intravedere *(tr)*	glimpse 101
introdurre *(tr)*	bring in, introduce 95
*intrudersi *(intr/refl)*	intrude 20, 7

intuire *(tr)*	sense 6
inumidire *(tr)*	moisten 6
*invecchiare *(intr)*	age 13
*invecchiarsi *(intr/refl)*	age, grow old 13, 7
inventare *(tr)*	make up, invent 3
investigare *(tr)*	investigate 11
investire *(tr)*	invest, run down/over (with car) 5
inviare *(tr)*	send 13
invidiare *(tr)*	envy 13
invitare a *(tr)*	ask, invite (to) 3
inzuccherare *(tr)*	sugar 3
ionizzare *(tr)*	ionize 3
ipotecare *(tr)*	mortgage 11
irrigare *(tr)*	irrigate 11
irritare *(tr)*	irritate 3
irrompere *(tr)*	break into a building 76
*iscriversi *(intr/refl)*	sign up 81, 7
isolare *(tr)*	isolate, shut off (water, gas) 3
ispessire *(tr)*	thicken 6
istruire *(tr)*	instruct 6
istupidire *(tr)*	stupefy 6

L

*lagnarsi di *(intr/refl)*	complain about 7
*lamentarsi di *(intr/refl)*	complain about 7
lampeggiare *(tr)*	flash, flash (lightning) 12
lanciare *(tr)*	throw (a bomb) 12
lanciare un razzo *(tr)*	launch, lift off (rocket) 12
*lanciarsi *(intr/refl)*	dart out 12, 7
languire *(intr)*	pine 6
lappare *(intr)*	lap 3
lasciare *(tr)*	leave, allow to remain 12
lasciare entrare *(tr)*	allow in, let in, allow to enter 12
lasciare passare *(tr)*	allow through, let through 12
lasciare per testamento *(tr)*	bequeath, will 12
lasciare vuoto *(tr)*	vacate 12
*lasciarsi cadere *(intr/refl)*	flop down 12, 7
lavare *(tr)*	wash 3
lavare a secco *(tr)*	dry-clean 3
*lavarsi *(intr/refl)*	wash oneself, get washed 7 **[M]**
lavorare *(tr)*	work 3
lavorare a maglia *(tr)*	knit 3
lavorare come uno schiavo *(tr)*	slave, work hard 3
lavoricchiare *(intr)*	potter about 13
leccare *(tr)*	lick 11
legalizzare *(tr)*	legalize 3
legare *(tr)*	bind, fasten, tie, band together 11
legare con corde *(tr)*	string 11

leggere *(tr)*	read 53 **[M]**
leggere ad alta voce *(tr)*	read aloud 53
levigare con carta vetrata *(tr)*	sand down 11
liberare *(tr)*	free, release, rescue, set free, rid of 3
*librarsi a volo *(intr/refl)*	soar (of bird) 7
licenziare *(tr)*	fire (s.one), sack, dismiss 13
limare *(tr)*	file (wood, metal) 3
limitare *(tr)*	keep to, limit 3
*limitarsi a *(intr/refl)*	confine to 7
liquefare *(tr)*	liquify, melt 10
liquidare *(tr)*	pay off debts 3
lisciare *(tr)*	smooth(e) 12
litigare con *(intr)*	fall out, quarrel 11
livellare *(tr)*	level 3
lodare *(tr)*	praise 3
*logorarsi *(intr/refl)*	wear out 7
lottare contro *(intr)*	struggle against 3
lottare per *(intr)*	struggle for, fight for 3
luccicare *(tr)*	gleam 11
lucidare *(tr)*	shine, polish 3
lusingare *(tr)*	flatter 11

M

macchiare *(tr)*	soil, dirty, spot, mark, stain, blur 13
macchinare *(tr)*	scheme 3
macellare *(tr)*	slaughter 3
macinare *(tr)*	grind, mill 3
magnetizzare *(tr)*	magnetize 3
maledire *(tr)*	curse 9
maltrattare *(tr)*	mistreat, misuse 3
*mancare *(intr)*	be missing, miss, lack 11
*mancare di *(intr)*	fail to do sth. 11
mandare *(tr)*	send 3
mandare *(tr)* **un fax**	fax 3
mandare a chiamare *(tr)*	send for s.one 3
mandare a prendere *(tr)*	send for sth. 3
mandare fuori *(tr)*	send s.one out 3
mandare per posta *(tr)*	mail 3
maneggiare *(tr)*	handle 12
mangiare *(tr)*	eat 12 **[M]**
mantenere *(tr)*	abide by/keep, maintain, support, provide for 92
mantenere la parola *(tr)*	stick to your word 92
mantenere le proprie posizioni *(tr)*	hold one's own, stand, maintain position 92

marcare *(tr)*	mark 11
marciare *(intr)*	march 12
marinare *(tr)* la scuola	play truant 3
martellare *(tr)*	hammer 3
massacrare *(tr)*	massacre 3
masticare *(tr)*	chew 11
*maturare *(intr)*	ripen 3
mentire *(intr)*	lie, tell a lie 6
*meravigliarsi di *(intr/refl)*	be amazed, wonder at 13, 7
meritare di *(tr)*	deserve 3
mescolare *(tr)*	jumble up, mix, mix up 3
mettere *(tr)*	place, put, stick 54 **[M]**
mettere all'aria *(tr)*	air 54
mettere alla prova *(tr)*	test 54
mettere da parte *(tr)*	put aside, put away, store 54
mettere fuori *(tr)*	catch out 54
mettere fuori combattimento *(tr)*	knock out 54
mettere fuori fase *(tr)*	phase out 54
mettere in comunicazione *(tr)*	put through (telephone) 54
mettere in disordine *(tr)*	make a mess of 54
mettere in fase *(tr)*	phase in 54
mettere in garage *(tr)*	garage (car) 54
mettere in moto *(tr)*	start car 54
mettere in ordine *(tr)*	put in order, tidy up 54
mettere in pensione *(tr)*	pension off 54
mettere in relazione a *(intr)*	relate to 54
mettere insieme *(tr)*	bond, put together 54
mettere per iscritto *(tr)*	set down on paper 54
*mettersi a *(intr/refl)*	begin to 54, 7
*mettersi a sedere *(intr/refl)*	sit down 54, 7
*mettersi al *(intr/refl)*	set in (of weather) 54, 7
*mettersi in contatto con *(intr/refl)*	contact 54, 7
*mettersi in piedi *(intr/refl)*	stand up 54, 7
*mettersi in piega *(intr/refl)*	set hair 54, 7
miagolare *(intr)*	mew 3
mietere *(tr)*	harvest, mow (corn), reap 4
†migliorare *(intr/tr)*	improve 3
minacciare di *(tr)*	threaten (to) 12
mirare a *(intr)*	aim at 3
mischiare *(tr)*	blend 13
misurare *(tr)*	survey, measure 3
modellare *(tr)*	model, mould/mold 3
modernizzare *(tr)*	modernize 3
modificare *(tr)*	modify 11
molestare *(tr)*	molest 3
moltiplicare *(tr)*	multiply 11
monopolizzare *(tr)*	monopolize 3

†montare	*(intr/tr)*	ride (bike, horse) 3
mordere	*(tr)*	bite 55 **[M]**
mordicchiare	*(tr)*	nibble 13
*morire	*(intr)*	die 56 **[M]**
*morire di fame	*(intr)*	starve 56
mormorare	*(tr)*	murmur 3
mostrare	*(tr)*	show, allow to be seen 3
motivare	*(tr)*	motivate 3
mudare	*(intr)*	moult/molt 3
muggire	*(intr)*	bellow (animals) 6
multare	*(tr)*	fine (law) 3
mungere	*(tr)*	milk 68
muovere	*(tr)*	move, stir 15 **[M]**
*muoversi	*(intr/refl)*	move oneself 15, 7

N

narrare	*(tr)*	narrate, relate (a story) 3
*nascere	*(intr)*	be born 57 **[M]**
nascondere	*(tr)*	conceal, hide, veil 75
naufragare	*(intr/tr)*	be shipwrecked, sink, go down, wreck 11
negare	*(tr)*	deny 11
negoziare	*(tr)*	negotiate, bargain 13
neutralizzare	*(tr)*	neutralize 3
†nevicare	*(intr)*	snow 11
nitrire	*(intr)*	neigh 6
noleggiare	*(tr)*	charter (plane), hire/rent (car) 12
nominare	*(tr)*	appoint, name, nominate 3
notare	*(tr)*	note, notice 3
notificare	*(tr)*	inform, notify 11
nuocere a	*(intr)*	harm 16 **[M]**
nuotare	*(intr)*	swim 3
nutrire	*(tr)*	cherish 6

O

obiettare	*(tr)*	object 3
obbligare a	*(tr)*	oblige s.one to 11
*occorrere	*(intr)*	be necessary *(Imp.)* 35
occupare	*(tr)*	occupy, take up (space) 3
occupare abusivamente	*(tr)*	squat, settle illegally 3
*occuparsi di	*(intr/refl)*	deal with, see about/to, organise 7
odiare	*(tr)*	hate, dislike 13
offendere	*(tr)*	disgust, offend 17
offrire	*(tr)* a qlcu.	bid, hold out, offer, treat s.one, give (present) to s.one 24
offrire alloggio a	*(tr)*	put up, accommodate 24
offrire di	*(intr)*	offer (to) 24
*offrirsi	*(intr/refl)*	volunteer 24, 7

omettere *(tr)*	leave out, omit 54
ondeggiare *(intr)*	flicker 12
operare *(tr)*	operate 3
opporre *(tr)*	oppose 64
*opporsi a *(intr/refl)*	oppose, be opposed to 64, 7
opprimere *(tr)*	weigh down, oppress 32
orbitare *(tr)*	orbit 3
ordinare *(tr)*	file (papers), order (food) 3
organizzare *(tr)*	organize 3
orinare *(intr)*	urinate 3
ornare *(tr)*	embellish 3
osare *(intr)*	dare 3
oscillare *(intr)*	oscillate, sway, range (in amount) 3
oscurare *(tr)*	darken 3
ospitare *(tr)*	accommodate, put up, entertain 3
osservare *(tr)*	notice, observe, remark 3
ossidare *(tr)*	oxydize 3
ostacolare *(tr)*	hold up (traffic), thwart 3
ottenere *(intr)*	come by, obtain 92
otturare *(tr)*	fill (a tooth) 3
oziare *(intr)*	idle about 13

P

pagare *(tr)*	pay, pay in 11
*pagare il conto *(tr)*	check out, pay bill/check 11
palleggiare *(tr)*	dribble (football/soccer) 13
paralizzare *(tr)*	paralyze 3
parcheggiare *(tr)*	park (car) 12
pareggiare *(tr)*	equalize (sport) 12
*parere di *(intr)*	appear, seem (to) *(Imp.)* 58 [M]
parlare di *(tr/intr)*	speak, talk (of) 3 [M]
parlare francamente *(intr)*	speak out 3
partecipare a *(intr)*	take part in, participate in 3
parteggiare per *(intr)*	side with, support 12
*partire *(intr)*	depart, set off, leave 5
*partire per *(intr)*	leave for 5
†passare *(intr/tr)*	spend (time) 3
*passare a *(intr)*	pass (an exam) 3
passare *(tr)* l'aspirapolvere	vacuum 3
passare a prendere *(tr)*	call for 3
passare a una velocità inferiore *(intr)*	change down (gear) 3
passare a una velocità superiore *(intr)*	change up (gear) 3
passare da *(intr)*	call in 3
passare per *(intr)*	pass by, pass through 3
passeggiare *(intr)*	stroll 12

pattinare *(intr)*	skate 3
peccare *(intr)*	sin 11
pedalare *(intr)*	pedal 3
†peggiorare *(intr/tr)*	worsen 3
pendere *(intr)*	slope, overhang 4
penetrare *(tr)*	penetrate, pierce 3
penetrare a forza *(tr)*	force one's way 3
pensare *(intr/tr)*	think 3
pensare a *(intr)*	think about 3
pensare di *(intr)*	plan, think of (opinion) 3
*pentirsi di *(intr/refl)*	regret, repent (of) 5, 7
percepire *(tr)*	detect, perceive 6
perdere *(tr)*	shed, lose 59 **[M]**
perdere *(tr)* **l'equilibrio**	throw off balance 59
perdere tempo *(intr)*	mess about 59
*perdersi *(intr/refl)*	lose one's way 59, 7
perdonare *(tr)*	forgive, pardon 3
perfezionare *(tr)*	perfect 3
perforare *(tr)*	punch (holes) 3
*perire *(intr)*	perish 6
permettere *(intr)*	permit, allow, let, enable 54
*permettersi *(intr/refl)*	be allowed 54, 7
*permettersi il lusso di *(intr/refl)*	afford 54, 7
perseguire *(tr)*	follow up, pursue, search for 5
persistere *(intr)*	keep at, persist 25
persuadere a *(tr)*	coax, persuade (to) 60 **[M]**
*pervenire *(intr)*	arrive at 102
pesare *(tr)*	weigh 3
pescare *(tr)*	fish 11
pestare *(tr)*	stamp (with foot) 3
pettinare *(tr)*	comb 3
*piacere a *(intr)*	like, be fond of, appeal to, please *(Imp.)* 61 **[M]**
piagnucolare *(intr)*	snivel, cry 3
piangere *(intr)*	cry, weep 62 **[M]**
piantare *(tr)*	pitch (tent), plant 3
picchiettare *(intr)*	patter (rain) 3
piegare *(tr)*	fold 11
pieghettare *(tr)*	pleat 3
pilotare *(tr)*	pilot 3
piluccare *(tr)*	peck at 11
†piovere *(intr)*	rain *(Imp.)* 63 **[M]**
piovigginare *(intr)*	drizzle 3
polverizzare *(tr)*	powder, pulverize 3
pompare *(tr)*	pump 3
porre *(tr)*	place, put 64 **[M]**
porre in scatola *(tr)*	box in 64

portare *(tr)*	bear, carry, bring, have on, wear 3
portare a *(intr)*	lead to 3
portare il lutto *(tr)*	mourn 3
portare via *(tr)*	carry off, take away 3
posare *(tr)*	lay, place 3
possedere *(tr)*	possess, own 14, 4
potare *(tr)*	prune 3
†potere *(intr)*	be able, can 65 **[M]**
pranzare *(intr)*	have lunch 3
praticare *(tr)*	practise/practice, put into practice 11
precipitare *(tr)*	precipitate 3
***precipitarsi** *(intr/refl)*	rush 7
***precipitarsi fuori** *(intr/refl)*	burst out 7
***precipitarsi in** *(intr/refl)*	burst in 7
precisare *(tr)*	specify 3
predicare *(tr)*	preach 11
predire *(tr)*	predict 9
preferire *(tr)*	prefer 6
pregare di *(tr)*	pray, beg, ask 11
premere *(tr)*	press (button) 4
prendere *(tr)*	take, catch (train, cold), have, eat 66 **[M]**
prendere a *(intr)*	begin to 66
prendere d'assalto *(tr)*	storm (a building) 66
prendere in considerazione *(tr)*	take into account 66
prendere in trappola *(tr)*	trap 66
prendere le difese di *(tr)*	stand up for 66
prendere nota di *(intr)*	minute, take down (in writing) 66
prendere parte a *(intr)*	take part in 66
prendere per *(intr)*	mistake for 66
prendersi la briga di *(intr/refl)*	take the trouble to 66, 7
prendersela con *(intr)*	be upset with 66, 7
prenotare *(tr)*	book, reserve 3
preoccupare *(tr)*	distress 3
***preoccuparsi di/per** *(intr/refl)*	worry, get worried about 7
preparare *(tr)*	get ready, prepare 3
preparare il terreno *(tr)*	pave the way 3
***prepararsi a** *(intr/refl)*	get prepared for, get ready for 7
prescrivere *(tr)*	prescribe 81
presentare *(tr)*	introduce, present, produce (show) 3
***presentarsi** *(intr/refl)*	arise 7
preservare *(tr)*	preserve 3
presiedere *(tr)*	chair meeting 4
prestare *(tr)*	lend 3
pretendere di *(tr)*	claim, profess (to) 91

puntare a *(intr)*	aim at 3
puntellare *(tr)*	shore up 3
purificare *(tr)*	purify 11
*putrefarsi *(intr/refl)*	rot 10, 7
puzzare di *(intr)*	stink of 3

Q

qualificare *(tr)*	qualify 11
quantificare *(tr)*	quantify 11
quotare *(tr)*	quote (prices) 3

R

racchiudere *(tr)*	contain 30
raccogliere *(tr)*	pick, pick up, rake up (leaves), summon up (courage) 31
raccomandare *(tr)*	recommend 3
raccontare *(tr)*	report, tell, narrate 3
raddoppiare *(tr)*	double 13
raddrizzare *(tr)*	straighten 3
radere *(tr)*	shave 69 **[M]**
*radersi *(intr/refl)*	shave oneself 69, 7
radiografare *(tr)*	X-ray 3
raffinare *(tr)*	refine 3
rafforzare *(tr)*	strengthen 3
*raffreddarsi *(intr/refl)*	get/catch cold 7
raggiungere *(tr)*	reach, attain, catch up with 52
ragionare *(intr)*	reason 3
*rallegrarsi *(intr/refl)*	rejoice 7
rallentare *(tr)*	slow down 3
*rammaricarsi di *(intr/refl)*	regret, feel sorry for 11, 7
rapinare *(tr)*	hi-jack 3
rapire *(tr)*	kidnap 6
rappresentare *(tr)*	represent, stage (a play) 3
*rassegnarsi a *(intr/refl)*	resign oneself to 7
rassomigliare a *(intr)*	take after, resemble 13
rattristare *(tr)*	sadden 3
razionare *(tr)*	ration 3
reagire *(intr)*	react 6
realizzare *(tr)*	accomplish, realize, make real 3
*recarsi *(intr/refl)*	go to 11, 7
recitare *(tr)*	act in theatre/theater, perform (a play) 3
redigere *(tr)*	draw up (document) 4, 25B
refrigerare *(tr)*	refrigerate 3
regalare *(tr)*	give as a present 3
reggere *(tr)*	rule, support 70 **[M]**
registrare *(tr)*	check in, register, record, video, store data 3

regolare *(tr)*	time, regulate 3
remare *(tr)*	row, paddle 3
rendere *(tr)*	return an object 71 **[M]**
rendere agro *(tr)*	sour 71
rendere conto di *(intr)*	account for 71
rendere duro come l'acciaio *(tr)*	steel, harden 71
rendere ridicolo *(tr)*	ridicule 71
rendere sicuro *(tr)*	make safe 71
***rendersi conto di** *(intr)*	realize 71, 7
resistere a *(intr)*	resist, weather 25
respingere *(tr)*	cast off (a boat), reject, turn down 86
respirare *(tr)*	breathe 3
***restare** *(intr)*	stay 3
***restare alzati** *(intr)*	wait up 3
***restare in casa** *(intr)*	stay in/indoors 3
restaurare *(tr)*	restore 3
restituire *(tr)*	restore, give back 6
restringere *(tr)*	shrink 88
rettificare *(tr)*	rectify 11
rianimare *(tr)*	revive 3
riassumere *(tr)*	sum up, summarize 26
***riaversi** *(intr/refl)*	come round/to (consciousness) 27, 7
***ribellarsi a** *(intr/refl)*	revolt against 7
ricamare *(tr)*	embroider 3
ricattare *(tr)*	blackmail 3
ricevere *(tr)*	receive, get (letter) 4
ricevere notizie da *(intr)*	hear from 4
richiamare *(tr)*	call back, call up, mobilize, recall 3
richiedere *(tr)*	demand, request 29
riciclare *(tr)*	recycle waste 3
ricompensare *(tr)*	compensate for, reward 3
riconciliare *(tr)*	reconcile 13
riconoscere di *(tr)*	spot, recognize 34
ricoprire *(tr)*	cover with, plaster, cover again, roof 24
ricordare a *(intr)*	remind 3
***ricordarsi di** *(intr/refl)*	remember 7
***ricorrere a** *(intr)*	resort to 35
ricostruire *(tr)*	reconstruct 6
ridere di *(intr)*	laugh (at) 72 **[M]**
ridurre *(tr)*	cut back, reduce 95
riempire di *(tr)*	fill, fill in with 5
***riempirsi di** *(intr/refl)*	cram with 5, 7
rifare *(tr)*	redo 10
***riferirsi a** *(intr/refl)*	refer to 6, 7

rifiutare di *(tr)*	decline, refuse (to) 3
riflettere su *(tr)*	reflect on, think over 22
rifluire *(intr)*	ebb 6
rigare *(tr)*	rule, draw line 11
riguardare *(tr)*	affect, concern 3
***rilassarsi** *(intr/refl)*	relax 7
rimandare *(tr)*	defer, put off, postpone 3
***rimanere** *(intr)*	remain 73 **[M]**
***rimanere indietro** *(intr)*	drop behind 73
***rimanere senza fiato** *(intr)*	gasp, be breathless 73
***rimanere valido** *(intr)*	stand, remain unchanged 73
rimbalzare *(tr)*	bounce 3
rimborsare *(tr)*	refund, reimburse 3
rimediare a *(intr)*	remedy, put right 13
rimorchiare *(tr)*	tow 13
rimpiangere *(tr)*	regret, feel sorry for 62
rimpinzarsi di *(intr/refl)*	guzzle 7
rimproverare *(tr)*	reproach 3
rimuovere *(tr)*	displace 15
rinchiudere *(tr)*	pound 30
***rincrescere** *(intr)*	regret *(Imp.)* 36
rinforzare *(tr)*	reinforce, steady, make firm 3
rinfrescare *(tr)*	cool, freshen, refresh 11
***rinfrescarsi** *(intr/refl)*	cool down 11, 7
ringraziare *(tr)*	say thank you for, thank 3
rinnovare *(tr)*	renew, renovate 3
rinunciare a *(intr)*	renounce, give up 12
rinviare *(tr)*	send back 13
riordinare *(tr)*	groom 3
riorganizzare *(tr)*	reorganize 3
riparare *(tr)*	mend, fix, repair, screen, shade, shelter 3
ripetere *(tr)*	repeat 4
ripiegare *(tr)*	fold up 11
riportare *(tr)*	bring back, take back 3
riposare *(tr)*	rest 3
***riposarsi** *(intr/refl)*	have a rest 7
riprendere *(tr)*	recover, get back 66
riprodurre *(tr)*	reproduce 95
***risalire a** *(intr)*	date back 77
riscaldare *(tr)*	heat, warm up 3
rischiare di *(tr)*	risk, be in danger (of) 13
risciacquare *(tr)*	rinse 3
riscuotere *(tr)*	raise (taxes), cash (cheque/check) 82
risentire *(tr)*	play back, hear again 5
riservare *(tr)*	reserve 3

risolvere *(tr)*	solve 74 **[M]**
*****risolversi di** *(intr/refl)*	resolve (to) 74, 7
risonare *(intr)*	resonate, resound 3
risparmiare *(tr)*	economize, save, spare 13
rispecchiare *(tr)*	reflect, mirror 13
rispettare *(tr)*	respect 3
risplendere *(intr)*	glow 17
rispondere a *(intr)*	answer, rejoin, reply, equivalent to 75 **[M]**
***risultare con** *(intr)*	result in, turn out 3
risuonare *(intr)*	rattle 3
ritardare *(tr)*	delay 3
ritenere di *(tr)*	retain, consider (doing) 92
ritirare *(tr)*	withdraw 3
ritirarsi *(intr/refl)*	drop out, flinch, pull back, stand back 7
***ritornare** *(intr)*	come back, go back, get back, hand back, return 3
***ritrarsi** *(intr/refl)*	cower 7
riunire *(tr)*	assemble, put/bring together, gather 6
riunire in mazzo *(tr)*	bundle up 6
***riunirsi** *(intr/refl)*	re-unite, meet/flock together 6, 7
***riuscire a** *(intr)*	manage to (do), succeed 99
rivedere *(tr)*	revise 101
rivelare *(tr)*	disclose 3
***rivivere** *(intr)*	live again, revive 104
***rivolgersi a** *(intr/refl)*	refer to, speak to 106, 7
rivoltare *(tr)*	turn inside out 3
***rizzarsi** *(intr/refl)*	sit up 3
rodere *(tr)*	gnaw 69
rombare *(intr)*	rumble 3
rompere *(tr)*	break 76 **[M]**
ronzare *(intr)*	buzz 3
rotolare *(intr/tr)*	roll 3
rovesciare *(tr)*	capsize, knock over, spill, upset 12
†rovinare *(intr/tr)*	ruin, spoil, harm, fall to ruin 3
rubare *(tr)*	pinch, steal 3
ruotare *(tr)*	wheel 3
russare *(intr)*	snore 3

S	**sacrificare** *(tr)*	sacrifice 11
	saggiare *(tr)*	sample 12
	salare *(tr)*	salt 3
	saldare *(tr)*	pay up, settle bill, weld 3
	†salire *(intr/tr)*	go up, climb, mount, come in

	(of tide) 77 **[M]**
†salire su *(intr/tr)*	get on, board (bus/train) 77
†saltare *(intr/tr)*	hop, jump, leap 3
*saltare (di valvola) *(intr)*	blow fuse 3
salutare *(tr)*	hail, greet, see off, say good-bye 3
salvare *(tr)*	rescue, salvage, save 3
sanguinare *(intr)*	bleed 3
sapere *(intr)*	know how to 78 **[M]**
sapere di *(intr)*	taste of, smack of 78
sarchiare *(tr)*	weed, hoe 13
sbadigliare *(intr)*	yawn, gape 13
*sbagliarsi *(intr)*	be mistaken 13, 7
sbalordire *(tr)*	stupefy 6
sbarcare *(intr)*	land, disembark 11
sbarrare *(tr)*	dam 3
sbattere *(tr)*	slam, whip (eggs) 4
sbloccare *(tr)*	unblock 11
sborsare *(tr)*	pay out, disburse 3
sbottonare *(tr)*	unbutton 3
sbriciolare *(tr)*	crumble 3
*sbrigarsi *(intr/refl)*	hurry up, make haste 11, 7
*scadere *(intr)*	expire (of credit card), fall due 28
scaldare *(tr)*	warm 3
*scalzarsi *(intr/refl)*	take off shoes 7
scambiare per *(tr)*	mistake for 13
scandalizzare *(tr)*	shock, scandalize 3
*scappare via *(intr)*	dash/rush away 3
scarabocchiare *(tr)*	scribble 13
scaricare *(tr)*	discharge, unload, download (IT) 11
scartare *(tr)*	scrap 3
*scatenersi *(intr/refl)*	storm (anger) 92, 7
scattare *(tr)*	snap (photo), trigger off 3
scaturire *(tr)*	well, well up 6
scavare *(tr)*	channel, dig, hollow out, mine, scoop 3
scavare *(tr)* **(un pozzo)**	sink (a well) 3
scegliere di *(tr)*	choose (to), pick select 31
†scendere *(intr/tr)*	come down, descend, go/get down 79 **[M]**
†scendere da *(intr/tr)*	get off, get down from 79
scheggiare *(tr)*	chip 12
scherzare *(intr)*	joke 3
schiaffeggiare *(tr)*	slap 12
schiantare *(tr)*	crack 3
schizzare *(tr)*	sketch 3
sciare *(intr)*	ski sports 12
scintillare *(intr)*	sparkle 3

segnare *(tr)*	score (sports), sign, tick off, mark 3
***segnarsi** *(intr/refl)*	cross oneself 7
seguire *(tr)*	follow 5
sellare *(tr)*	saddle 3
***sembrare** *(intr)*	appear, seem *(Imp.)* 3
***sembrare di** *(intr)*	look, seem, sound (like) 3
seminare *(tr)*	sow (seed) 3
sentire *(intr)*	feel, hear, smell 5
***sentirsi di** *(intr/refl)*	feel (well/unwell) 5, 7
sentirsi girare la testa *(intr/refl)*	feel dizzy 5, 7
separare (da) *(tr)*	separate (from) 3
seppellire *(tr)*	bury 6, 25B
servire *(tr)*	serve, wait on, bowl (cricket) 5
***servire da** *(intr)*	serve as 5
***servire per** *(intr)*	be used for 5
***servirsi di** *(intr/refl)*	help oneself, use 5, 7
setacciare *(tr)*	sieve 12
***sfasciarsi contro** *(intr/refl)*	smash into 12, 7
sfidare a *(intr)*	challenge to, defy to 3
sfigurare *(tr)*	deform 3
sfiorare *(tr)*	brush against, graze, sweep past 3
sfogare *(tr)*	vent (anger) 11
sfogliare *(tr)*	leaf through 13
***sforzarsi di** *(intr/refl)*	try hard (to) 7
sfrecciare via *(intr)*	shoot off quickly 12
sfregiare *(tr)*	deface 12
sganciare *(tr)*	unhook, uncouple 12
sgattaiolare *(intr)*	slip away 3
sgelare *(tr)*	defrost, thaw 3
sgobbare *(tr/intr)*	swot (for exam) 3
sgonfiare *(tr)*	deflate 13
sgranare *(tr)*	shell (peas etc) 3
sgranocchiare *(tr)*	crunch 13
sgridare *(tr)*	scold 3
sgusciare *(intr)*	slip 12
sgusciare *(tr)*	shell, hull 12
sibilare *(tr)*	hiss 3
sigillare *(tr)*	seal 3
significare *(intr)*	denote, mean, signify, represent 11
singhiozzare *(intr)*	sob 3
sintetizzare *(tr)*	synthesize 3
sintonizzare *(tr)*	tune in 3
slacciare *(tr)*	unfasten 12
slegare *(tr)*	loosen 11
slogare *(tr)*	dislocate 11
smaltire *(tr)* **la sbornia**	sober up 6

spaccare *(tr)*	chop, hew, split (wood) 11
spalancare *(tr)*	open wide (door) 11
sparare *(tr)*	shoot, shoot a goal 3
sparare a *(intr)*	shoot at 3
sparecchiare *(tr)*	clear away 13
spargere *(tr)*	scatter, spread, sprinkle 84 **[M]**
***sparire** *(intr)*	pass away, die, vanish 6
spaventare *(tr)*	frighten, scare, startle, terrify 3
***spaventarsi di** *(intr/refl)*	to be alarmed/startled at 7
spazzare *(tr)*	sweep (chimney) 3
spazzolare *(tr)*	brush 3
***specializzarsi in** *(intr/refl)*	specialize 7
specificare *(tr)*	specify 11
speculare *(tr/intr)*	speculate 3
spedire *(tr)*	send off, despatch 6
spegnere *(tr)*	put out, extinguish, turn off light 85 **[M]**
spegnersi *(intr/refl)*	go out (of light) 85, 7
spendere *(tr)*	spend money 17
sperare di *(intr)*	hope (to) 3
sperimentare *(tr)*	experiment 3
***spettare a** *(intr)*	be up to, be the duty of *(Imp.)* 3
spezzare *(tr)*	snap, break 3
spiacere *(intr)*	mind (disinterest) 61
spiare *(tr)*	bug, spy on 13
spiccare *(tr)*	stand out (against background) 11
spiegare *(tr)*	explain, give reasons (for), open out (map), spread out (newspaper) 11
spingere a *(tr)*	push, shove, urge (to), jostle 86 **[M]**
splendere *(intr)*	shine (of sun) 17
splendere *(tr)*	flare 17
spogliare *(tr)*	strip, undress 13
***spogliarsi** *(intr/refl)*	get undressed 13, 7
spolverare *(tr)*	dust 3
sporcare *(tr)*	dirty 11
sporgere *(tr)*	jut out 80
***sporgersi** *(intr/refl)*	lean out 80, 7
sposare *(tr)*	marry 3
***sposarsi con** *(intr/refl)*	get married to 7
spostare *(tr)*	shift, move 3
sprangare *(tr)*	bar (door) 11
spremere *(tr)*	squeeze 4
spulciare *(tr)*	rid of fleas, examine, debug (IT) 12
spruzzare *(tr)*	splash, spray 3
spumeggiare *(intr)*	foam 12

*struggersi *(intr/refl)*	pine away 89, 7
strutturare *(tr)*	structure 3
studiare *(tr)*	study, learn 13
*stufarsi di *(intr/refl)*	get fed up of 7
stupire *(tr)*	amaze 6
*stupirsi di *(intr/refl)*	wonder, be amazed at 6, 7
subire *(tr)*	suffer, undergo 6
*succedere *(intr)*	occur, happen, take over *(Imp.)* 33
*succedere a *(intr)*	come after 33
succhiare *(tr)*	suck 13
sudare *(intr)*	sweat 3
suggerire *(tr)*	convey, suggest 6
suggerire a qlcu. di fare *(intr)*	suggest to s.one to do sth. 6
†suonare *(intr/tr)*	sound, produce sound, play (an instrument), hoot (car), ring (bell) 3
suonare il tamburo *(tr)*	drum 3
superare *(tr)*	exceed, overcome, top, surpass 3
supporre *(intr)*	suppose 64
susseguire *(intr)*	succeed, come next 5
sussultare *(intr)*	jump up 3
svaligiare *(tr)*	burgle 12
svalutare *(tr)*	depreciate, devalue 3
*svanire *(intr)*	vanish, die away, wear off (of sensation) 6
svantaggiare *(tr)*	handicap 12
svegliare *(tr)*	arouse, awaken, wake (s.one) 13
*svegliarsi *(intr/refl)*	wake up 13, 7
svelare *(tr)*	reveal, disclose 3
svendere *(tr)*	sell off 4
*svenire *(intr)*	pass out, faint 102
sviluppare *(tr)*	develop 3
svitare *(tr)*	unscrew 3

T

tacere *(intr)*	be silent 90 **[M]**
tagliare *(tr)*	cut, crop, shear 13
tagliare a fette *(tr)*	slice 13
tamponare *(tr)*	stop (wound) 3
tappare *(tr)*	plug, stop up 3
tappezzare *(tr)*	paper (wall) 3
tardare a *(intr)*	delay (in doing sth.) 3
tassare *(tr)*	tax 3
telefonare a *(intr)*	ring up, telephone 3
temere di *(tr)*	fear, dread 4
tendere *(tr)*	extend, strain (to limits), tense (muscles) 91 **[M]**
tendere a *(intr)*	tend to 91

tendere un'imboscata a *(intr)*	ambush 91
tenere *(tr)*	hold, grasp 92 **[M]**
tenere a *(intr)*	be eager to 92
tenere il broncio *(tr)*	sulk 92
tenere un discorso a *(tr)*	address, give a talk to 92
tenere a freno *(tr)*	bridle 92
tenere conto di *(tr)*	allow for 92
tenere in debito conto *(tr)*	make allowance for 92
tenere indietro *(tr)*	keep back, withhold 92
tenerci a *(intr)*	care a lot about 92
*tenersi lontano *(intr/refl)*	keep away, abstain 92, 7
tentare di *(tr)*	attempt (to), try, tempt 3
†terminare *(intr/tr)*	end, terminate 3
tessere *(tr)*	weave (threads) 4
testimoniare *(tr)*	bear witness, witness 13
timbrare *(tr)*	frank (letters) 3
tingere *(tr)*	dye 93 **[M]**
tirare *(tr)*	draw, pull, haul, stretch, extend 3
tirare di scherma *(intr)*	fence (sport) 3
tirare giù *(tr)*	pull down, take down (tent etc.) 3
tirare in lungo *(tr)*	linger 3
tirare vento *(tr)*	be windy 3
toccare *(tr)*	touch 11
*toccare a *(intr)*	take (turn), be up to *(Imp.)* 11
togliere *(tr)*	draw out, extract, remove, take off (clothes) 31
togliere il nocciolo a *(tr)*	stone (fruit) 31
togliere di mezzo *(tr)*	do away with 31
togliere la comunicazione *(tr)*	ring off 31
tollerare *(tr)*	tolerate 3
torcere *(tr)*	twine, wring 94 **[M]**
tormentare *(tr)*	harass, torment 3
*tornare (a casa) *(intr)*	go home, turn back 2
torturare *(tr)*	torture 3
tossire *(intr)*	cough 6
tracciare *(tr)*	plot, trace 12
tradire *(tr)*	betray 6
tradurre in/da *(tr)*	translate (into/from) 95 **[M]**
*tramontare *(intr)*	set (of sun, moon) 3
trangugiare in fretta *(tr)*	gobble up 12
trapanare *(tr)*	drill a hole 3
trarre *(tr)*	pull 96 **[M]**
trarre il massimo vantaggio da *(tr)*	make the best of 96
trasalire *(intr)*	start (startled) 77
trascinare *(tr)*	trail, drag 3
trascorrere(intr)*	pass (of time) 35
trascrivere *(tr)*	transcribe 81

trascurare *(tr)*	neglect 3
trasferire *(tr)*	transfer 6
trasformare in *(tr)*	transform (into) 3
trasgredire *(tr)*	infringe 6
traslocarsi *(intr/refl)*	move (house) 7
trasmettere *(tr)*	pass on, send on (orders) 54
trattare *(tr)*	use, treat (person) 3
trattare con *(intr)*	deal with 3
***trattarsi di** *(intr/refl)*	be a matter of, be about 7
trattenere *(tr)*	detain 92
***trattenersi** *(intr/refl)*	holdback, stay, remain 92, 7
travestire *(tr)*	disguise 5
trebbiare *(tr)*	thresh 13
tremare *(intr)*	quiver, tremble 3
trionfare *(tr)*	triumph 3
tritare *(tr)*	mince 3
trovare *(tr)*	find, think out (a solution) 3
trovare per caso *(tr)*	chance upon 3
***trovarsi** *(intr/refl)*	stand, be situated/located 7
***truccarsi** *(intr/refl)*	make up (cosmetics) 11, 7
***tuffarsi** *(intr/refl)*	plunge, dive 7
tumultuare *(intr)*	riot 3
tuonare *(intr)*	thunder 3
turare *(tr)*	cork 3

U	**ubbidire a** *(intr)*	obey 6
	***ubriacarsi** *(intr/refl)*	get drunk 11, 7
	uccidere *(tr)*	kill 97 **[M]**
	udire *(tr)*	hear 98 **[M]**
	uguagliare *(tr)*	equal, equalize 13
	umiliare *(tr)*	humiliate 13
	ungere *(tr)*	grease, oil 68
	unire *(tr)*	annex, join, combine, pool (resources), unite 6
	***unirsi a** *(intr/refl)*	join, unite, team up, link up 6, 7
	urlare *(intr)*	roar, hoot, howl, scream 3
	usare *(tr)*	use 3
	***uscire** *(intr)*	come out exit, go/get out of 99 **[M]**

V	**vagabondare** *(intr)*	hike 3
	vagare *(intr)*	ramble, stray 11
	vagliare *(tr)*	sieve, riddle, screen 13
	***valere** *(intr)*	be worth 100 **[M]**
	***valere la pena** *(intr)*	be worth the trouble *(Imp.)* 100
	valutare *(tr)*	evaluate, rate, value 3
	***vantarsi di** *(intr/refl)*	boast about 7

variare *(tr)*	vary 13
vedere *(tr)*	see, view 101 **[M]**
non vedere l'ora di *(intr)*	look forward to 101
veleggiare *(intr)*	sail 12
vendere *(tr)*	retail, sell 4 **[M]**
vendere al mercato *(tr)*	market 4
venerare *(tr)*	worship, venerate 3
*venire *(intr)*	come (motion) 102 **[M]**
*venire a *(intr)*	come to, come and 102
*venire a vedere *(intr)*	come and see 102
*venire in mente *(intr)*	occur (of idea) 102
ventilare *(tr)*	ventilate 3
*vergognarsi di *(intr/refl)*	be ashamed of 7
verificare *(tr)*	audit, check, verify 11
verniciare *(tr)*	paint (house) 12
versare *(tr)*	pour, shed, pay in (money) 3
vestire *(tr)*	clothe 5
*vestirsi *(intr/refl)*	dress, get dressed 5, 7
vezzeggiare *(tr)*	fondle, pet child/animal 12
viaggiare *(intr)*	travel 12
vibrare *(tr)*	vibrate 3
vietare di *(tr)*	forbid (to) 3
vincere *(tr)*	win 103 **[M]**
violare *(tr)*	violate 3
violentare *(tr)*	rape 3
visitare *(tr)*	visit places 3
visualizzare *(tr)*	display (IT) 3
†vivere *(intr/tr)*	live, be alive 104 **[M]**
†vivere di *(intr/tr)*	live on 104
viziare *(tr)*	spoil (child) 13
vogare *(intr)*	stroke (of oars) 11
†volare *(intr/tr)*	fly 3
†volare via *(intr/tr)*	fly away 3
†volere *(intr/tr)*	like, want 105 **[M]**
†voler bene a *(intr/tr)*	be fond of, love 105
*volerci	take, require (time) 105
volgere *(tr)*	turn 106 **[M]**
*volgersi *(intr/refl)*	turn around 106, 7
voltare *(tr)*	switch (direction) 3
*voltarsi *(intr/refl)*	turn around 7
vomitare *(intr/tr)*	be sick, vomit 3
votare *(tr)*	vote 3
vuotare *(tr)*	empty 3

Z

zoppicare *(intr)*	limp 11